"Speak
Well of
Me"

RONALD HARWOOD

"Speak Well of Me"

The Authorized Biography

by W. Sydney Robinson

OBERON BOOKS
LONDON

WWW.OBERONBOOKS.COM

First published in 2017 by Oberon Books Ltd
521 Caledonian Road, London N7 9RH
Tel: +44 (0) 20 7607 3637 / Fax: +44 (0) 20 7607 3629
e-mail: info@oberonbooks.com
www.oberonbooks.com

A catalogue record for this book is available from the British Library.

HB ISBN: 9781786820433
E ISBN: 9781786820440

Cover photo credit: Jay Brooks http://www.jaybrooks.net/

Printed and bound by 4edge Limited, UK

Visit www.oberonbooks.com to read more about all our books and to buy them. You will also find features, author interviews and news of any author events, and you can sign up for e-newsletters so that you're always first to hear about our new releases.

Contents

To my subject

Talk of me sometimes. Speak well of me. Actors live on only in the memory of others. Speak well of me.
The Dresser, *Act Two*

Prologue

'You will always get a decent screenplay out of Ronnie Harwood,'
an American movie mogul once declared, '– but I wouldn't
give him Jurassic Park IV.'

To the author of *The Pianist*, *The Dresser* and *Quartet*, there could be few higher accolades. For Sir Ronald Harwood – playwright, screenplay-writer, novelist, biographer and Grand Old Man of the Garrick Club – has always believed drama to be about more than computer gimmickry and fist-pumping action. In a career spanning over six decades, he has held fast to those often-reviled traditions – those of Coward and Rattigan, Shakespeare and Jonson, Sophocles and Euripides – in striving, above all else, to effect the union of dramatist, actor and audience through the magical deployment of ordinary characters thrown into the most extraordinary circumstances.

This self-conscious rootedness in the past has frequently alienated Sir Ronald from his contemporaries. Not a man for the 'graduate seminar' or 'Eng. Lit.', he shares little obviously in common with writers of the experimental school such as Sir Tom Stoppard and the late Harold Pinter. Still less does Sir Ronald resemble those faded 'angry young men', Sir Arnold Wesker and John Osborne, who achieved such prominence at the outset of their careers by railing against 'the Establishment'. When, in the summer of 2016, the veteran playwright used an interview in *The Times* to lament the 'astonishingly stupid' modern practice of casting female actors for male roles, he found himself condemned in the same newspaper for succumbing to a 'strange pedantic realism'. Harwood prefers to hark back to the unashamedly uncomplicated theatre of the eighteenth and nineteenth centuries; before

George Bernard Shaw – 'a pernicious influence' – began the trend of preaching politics to squirming audiences.[1]

To glance at the listings of almost any theatrical journal is to see the quiet success of Sir Ronald's lonely counter-revolution. His most celebrated play, *The Dresser*, has been adapted for both television and cinema, and has recently enjoyed its sixteenth major stage production in Britain (at the Duke of York's Theatre starring Ken Stott and Reece Shearsmith); its fifth in Japan, and its third in Mexico. His screenplays and TV dramas, meanwhile, have delighted millions of viewers across the globe, winning him in the process a host of prizes, including a BAFTA for *The Diving Bell and the Butterfly* and an Academy Award for *The Pianist*.

With these remarkable achievements in mind, it seems incredible that, in this age of celebrity, Sir Ronald remains something of an outsider in the country to which he emigrated in 1951. But the British have never felt a personal affinity with the glitterati of Hollywood. From Charlie Chaplin to Robert Pattinson, the stars which these islands have exported are usually lost forever: 'citizens of the world', they might grandly say – but in truth the majority have simply assumed an American identity.

Not so Sir Ronnie. A man of obsessions, he has no greater love than for England and her people – especially, it must be added, her 'well-born' people. Yet this betokens no overnight transformation. Even as a child growing up in an insalubrious corner of Cape Town, South Africa, he was always sure to dress smartly, 'speak proper' and generally conduct himself in the manner in which he intended to go on. When he later achieved fame in the movies, he never considered, as have so many before him, relocating to the city described by those alien to its magnetism as 'Tinseltown'. To this day he remains surprisingly little known even in that bastion of all things showbiz.

Such is the lot of many a solitary screenplay-writer. 'Before it's written,' he has revealingly lamented, 'you are everything; as soon as it's handed in you are no one.' But the list of his collaborators is legion: practically every major dramatist from J. B. Priestley to Roman Polanski, and every film star from Laurence Olivier to Sheridan Smith, has at some stage crossed his path professionally. I confess that all this has sometimes overwhelmed his biographer: the length and breadth of Sir Ronald's activities would crush even a literary Hercules. How many writers of note today, one wonders, have press cuttings stretching back to the summer of 1954? It is sobering to reflect that even at that time Harwood was a veteran of the theatre company founded by the legendary actor-manager Sir Donald Wolfit. More than six decades on, the wizened playwright shows no sign of slowing down.

This energy and enthusiasm has been invaluable in the writing of this book, but neither its subject nor its author has sought to create a work of hagiography. At our first meeting – about my critical biography of the Victorian investigative journalist W. T. Stead, *Muckraker* – Sir Ronald casually mentioned that he had been asked to write his memoirs, but had lost the desire to go on with them. We both came to the conclusion that it would be better to allow a biographer to work his material into a different kind of book. Since I happened to have been on hand at the right moment, he agreed to delegate this task to me. 'You can write whatever you like,' he said bravely: 'I have never done or written anything which I would like to have covered up,' he continued, '– except perhaps that libretto I did for André Previn.'

That generous sentiment provides the keynote for this biography. While there will doubtless be successors to *Speak Well of Me*, no one will be able to say that material was actively hidden from Sir Ronald Harwood's first biographer. And, whatever the skill and ingenuity of those future critics may be, they will not have access to the greatest source of all – the man himself. To him, and those who so generously shared their memories of this theatrical titan, this book is dedicated.

Act One:

WALKING THE BOARDS

1

A Man from the Colonies

We are talking about a city, about Mecca, about Jerusalem, about London, about England.
Another Time, *Act One*

It was a bleak, wet day in post-war London. A tanned seventeen-year-old named Ronnie Harwood stood gazing at the bright hoarding outside the Wyndham's Theatre in London's West End. '*The Love of Four Colonels* by Peter Ustinov', he baldly read. Although he had only been in the country for twenty-four hours, the youth already knew that this was something he wished to be a part of. It did not matter that the building was black with soot, that its windows rattled as the buses heaved along the Charing Cross Road, or that the flower girls mobbed every passer-by. Ronnie was home at last. He was going to the theatre.

Nothing could have upset this adventure – not even the solemn face at the box office which informed him that the matinee was already sold out. *Surely, but surely, there was a seat somewhere?* 'Of course,' the gentleman suggested, 'we do have boxes available. Price: seven pounds.' *Seven pounds!* That was nearly all the money Ronnie had in the world: a third of the annual fees for the Royal Academy of Dramatic Art, enough to live on for months – almost as much as the cost of his ticket to England. But the young man was loath to appear fazed. 'That would be fine,' he blithely responded, before emptying the entire contents of his wallet onto the counter. A lifetime later the visitor would sit in the same box to see one of his own plays performed by some of the most distinguished actors of his generation.

The tale rivals Dr Johnson's assertion to David Garrick that he had come up to London with more half pence in his pocket than the impecunious actor.

This is of a piece with Sir Ronald Harwood. For he belongs, both spiritually and artistically, more to the bohemian world of the eighteenth century than to that of *Celebrity Big Brother*, *X Factor* and *The Graham Norton Show*.

His journey has been a long one. Born on 9 November 1934 at Sea Point, a modest suburb to the north-west of Cape Town, he was known for the first seventeen years of his life as Ronald Horwitz. His parents, Ike and Bella, were first-generation Jewish immigrants who had, either personally or by parentage, fled the notorious pogroms which engulfed Eastern Europe during the closing years of the nineteenth century. In the case of Ike this had entailed being placed in a coffin in order to be smuggled out of his native village of Plungé, Lithuania, as a young man at the turn of the century. Around the same time his future wife, the daughter of Polish refugees, Adolph and Eva Pepper, was born in the East End of London. Shortly thereafter Bella and her family emigrated to the Cape, where she grew up in an atmosphere of genteel poverty before marrying Ike, a commercial traveller ten years her senior, in the last year of the First World War. The couple went on to have two children, Eve ('Evvy') Leonora and Harold Ralph, before the birth of Ronnie almost two decades after their nuptials. The Benjamin of the family was known simply as 'the afterthought'.

Ike and Bella had little in common besides being Jewish, but even this oddly served as a barrier. For the Horwitzes were both *frum* – strict, Yiddish-speaking and Orthodox – as well as *Litvaks* – uneducated, rural and non-European. The Peppers could scarcely refrain from looking down on such people. 'They aspired to the culture of Europe,' recalls Harwood, 'and were highly educated.' Whereas the most distinguished of Ike's forebears had been a Chief Rabbi with an eccentric distaste for turkey – he believed this meat to be unclean after seeing a large bird eating from the ground like a pig – the Peppers listed among their kith a Nobel Laureate, Dr Paul Ehrlich. This world-famous scientist, a cousin of Bella's mother, had received his prize in recognition of his pioneering cure for syphilis – the so-called 'silver bullet' technique. It may be supposed that some of the liberalism and sophistication native to the Peppers derived from Dr Ehrlich's mature approach to all matters sexual. So uninhibited was the good doctor that he once explained the nature of his research to a half-deaf countess. 'Ah, syphilis,' she finally grasped: 'What a shame – if you had discovered the cure earlier my poor husband would still be alive.'

The unhappy family lived in a small ground-floor apartment on a main road, Victoria Street, overlooked by the Lion's Head mountain. Harwood would later recreate the exact dimensions of this cramped home in his most autobiographical play, *Another Time*. 'The likeness was uncanny,' reflects one of Harwood's oldest companions. Visitors approached the maisonette through a scraggy front garden, which abruptly ended where the veranda had been converted by means of frosted glass panes into a makeshift bedroom. Beyond the front door there was a dark, hexagonal entrance hall – the dining room and living area – from whence there followed two more bedrooms and a tiny kitchen. 'We lived on top of each other,' recalls Harwood morosely, 'and the atmosphere in the flat was sometimes unbearable.' But of all the inconveniences of this cheek-by-jowl arrangement, the greatest was the refusal of Ike and Bella to exchange even the simplest conversation with one another. The words 'ask your father' became painfully familiar to young Ronnie, and it was not long before this human carrier-pigeon was told to bunk down with his father on account of his mother being kept awake by his snoring. 'I now assume,' reflects Harwood, 'that she had other reasons for not wanting to share a room with my father.'

For Ike was not an ideal husband. When his commanding mother, Sarah (known to his wife as 'the octopus'), died shortly after his marriage he had a severe nervous breakdown from which he never fully recovered. As well as making it almost impossible for him to continue working, the trauma exacerbated an undiagnosed cerebral condition which manifested itself in his gammy left hand. Hereafter it fell to Bella, a clerk at the Electricity Board, to provide for the family. The displaced paterfamilias passed out the remainder of his days loitering in the streets, drinking cold cups of tea and thumbing through ancient encyclopaedias. Always short of cash, he once appeared faint with hunger at his daughter's workplace, a dance studio, pleading for money to buy himself lunch. 'His sense of failure must have been immense,' says Harwood ruefully. But there were times when Ike showed traces of a steelier determination. To the amazement of his wife and children, he enlisted in the Army at the outbreak of the Second World War – 'Didn't they see your bad hand?' asked his incredulous wife; 'They didn't ask, so I didn't show,' came the laconic reply. On another occasion Ike snubbed the haughty rabbi of the Orthodox synagogue on Marais Road by removing himself and his children to the new Reform synagogue, headed by a young American named Dr David Sherman. Such actions showed that, despite his obvious limitations, Ike took pride in himself and his family.

This was all to the good for little Ronnie. 'I was spoilt rotten,' he recalls with a toothy grin. Celebrated in the family circle for his 'film-star' appearance, the child was petted and complimented almost continually from the first. Even with the family's strained finances, nothing from piano lessons to the finest clothes was denied to him. Only from the vantage of the present does Harwood recognize the sacrifices which these small luxuries must have entailed for his parents. 'It never crossed my mind that we were poor,' he recalls sadly. 'I've always been insanely self-confident,' he continues more cheerfully, 'and even as a child regarded myself as being extremely lucky.' A photograph of young Ronnie strumming a toy guitar in his aunt's front garden suggests this to be no exaggeration. Neatly dressed and exceptionally well-groomed, the merry three-year-old exudes the same impish mirth that he retains even today.

By far the most significant of the indulgences heaped upon the future playwright were the elocution classes arranged by his mother with a local actress and voice coach, Mrs Sibyl Marks. Without the influence of this cultured British émigré it is hard to envisage that Harwood would ever have moved to England or pursued a career in the theatre. 'Everything she said,' he recalls today, 'was either dramatic or seductive' – a winning combination for the impressionable boy who fast became one of her star pupils. Encouraged by her and his mother to enter various recital competitions, the born performer first won a degree of acclaim with a rendition of 'There's a mouse in the house' at the age of seven. A few years later he found himself acting out scenes from Shakespeare's *King John* alongside another local starlet, the future Sir Nigel Hawthorne of *Yes, Minister* fame. 'So dazzled was I by my own brilliance,' boasts Harwood disarmingly, 'that he made little impression on me as an actor, but I liked him a good deal and enjoyed working on our scenes.' The pair would next meet amid the pomp and ceremony of Buckingham Palace.

But this is anticipating. For the time being, Ronnie Horwitz lived in a world of Boers and Afrikaners; English-speakers and colonialists, blacks and Bantu. Even for a boy with little awareness of politics, the grim shadow of apartheid, which was to be introduced by the Nationalist Government in 1948, was already discernible in the Cape. This was largely the doing of the country's Dutch-speaking elite, the Afrikaners, who regarded the black majority as 'children' needful of protection and subjugation. Throughout the 1920s and 1930s, the last pro-British president, General Smuts, appeased his more hard-line colleagues by keeping the native population in a state of near-total servitude. So extreme was the resulting economic disparity that even the poorest European families, such as the Horwitzes, could afford a black maid to help with the housework. In later years Harwood would particularly recall one of these women, Annie, who unwittingly became a major influence. The only words on the subject of racial politics uttered at home were Ike's: 'Thank God it's not us!' – a view common among the various white minorities of the Rainbow Nation.

Harwood does not claim retrospective virtue when discussing these matters. 'People say that they opposed apartheid,' he sighs, 'but the truth is that few whites of my age were even conscious that it existed.' It was the banality of the discrimination – the overcrowded 'coloured' railway carriages and the informally segregated shops and restaurants – which most affected the future dramatist. As a member of the racial elite only by default, the child had other worries to contend with. Among the most oppressive of these was the attempt by a teacher at his junior school, a Mr van der Merwe, to convert him and the other Jewish pupils to Christianity. 'He threatened us with hellfire and eternal damnation if we resisted,' remembers Harwood, '– which of course we did.' This plucky defiance, much encouraged and admired by his proud mother, not only sharpened the boy's inner resolve, it also developed his latent wit. Asked to select a favourite passage from the Old Testament, Ronnie could always be relied upon to furnish the overzealous pedagogue with a suitably absurd text. Particularly he recalls Isaiah, chapter 36, verse 12: '… [H]ath he not sent me to the men that sit upon the wall, that they may eat their own dung, and drink their own urine?' A little later Harwood got even more laughs by directing the unfortunate van der Merwe to the passage in Genesis in which Onan is struck down for spilling his own seed. 'He fell for it every time,' chuckles Harwood dryly, '– he was not the brightest of men.'

Having survived these ordeals, Ronnie progressed to the senior school, Sea Point Boys High, where he continued to make an impression as a joker, Anglophile and aspiring intellectual. It was to be predicted that given the opportunity to acquire the accoutrements of a classical education, the young man would seize it with eager hands. But his Latin master, Mr Thompson, proved to be a far more considerable adversary than the simple van der Merwe. At a time when his countrymen had only recently been ostensible allies in the war against Hitler, this defiant Afrikaner thought nothing of sporting a toothbrush moustache in honour of the German dictator. Needless to say, 'Tommy' – as he was known behind his back – did not take to Ronnie Horwitz. Trouble began almost straightaway when the master introduced the class to the verb 'amo'. 'Puellam amo,' he intoned: 'I love the girl.' Ronnie sniggered. Even today Harwood shudders as he recalls Tommy's sharp reaction. Striding over with a clenched fist and bulging eyes, the brutish man screeched: 'You think it's funny, hey? Well I'll tell you what's very funny. You haven't stopped sucking from your mummy's titties, that's what's very funny!'

before savagely clipping the child across the head. Another boy caught gazing out of the window was suspended from that aperture by his ankles until he wet himself. 'You've got a better view of the view now!' boomed Tommy, 'hey, hey, hey?'

It was not long before a formal complaint was lodged against Mr Thompson. This came from the parents of Ronnie's closest friend at the school, Gerald Mosselson, who lived in a more luxurious home nearer the top of the Lion's Head. Even more than his introduction to Mrs Marks, this was a turning point for the future playwright. For it brought him into the orbit of the theatrical director and most influential English teacher in the school, Mr Quinn, who was known, on account of his rough appearance and accent, as 'Cowboy Quinn'. While their fellow students were plodding through their Latin declensions with Tommy, a group of boys dominated by Ronnie and Gerald studied literature – mostly English literature. It was an awakening. A true aficionado, Harwood devoured the works of the Brontë sisters, Washington Irving and Charles Dickens with the same gusto with which he approached such staples as *The Famous Five* and *Biggles*. 'I cannot pretend it was the elegant writing that first caught my attention,' he remembers of his first rapturous embrace of the Western canon. Instead it was the intriguing openings, followed by gripping narrative, which ensnared him. 'A shot rang out!' he explains – 'And then? And then? And then?' Almost unconsciously, the schoolboy began to grasp the meaning of plot and characterization. In later years he would find his intuition rationalized most eloquently by E. M. Forster: '"The King died and then the Queen died" is a story. "The King died and then the Queen died of grief" is a plot.' For over sixty years that has been a guiding principle in all Harwood's work.

Forster's kingly lesson could not have been more apt for the author whose obsessive love of the theatre can be traced back to the most famous of all plays royal: *Hamlet*. This tragedy entered his miniature universe unexpectedly when the film version, directed by Sir Laurence Olivier, appeared in the year 1948 at his favourite cinema, the Alhambra on Riebeeck Street. Although the young man went along with his mother hoping to see a detective story – 'Who killed the king?' – he fast became aware that he had come into contact with something of a hitherto unimaginable brilliance. 'It was electrifying,' reminisces Harwood of the occasion. 'The actors ceased to be actors – Basil Sydney *was* Claudius, Eileen Herlie, a real-life Gertrude; the others, too: Jean Simmons, Terence Morgan, Norman Wooland, Stanley Holloway, Peter Cushing …' he reels off without pause. But it was the lead role, played by Olivier himself, which really stuck in the boy's imagination. Before the cinema managers had reverted to their standard fare of spaghetti Westerns and Hollywood romances, the fourteen-year-old had seen the film seven or eight times; sometimes with Gerald Mosselson, but more often alone.

Gerald and Ronnie were soon to embark on careers as actor-directors of their own. This was encouraged by Gerald's father, an agent for 20th Century Fox, who built them a model theatre in which they performed scaled-down versions of the plays they had discussed with Cowboy Quinn. 'The Royal Acropolis', as their toy playhouse was known, was fitted with fairy lights, glittering cardboard and a range of elaborate props scarcely unworthy of the theatre's triumphant name. Upon its boards plaster figurines controlled by Gerald were given the breath of life by Ronnie, who read aloud from their school editions of works by playwrights as various as Sophocles, Shakespeare and Shaw.

Harwood is the first to acknowledge that there were some drawbacks to learning so much of the classical repertoire in this way. When, for instance, Tom Stoppard burst onto the London theatre scene in 1967 with *Rosencrantz and Guildenstern are Dead*, his as yet little-known South African-born contemporary was mortified after admitting his bafflement about the play's title – the characters, it emerged, had been cut from Olivier's seminal film. Yet Harwood has never been embarrassed or inhibited by these occasional blots in his copybook. 'Once I had devoted myself to being an author,' he elucidates, 'I read everything – even books like *Ulysses*, which I soon discovered few well-educated people had actually read.' Still later, Harwood remembered his *Rosencrantz* gaffe when making the major cuts which are necessary when adapting any novel or play for the big screen.

But of all the influences on the latent dramatist, the greatest was a modest publication entitled *Theatre World*. His subscription to this journal was another small extravagance made by his mother, who could already see that her son's future was likely to be on the stage. 'It's easy to be a big fish in a little pond,' she said after one of his early theatrical triumphs, 'but if you really want to know how good you are, you will have to go to London.' Such a prospect was by now becoming a serious possibility: 'If I have to eat one meal a week, you'll go,' declares a thinly disguised version of Bella in *Another Time*. This encouragement doubtless added to the excitement of thumbing through the pages of *Theatre World* in the glass-plated stuffiness of Ronnie's makeshift bedroom, his father snoring all the while. Breathlessly the fanatic gazed at the monochrome photographic essays of such notable West End productions as Ralph Richardson's *Richard II* starring Alec Guinness as the king and Donald Wolfit's career-defining *Tamburlaine the Great*. Little did the reader know that before long these giants would be counted among his colleagues.

Ronnie's yearning for England impacted on his daily life in various ways. For one thing, he ceased taking much interest in school or schoolwork. 'My discontent had its source partly in what I now see as unjustifiable arrogance,' reminisces Harwood, 'believing instinctively that what I was being taught was of no earthly use to me.' He also became increasingly remote from his small circle of friends, who were now focusing their attentions on passing their School Certificate examinations. Only the occasional evening tinkering with the Royal Acropolis interrupted the young man's relentless circuit of elocution classes and amateur dramatics – sometimes he was even called upon to take a role in a semi-professional show. While his classmates sweated over their textbooks, the loner preferred to dream of London and the theatre. On free afternoons he would often wander down to the docks and gaze at the names on the ships – Southampton, Portsmouth and Liverpool. 'Somehow,' he says today, 'I believed myself to have been born in the wrong country – I desperately wanted to go to

England, where I thought I could make a name for myself.' Mournfully, the young Hamlet would spit into the sea, dreaming of the distant shores upon which his spittle would be washed up.

As Ronnie reached the end of his final year at school, two life-changing events took place which helped make this fantasy a reality: the death of his father and his invitation to be interviewed at the Royal Academy of Dramatic Art in London. Harwood contends that the first of these developments did not at the time seem likely to further his chances of leaving South Africa, but in retrospect it clearly allowed both him and his mother to leave the colony – within only a few years Bella would follow her son to the centre of Britain's crumbling empire. In any case, Ike's passing marked the end of an era in the Horwitz household in other ways. The dreaded, long-anticipated event occurred within only a few days of the marriage of the eldest child, Ralph, who had served as an RAF pilot during the war, to an attractive young woman called Nola Oliver. On the evening of the celebration, Ike collapsed in a fit of coughing, and was duly diagnosed with acute bronchitis. A few days later a psychologist suggested that there was something more seriously wrong with Ike. After years of being told that his afflictions were 'mind over matter', he was now sent to a specialist who found his brain to be encrusted with a non-malignant tumour known as meningioma. The patient was last seen by his family shortly after enduring the arduous and dangerous procedure of trepanning. Drowsily but sweetly, he said to his wife: 'Bella, get some sleep; you have very black rings under your eyes.' In all their years of marriage, the fifty-nine-year-old had never commented on this distinctive feature of his long-suffering spouse.

The invitation from RADA followed soon after Ike's demise. It provided the impetus needed to justify Ronnie's long and expensive journey overseas. At the behest of Mrs Marks, a fund-raising concert was organized which raised over £90 to help her protégé on his way. A well-meaning teacher, meanwhile, took the boy aside to suggest that it would be advisable to adopt a less 'foreign' surname for his new life in England. After consulting Cowboy Quinn on the matter, Ronnie selected Harwood, remembering the precedent of Laurence Harvey, the famous South African actor who had been born Laurence Skikne. Considering these matters today, Harwood has no regrets. 'I have been reproached for changing my name,' he declares angrily, 'as though I were trying to hide my Jewish origins; an accusation I find offensive.' Besides the simple truth that there were, at that time, few working actors in Britain, or anywhere, with Jewish surnames, Harwood points out that these names are, in any case, arbitrary. Quoting the author Joseph Roth, he has written:

> Don't be surprised at the Jews' lack of attachment to their names. They will change their names with alacrity … For Jews their names have no value because they are not their names. Jews, Eastern Jews, have no names. They have compulsory aliases. Their true name is the one by which they are summoned to the Torah on the Sabbath and on holy days: their Jewish first name, and the Jewish first name of their father. Their family names, however, from Goldberg to Herschl, are pseudonyms foisted upon them. Governments have commanded Jews to have names. Does that make the names their own? If a Jew's name is Nachman and he changes it to Norbert, what else is Norbert but camouflage? Is it anything more than a falsification? Does the chameleon feel any respect for the colours he continually keeps changing? The Jew changes Grünbaum to Greenboom. The shift in the vowels doesn't upset him.[2]

So Ronnie Harwood he became. Boarding the *Edinburgh Castle* on the morning of 7 December 1951, the young man kissed farewell to each of his relations in turn – but not his devoted maid, Annie. Harwood has never forgiven himself for this concession to the social practices of the time. 'It must have broken her heart,' he bitterly sighs. Standing beside her on the quayside, Ronnie's mother looked just as sad. 'I cannot now remember if she waved me goodbye,' he whispers.

As Harwood leaned over the bow of his mighty ship, he clapped eyes for practically the last time on South Africa. Only the sight of his brother pointing ostentatiously to his backside and forearm on the shore threatened to undermine the poignancy of the occasion. The gesture was a reminder of Ralph's oft-repeated judgement upon his youngest sibling: 'The trouble with Ronnie is that he doesn't know his arse from his elbow.' The lonely voyager would have to learn such things fast – for he was about to enter into a larger, fiercer, brave new world.

2

Uncle Lionel

IRENE: Scorpio…
SIR: Good. Ambition, secretiveness, loyalty and capable
of great jealousy. Essential qualities for the theatre.
The Dresser, *Act Two*

Aristotle held that art imitates life. So, too, does Ronnie Harwood. That might be all the famous playwright has in common with the immortal philosopher, but the fact is essential. 'Me, me, me,' he muses cheerfully, '… I cannot help always writing about myself.' To call this vanity would be an over-simplification. For no one who has travelled as far in life as Harwood could fail to make others aware of his experiences. Each of his plays and novels has been torn from a Nessus' shirt of hardship, disappointment and failure.

These semi-autobiographical fragments are most illuminating when they are least obvious. Harwood has never been so blatant as to invent a character who longs for England, only to find himself lost and alone in his adopted homeland. We have instead to consider the case of Leonard Levine, who appears in his 1973 novel *Articles of Faith*. This character wishes to overcome the obstacle of his humble origins to win acclaim as a state prosecutor in Cape Town. He plays his part faultlessly: after racking up legal qualifications and setting up his own practice, he joins the Attorney-General's office, where he quickly establishes himself as one of the most capable lawyers in the colony. Yet, when he falls in love with the daughter of a high-ranking judge, the thrusting young upstart is hurled back into the ghetto. 'You are no longer employed here as of *now!*' yells his boss on hearing that the young lady has fallen pregnant. Once again, Lennie has nothing.

The parallels with Harwood are painfully apparent. Although he kissed the ground when he disembarked from the *Edinburgh Castle* on his arrival at Southampton on Friday 21 December 1951, it was not long before the young South African realized that England was not exactly the country of his dreams. His brief conversations with the gruff officials on the quayside taught him first-hand that the subjects of King George VI were not universally welcoming towards foreigners. For, despite all his training and expectations, this is undoubtedly what Ronnie Harwood was.

He knew only one person in the country. This was Gerald Mosselson's uncle, Lionel Bowman, who came to meet Harwood at Waterloo station that wet December morning. It was the beginning of one of the most important relationships of the future playwright's life; one which would, in time, clear his way into the world of the theatre. Yet few could have predicted that this failed concert pianist, who had himself only recently emigrated to England, had it in him to set the ugly duckling on his way. 'I don't think he ever made any money from his vocation,' opines Harwood, 'nor did it ever cross my mind that I would either.' Worse, by the standards of the time, was the fact that Uncle Lionel was a homosexual, living with another man, Raymond Marriott – an arrangement deemed criminal under English law for a further sixteen years. But Harwood was as yet unaware of Lionel's sexuality. Even his unsqueamish mother could not have broached such a matter with him. 'He's effeminate,' explained Bowman's relations in the Cape. Considering this today, when even senior members of the judiciary can be married to persons of the same sex without comment, the veteran breaks off in bewilderment: 'It was a different world.'

The irresistible question looms: was Harwood tempted to join the gay avant-garde? 'No,' he says firmly. For while his conversation is littered with as many 'my dears' as a vicar's tea party, Harwood has always been exclusively attracted to what the French call *le beau sexe*. 'We in the theatre used to have a way of saying that someone was gay,' he says cheekily. In what the listener assumes to be an unrelated action, Harwood removes his glasses and licks his middle finger. 'He's a nice boy,' he says, as he glides the moistened digit over one of his eyebrows. According to Harwood, many of these homosexual actors themselves preferred to be known as 'queer'. 'It gave them a secret identity,' he explains without condescension. When it came to Lionel Bowman and Raymond Marriott, the young man accordingly presumed little and said less.

It was, however, fortunate that Uncle Lionel lived with another man. Had he been a successful pianist living quietly in the suburbs with a housewife, it is unlikely that the world would have heard any more of Ronnie Harwood. The reason was that R. B. Marriott, as Bowman's partner was professionally known, happened to be the theatre critic for *The Stage*. This meant that Harwood's unofficial guardian was scarcely less knowledgeable about the theatre than his esteemed companion. On their way to the YMCA off the Tottenham Court Road, where Harwood was to be staying, the two men discussed the latest plays. As landmarks such as Nelson's Column flew past, it became apparent that the wide-eyed visitor knew a thing or two about the theatre himself. Suddenly aware of the young man's precocity, Lionel explained with some embarrassment that he and Raymond had booked tickets for them to see a pantomime that evening – *Cinderella*. 'Not what I would have selected,' recalls Harwood haughtily. But it could not be helped. At the end of the show, Raymond tried to make up for the blunder by taking his guest backstage to meet a well-known double act known as the 'Ugly Sisters', Vic Ford and Chris Sheen. Bashfully, the novice explained that he was shortly going for an audition at RADA. 'RADA?' one of the unhandsome pair echoed, '– Oh, la-di-da!' 'La-di-definitely-da!' the other chirped. Humiliated, Ronnie fled.

While *Cinderella* did not overwhelm Harwood, his memories of his first night in the West End remain fresh. 'It was already dark,' he recalls of meeting Lionel and Raymond before the show, 'with the lights of the buses, the taxis and theatres glowing, flaring, sparkling, creating expectation for whatever excitement might lie ahead – like an orchestra tuning up for the overture.' There were not in those days the now-familiar crowds of tourists and pleasure-seekers, and even amid the wreckage of the Blitz few Londoners walked the streets without a collar and tie. Least negligent in these sartorial matters was Harwood, whose mother had firmly instructed him that a tie was the 'respect one paid to a great city.'

But there were signs, too, that the West End was modernising. Only three years previously the first musical, *Oklahoma!*, had been produced by the doyen of theatreland, Hugh 'Binkie' Beaumont – a spectacle considered by one R. B. Marriott of *The Stage* to herald the onset of an 'American invasion'. This deluge, however, was not to come for some years yet. For the time being it was principally the deaths of the two biggest names in the theatre which rocked the West End. The first of these was entirely expected: on 2 November 1950 died George Bernard Shaw at the age of ninety-four. He left behind him a school of followers determined to make the theatre a place of politics and irreverence towards 'the system' and 'the Establishment'. The other playwright to die shortly before Harwood's arrival was Ivor Novello. Although little more than a name today, this multi-talented writer, actor and musician was at the time of his unexpected death, aged fifty-eight, one of the most beloved figures in Britain. By contrast to the intellectual Shaw, his plays and melodramas appealed to the senses, transporting audiences to lost worlds crowded with poignant scenes. This was the school to which Harwood was instinctively drawn.[3]

Novello's last play, *King's Rhapsody*, showed what the public yearned for in those grim years of ration books and austerity. An extravaganza written, composed and also starring Novello, the story concerns a monarch forced to abdicate in favour of his son. Interspersed with music, pageantry and high drama, it was unashamedly entertainment on a massive scale. But to call it frivolous or lightweight would be mistaken: the plot has clear parallels in Shakespearean, to say nothing of Shavian, drama. At the end of the play the ex-king, inevitably played by Novello, steals unobserved into the cathedral in which his son has just been crowned. Broken and alone, he falls to his knees clutching a white rose to his breast.

The applause on the first night of this production was matched only by the deafening silence of the theatre critics. One of these disgusted onlookers was Harold Hobson of the *Sunday Times*. In later years he would remember Novello's last hurrah as a watershed in British theatre. 'The final scene of *King's Rhapsody*', he wrote in 1984, 'gives some idea of what "relevant" drama has released the public from; or, as many would prefer to put it, what it has deprived the public of.' Ronald Harwood unquestionably belongs to the latter camp. This owes almost everything to the time of his entry into the theatre. Had he arrived in London just five or six years later, when *Waiting for Godot*, *Look Back in Anger* and other examples of the 'New Theatre' were all the rage, he might have never known what he was missing. 'There was no subsidised theatre in those days,' recalls Harwood nostalgically: 'If a play did not entertain the public, it failed on the first night.' Even the relatively unsophisticated comedy that he saw on his second day in the capital, Peter Ustinov's *Love of Four Colonels*, had more in common with Homer than it did with the new wave of drama that would shortly sweep the capital.[4]

For the meantime, however, Harwood had more pressing worries: he needed to find somewhere to live. After a few nights at the YMCA, he settled down as a lodger at the home of some of Bowman's friends, a doctor and his wife named Percy and Ethel Helman. While flats such as theirs in Charleville Mansions, West Kensington, now change hands for upwards of two million pounds, neither the neighbourhood nor the living quarters were especially agreeable when Harwood first lugged his trunk up the building's stone staircase. 'It was a rundown Edwardian block,' he recalls unemotionally, 'with cold, oddly-shaped rooms and high ceilings.' Shortly after moving in he handed over his ration book to his hosts and assumed the role of babysitter to their young child. But Harwood remained quietly optimistic. Although confined to a camp-bed in a box room, he had landed on a new and exhilarating planet.

His guides, Lionel and Raymond, could not have been more ideal. Shepherded by these bohemians, he was introduced to a *demi-monde* which was, even then, passing into history. In the pubs and cafes of Soho – 'raffish rather than offensive as it later became' – Harwood saw the lingering vestiges of the society of Evelyn Waugh and the Roaring Twenties. Propped against stinking bars and mouldy wall-paper, these glassy-eyed men and women, badly dressed and always clumsily made up, waited to be bought drinks by the likes of Lionel and Raymond. Ronnie was never excluded. On one famous occasion at The Salisbury public house in St Martin's Lane he recalls Raymond telling him that Dylan Thomas was downstairs in the gents, covered in his own vomit. Did he wish to be introduced? Aside from being ignorant of this 'greatest of living poets', the prissy youth instinctively held back. 'I don't really regret it,' he winces. A few months later Thomas was dead.

But Harwood did agree to meet a more agreeable jewel in the crown of the London underworld. This was the so-called Queen of Bohemia, Nina Hamnett. Although by then wrinkled and grey-haired, she retained much of the charm and allure which had, in former years, brought her into the circles of Amedeo Modigliani, Walter Sickert, Roger Fry and Augustus John. 'She flirted outrageously,' recalls Harwood of their conversation at the Fitzroy Tavern, 'and was entertained by my embarrassment.' Unused to the full, frank attention of a woman, the young man felt, for the first time, his energy and enthusiasm to be overwhelmed by another personality. Sadly, however, Nina was shortly to follow her friend Dylan Thomas to the grave. On 16 December 1956 she threw herself onto the railings outside her London home and died in agony. No one is sure if it was suicide, but her last words were, 'Why won't they let me die?'

Surrounded by such drama, Harwood's interview at RADA the following January was slightly anticlimactic. After a few weeks of coaching from Miss Vivienne Guignard in Westbourne Grove, he made his way to the famous building in Gower Street where, he hoped, destiny awaited him. Harwood recalls the ordeal as though it were yesterday. It began inauspiciously with the sight of a young Scot with a broken nose and an incredibly small mouth – a fellow hopeful, clearly. This was Ronald Fraser, later to become famous as an actor specializing in pugnacity and pomposity. The pair uttered few words before the Scotsman was ushered away for his audition. Harwood waited for what felt like an eternity. When Fraser finally returned he was followed back into the waiting room by a tall stranger. 'Mr Fraser?' this character announced in a glorious velvet brown monotone, 'Would you please come back a moment?' Obediently, the young man disappeared again. Harwood craned his neck to see what was happening through the half-closed door. What he saw startled and alarmed him. Taking Fraser's head into his hands as though he were about to kiss him, the man said, 'Please would you open your mouth?' The tiny slit above Fraser's chin expanded a milometer. 'Wider,' the clipped voice commanded. But the slither barely dilated. 'Extraordinary,' the man continued before hurrying back into the audition room. A moment later young Harwood was called thither.

He was confronted by a silhouetted group of people illuminated by the occasional glow of a cigarette – 'like a Rembrandt painting in need of cleaning,' he reflects. Behind them were poised a collection of stage lights directed at the space in which Harwood hoped to work his magic. For his Shakespeare he had selected Hamlet's soliloquy, 'O, what a rogue and peasant slave am I!'; for his modern piece, he had plumped for the equally brooding *The Journey of the Magi* by T. S. Eliot. The audition, though, did not go especially well. Whatever Harwood had imagined he sounded like under the direction of Mrs Marks back in Cape Town, to the refined ears of RADA the young man sounded offensively guttural. This was compounded by something even more alarming – a faint lisp, of which he had scarcely been conscious. At the end of his soliloquy there was an unmistakable sound of laughter – slow, monosyllabic and superior: 'hoh – hoh – hoh'. The forecast was not good.

But Harwood remained as sure of himself as ever. His fellow applicant, Ronald Fraser, would never forget his new friend's triumphant account of his recital. Over a pint of beer at a local pub after their auditions, the young South African began outlining grandiose plans for his career at RADA: the plays he would be in, the classes he most wished to take, and so forth. Fraser, meanwhile, felt as bad inside as he looked from the outside. His audition, he confessed, had been a disaster. As the pair departed, Harwood implored Fraser not to feel too downcast – there were, after all, other careers. Needless to mention, when the pair next met, Fraser had been admitted to RADA; Harwood had not.

This is where the embryonic playwright showed his true worth. Sure that his future remained in the theatre, he enrolled at RADA's preparatory school, PARADA, in Highgate. For two terms he underwent intensive training to obliterate whatever remained of his South African accent. It was a success. By the end of this process he was proud to be told that he spoke like an undertaker. But, as there were few parts for undertakers, Harwood went the extra mile by perfecting the certified RADA accent. His efforts were rewarded when the theatrical director of PARADA, Richard ('Dicky') Scott, cast him as the lead role in a student production of Noël Coward's 1942 play, *Present Laughter*. The character, Garry Essendine, had been created for the stylish playwright himself, and Harwood reflects that he took to the role of the dapper English gentleman like a duck to water. By the autumn of 1952 he was among the greats at RADA.

The president of the college, Sir Kenneth Barnes, had been born in 1878. After an undistinguished career as an actor and journalist, he was appointed head of RADA in 1909 and set about transforming it from a small school for young actors into the leading centre for theatrical training in the world. The year of Harwood's entry proved to be the last of Sir Kenneth's long reign. This was more than slightly unfortunate for the would-be theatre star. 'It was the last year in this history of RADA,' explains Harwood somewhat bitterly, 'in which Received English was obligatory – had I entered just one year later my South African accent would have been treated as a great asset.' In the event, Harwood recalls spending most of his time at RADA perfecting his pronunciation with the voice coach, Clifford Turner, whom he had first encountered inspecting Ronald Fraser's mouth. He was also the shady figure who had broken out in staccato laughter at the end of his audition. The pair soon became great friends.

On his first day at RADA Harwood and the other new boys and girls were treated to a welcome speech from Sir Kenneth himself. 'The most important thing in acting,' he solemnly pronounced, 'is to become familiar with each other's parts.' There was a sound of stifled laughter as young Harwood cast a mischievous eye around the auditorium. 'We took his advice enthusiastically,' he beams, '– if not always in the way he intended.' Outnumbered by females by almost two to one, Harwood and the other young men were given ample opportunity to play the role of Lothario both on the stage and off. 'I ran riot,' he reminisces delightedly. Handsome and garrulous, he enjoyed a series of tempestuous romances – but not, to his great regret, with the one girl at RADA who went on to make it big in the movies, Belinda Lee. Famous in the late 1950s and early 1960s for playing sultry temptresses, Lee was far and away the most beautiful woman Harwood had ever known. 'I fell in love with her,' he sighs, 'but, alas, she was not aware of it.' After a controversial love affair with a high-ranking Vatican official, Prince Filippo Orsini, she was killed in a car crash in Los Angeles in 1961, aged just twenty-six.

'We were a pretty undistinguished bunch,' recalls Harwood of the rest of that year's intake. This is perhaps an overly-harsh judgement on the likes of Keith Baxter, who co-starred with Elizabeth Taylor in *Ash Wednesday* (1973), and Sylvia Syms, who went on to appear in over forty films, including *The Queen* (2006). But there were certainly no future Oliviers or Ashcrofts at RADA that year. Least likely of all to join this pantheon was Harwood. 'I was a lousy actor,' he calmly explains, 'but I stuck at it, and that is always half the battle in life.' What defined his performances was their unrestrained exuberance, particularly his Petruchio in the academy's 1953 production of *The Taming of the Shrew*. Although his acting coach, Nell Carter, regretted this 'tendency to over-elaborate his performances', she believed that he could make it if he persisted. 'He has considerable talent,' she wrote in his final report, 'plenty of vitality and keen humour.'[5]

Such a mild endorsement was enough to convince Harwood that he could, in time, take to the stage as a professional. Contrasting this blind determination with the attitude of the drama students who tell him today that their greatest ambition in life is to star in a soap opera and have a regular income, Harwood laments the passing of grit in the theatre. 'To find work in the theatre for work's sake was the driving force,' he continues with a shake of his fist, '– but how ridiculously old-fashioned and pompous does that sound now?'

One student who shared Harwood's commitment to walk the boards was his greatest friend at RADA, Robin Ray. The son of one of the most famous comedians of the time, Ted Ray of *Ray's a Laugh*, he was noticeably the most well-dressed and affluent of all the students at the academy. 'His clothes even in those days came from Harrods,' recalls Harwood of the future star of panel shows such as *Call My Bluff* and *Face the Music*. Short and slender, with a boyish charm and bravura which thrilled the young South African, they became inseparable companions. 'He was wonderfully generous,' continues the proud playwright, 'and used to take me to see lots of shows.' These ranged from theatrical outings in the West End to Ronald Strong's public séances at the Wigmore Hall. But what the two friends most enjoyed were the classical concerts which were held at this venue during the week. Harwood's first taste of orchestral music had been in Cape Town, where he had been mesmerized by a warped recording of Mozart's famous G Minor symphony played on his sister's gramophone. Ray's knowledge of the classical repertoire was undoubtedly more sophisticated than his companion's, but the future playwright, as ever, proved to be an extremely retentive pupil. After being taken by his moneyed friend to hear a recital by Benedetti Michelangeli – a new name for Harwood – the budding musicologist discerned a slight tremor in the virtuoso's left hand. 'He did become ill,' remarks the octogenarian with a little satisfaction, 'stopped playing for a while, but thankfully returned in later years to the concert platform.'

As RADA students, Harwood and Ray also went to see many plays. 'The West End glittered with stars,' recalls the playwright happily. Notable performances by Katharine Hepburn and Robert Helpmann in Bernard Shaw's *The Millionairess* and Rex Harrison in *Bell, Book and Candle* remain vivid. But by far the most dazzling of all these greats was John Gielgud.

His acclaimed Leontes in *The Winter's Tale* gave the student-actor his first experience of Shakespeare performed on the stage by a master. 'Gielgud's genius for exploring the architecture of Shakespearean verse,' he explains with the insight of experience, 'his faultless phrasing and preference for the music of the words was a revelation.' At the end of many of these displays of theatrical verisimilitude, Harwood would wait by the stage door to catch a glimpse of his hero disappearing into the night with his hat tilted at a rakish angle. Did he ever ask for an autograph? 'Certainly not,' he says disdainfully: 'I was not a "fan" – I wished to be a part of it all.'

But without Gielgud's privileged background, it was hard to imagine how Harwood could scale the dizzying ladder of the West End. So short of funds was the young fantasist that he soon began working at the Lyon's Corner House on the Strand. In the days before extensive employment legislation, Harwood would begin his shift at 10 p.m. and work through the night until 4 a.m., when he would hurry home for a few hours of sleep. 'Most of the customers,' he recalls, 'looked as if they were criminals having something to eat either before or after doing a job.' Harwood's co-workers were no less offensive to the debonair bottle-washer. One of these individuals particularly stands out in his memory. 'He was round and bald with rouge on his cheeks,' he cringes, 'and wore open sandals, toenails painted blood red.' Early one morning, just before finishing, this character appeared in the kitchen in a state of great agitation. 'What's up?' asked Ronnie. It transpired that a customer had pinched his bottom. 'I may be bohemian,' continued this rather camp Cockney, 'but I'm not a fourpenny-fuck!'

Two memories of the theatre in these years are especially precious to Harwood. The first was the evening he found himself in the same audience as Noël Coward. 'There was a discernible hush,' he remembers, 'as he chatted with his friends in the stalls – there he was; and me, breathing the same atmosphere – it was exhilarating.' Of scarcely less importance was the occasion upon which Harwood was in the theatre with the prime minister, Sir Winston Churchill. 'The moment the play began,' he chuckles, 'Churchill's sonorous tones could be heard saying the lines not so *sotto voce* with the actors.' The former war leader was apparently reading from his own text of *Romeo and Juliet*, but was not aware of the cuts made for that particular production. 'When the curtain descended on the first part of the play,' continues Harwood excitedly, 'he was still reciting lines from the previous scene.' At the close of the final act, Harwood and a band of fellow-admirers rushed down to see Churchill depart. 'He paused to light his cigar,' he beams, 'waved, smiled and gave us his V-sign before climbing into his car.' The young man then scampered off to Lyon's Corner House to start his shift.

Life, then, was going tolerably well for Harwood. But towards the end of 1952 came a bombshell. His mother wrote to inform him that she was no longer able to manage his fees at RADA – £21 per year. He would either have to find a better-paid job or, more likely, arrange a berth back to Cape Town. Once again, however, Harwood's *chutzpah* intervened to solve the problem. For it so happened that in one of his last ever classes at RADA he met an actor named Joseph O'Conor. The guest mentioned, a little boastfully, that he was a great friend of the famous actor-manager Donald Wolfit. This gave Harwood an idea. At the end of the session he sidled up to O'Conor and explained his circumstances. Would he mind if he wrote to Wolfit using his name? Predictably O'Conor prevaricated, but the young actor nevertheless wrote to Wolfit mentioning his new friend, he recalls, 'a little more forcibly than I should have done.' Eagerly the bold supplicant awaited Wolfit's reply.

A romantic such as Harwood might have imagined that this was all it took to secure a job in the theatre. Alas, things were not so easy. From a grubby office somewhere above a provincial playhouse, Wolfit sent back a little card informing the young hopeful that his company was already fully cast. Crushed, Harwood went for dinner with his theatrical mentors to tell them that he had received his first letter of rejection. 'You fool!' responded Raymond sympathetically, 'I know Wolfit very well, and I'll write to him for you.' Now this was a development. Only a few words murmured under Uncle Lionel's breath portended future malaise – 'But the trouble is Wolfit's mad.'

3

'Clean My Boots!'

'What do we play tomorrow, Norman?' I told him King Lear *and he said,*
'Then I shall wake with the storm clouds in my head.'
The Dresser, *Act One*

A noted Viennese psychologist once suggested that, alongside killing one parent and sleeping with the other, all real men seek a father substitute. For the future Sir Ronald Harwood this person was unquestionably Sir Donald Wolfit. Virtuoso, tyrant, maverick, bully, genius, Wolfit was the last of the great Victorian over-actors. An outsider in the twentieth century, he took his acting style from mentors such as Fred Terry and, indirectly at least, the great Sir Henry Irving himself. Whenever he passed between the wings and the stage he expected a rapturous applause – an effect he sometimes encouraged with a light pat of his own hands. Since he disliked sharing the limelight with anyone, he only ever worked with actors of lesser quality than himself. And it was taken as a matter of course in his theatre company that the best costumes and brightest spotlights would be reserved for him alone. All this was not simply because Wolfit was inordinately vain: it was also because he believed drama to depend entirely on the brilliance of the star performer. *'Le theatre,'* ran his unofficial tag line – *'c'est moi!'*

Harwood was told to present himself for his interview with Wolfit at 3 p.m. at the Waldorf Hotel, Aldwych, on Sunday 7 December 1952 – a year to the day since his departure from South Africa. The weather that afternoon was particularly bad: a thick 'pea-souper' weighed down on the capital, making it impossible to see more than a few feet ahead. It was the first time Harwood had experienced this unpleasant phenomenon, but he revelled in it. 'This was the London of my imagination,' he recalls, 'the London of Sherlock Holmes,

Jack the Ripper and Fagin.' Through the sickly haze, wearing his only suit and ill-repaired shoes, young Harwood hurried to his destination.

His eagerness was clear from his arrival at the Waldorf Hotel a full hour before his interview. While he sat nervously in the entrance hall, he took in his palatial surroundings: marble floors, smartly attired concierge, and important-looking guests sweeping in and out of the revolving doors. This was where he wanted to be. Scarcely had Harwood's socks dried, however, than he saw a dark young man bound down the staircase and embrace a lithe redhead. 'I've got it! I've got it!' he yelped. This, Harwood soon discovered, was Harold Pinter. 'My initial impression of him,' says Harwood, 'was how handsome he was.' Also present at the auditions, it transpired, was John Osborne – the only one of the future playwrights not taken on by Wolfit that day.

When Harwood was finally called for his audience with the famous actor, he found himself in the presence of what he took to be an extremely tall man wearing striped trousers and a frock-coat – evidently, imagined Harwood, the usual attire of an actor-manager. Both these impressions were completely mistaken. Not only was Wolfit only 5'8" (the exact height of Harwood), his formal dress betokened nothing more than the fact that he had been at a memorial service that morning. Yet Wolfit carried off his part no less brilliantly than he did upon the stage. 'He exuded a brute strength,' says Harwood as though still locked in the actor's gaze, 'and looked out from heavy eyebrows in a way that made his mood unpredictable.' Beside him there sat an extremely dignified gentleman – 'no other words to describe him,' rattles off Harwood – who might have been a High Court judge or an archbishop. 'This is Mr Llewellyn Rees, my administrator,' said Mr Wolfit in the hushed tone that Harwood would later recognize as the one he reserved for times when he wished to impress. There was a brief pause while Wolfit read the letter he had received from Raymond Marriott. Handing this document to Mr Rees with a nod, he said in one breath to the dishevelled applicant: 'I can pull you into the crowd, thirty shillings a week, student rate, the season begins in February, goodbye.' The most important interview of Harwood's entire career was over.

Optimistic to a fault, Harwood had not yet mentioned his parlous financial circumstances to RADA. 'Micawber-like,' he continues cheerily, 'I hoped something might turn up.' But not even a job with Wolfit was enough to save him: as he was well aware, student-actors were expressly forbidden from working in the theatre. For this reason, Harwood soon arranged an interview between himself and Sir Kenneth Barnes to explain his situation. Was there, he asked, any chance of obtaining a scholarship to stay at RADA? Sir Kenneth looked grave. No, there was not. So that decided it. Ronnie would leave RADA for Donald Wolfit.

In later years this action would help make Harwood one of Sir Donald's favourites. Having himself risen in the profession without the assistance of RADA, his parents or even his fellow actors, Wolfit delighted in his reputation as a lone wolf. Fanatically conservative, he was prominent in an association known as the Society for Individual Freedom. But what most endeared Harwood to the last great Shakespearean actor-manager occurred shortly after the young man's decision to break with RADA. Concerned that he had not heard anything more about his engagement in mid-January, the intrepid youth obtained Wolfit's home telephone number and gave him a call. 'He did not seem pleased,' recounts Harwood bashfully, 'and said somewhat brusquely that I should attend at the King's Theatre for the last week of rehearsals at the end of January.' Years later Wolfit would explain that this daring action had reminded him of his own youthful impertinence when he had entered the theatre in the early 1920s.

Wolfit's programme at the King's Theatre, Hammersmith, in Coronation Year was of a measure with Harwood's wild audacity. As well as facing stiff competition from the all-powerful theatre company of Hugh 'Binkie' Beaumont – which was producing a season of Shakespeare with John Gielgud and Paul Scofield just a quarter of a mile away at the Lyric – Wolfit decided to take on more parts than a Tolstoy novel. Committed to giving a matinee and an evening performance (often of a different play) six days a week, it was a recipe for financial and physical exhaustion. Even with Wolfit's long experience of touring provincial England as Hamlet, Macbeth, King Richard III and all the other great parts of Shakespeare, this was a new kind of strain. The plays he selected for the King's Theatre were not even part of his usual repertory. He began with a double bill of Oedipus – *Oedipus the King* and *Oedipus in Exile* – which was the first time both of these plays of Sophocles had been played back-to-back by a major company. In the second part of his residency he revived *The Wandering Jew* by E. Temple Thurston, before trying to draw in yet larger audiences with a run of *School for Scandal* and *Henry IV, Part 1*. And throughout all these scene changes, Wolfit continued to appeal to his hinterland with frequent performances of his signature role – King Lear.[6]

It was in connection with *King Lear* that young Harwood first came to Wolfit's attention. The storm scene had long proved difficult to engineer in the surroundings of a modest West London theatre. A troupe of zealous theatre-hands had been told to simulate thunder with a variety of contraptions including a giant steel sheet. After a few performances conducted in this way, Wolfit summoned the storm-makers to indicate his displeasure. In an almost unheard of act of defiance, one of these individuals declared that it was impossible to provide any more noise – if he shook that steel sheet any harder he would cut himself in two. Wolfit looked aghast. 'I see,' he said at last, '– not man enough.' In the aftermath of this denouement, a technician mentioned that there was an old water tank in the basement which might be employed in some capacity. A coffee break was taken while this contraption was suspended from one of the high beams over the stage. 'Harwood!' barked Wolfit to one of the bystanders, 'Get up there and see if you can give us some thunder.'

And did he. At the performance that evening Harwood beat that tank with a sawn off broom-handle as though his life depended on it. Taking Wolfit's advice of placing his head inside the tank and beating the sides with all his might, Harwood became almost delirious. 'Encased in the water tank,' he recalls, 'besieged by wave upon wave of reverberating sound, I lost all sense of time and space.' Yet his efforts did not go unacknowledged. After the performance the great man approached him. 'The storm, my boy,' he said: 'very fine tonight.' 'Thank you, Sir,' responded Harwood as meekly as he could muster. Wolfit continued nodding, 'as though Lear had palsy', before saying rather regretfully: 'You're an artist.' Overcome with self-satisfaction, Ronnie melted.

The young man had every reason to. After all, 'Sir' – as Wolfit was known long before receiving his knighthood in 1957 – was not exactly a flatterer. Not, at least, to those subordinate to him in the theatre. The stories of him losing his rag were legion. Even on stage he could display his ferocious pique: anyone fool enough to cast a shadow upon him would be liable to be struck in the face by a projectile (usually a cherry stone) fired through Wolfit's pursed lips. But in cases in which the miscreant was suitably contrite, Sir was not without a certain imperial magnanimity. On one occasion, Harwood recalls a young stage manager on her knees pleading for forgiveness – she had inadvertently misplaced a vital prop. At length, Sir raised his hand and said, 'I absolve you.'

An even more classic example of Wolfit's grand manner involved the actor Sir Lewis Casson, who briefly joined Wolfit's company during the King's Theatre season. 'Tell Sir Lewis I want to see him!' he screamed to a crowd of assistants: 'His wig join is a disgrace!' A stickler for theatrical hierarchy, Wolfit instantly gave a look of unease. He had inadvertently committed himself to delivering a reprimand to one of the actor-knights he so worshipped. How to get out of it? Remembering that Sir Lewis professed to hold left-wing sympathies, and that a certain Soviet premier had recently died, Wolfit corrected himself: 'No, no,' he said gravely: 'it's too soon after Stalin's death.'

For all that, Wolfit's season at the King's Theatre got off to a flying start. 'NOW WOLFIT HAS GOT THAT WEST END GLAMOUR', boomed a banner headline in the *Daily Express*. Equally gratifying was the headline in the *Star*: 'West [London] may have own "Old Vic"'. Smart limousines were reported to be fighting for parking spaces in the area, while large groups from the provinces – a nice reversal for Wolfit – were said to be descending on the capital. The upshot was that Wolfit's season promised to be a modest financial success: advance bookings topped £3,000, and every night the packed 650-seat theatre reverberated with cries of, 'Donald! Donald!'

But there were signs, too, that all was not well with Sir. It had long been a vital part of his act to appear at the curtain call, often in evening dress, to milk his applause in the guise of a bashful invalid. At the King's Theatre, however, Wolfit actually began to look dangerously ill. Harwood particularly remembers a party of ladies remonstrating with the cashier at the box office: they had just seen the veteran actor hobble onto the stage after the matinee of *King Lear* and were certain that he could not re-emerge later that evening as King Oedipus.

But Sir never let his audience down. It was this unconquerable dedication to the theatre which most inspired the young man who was soon invited to become his dresser. Audiences of *The Dresser* and readers of Harwood's equally poignant biography of Wolfit need not be reminded whom this devotee happened to be. But the aged dramatist likes to point out that his portrayal of 'Sir's' dresser – the camp and motherly Norman – is not at all a self-portrait. 'He was based on Paul Scofield's dresser,' he explains somewhat grumpily, '– and even the character of "Sir" is only partly based on Wolfit.'

True though this may be for Harwood, *The Dresser* evokes the setting, feel and dynamic of Wolfit's company almost exactly. Adoring and protective, the young man was the only member of the company who truly loved Sir – and equally wished to be loved by him. Unlike Harold Pinter, who could not abide the faded star's prejudice and conceit, young Harwood relished playing the role Jacob to their theatrical Abraham. When he later caricatured his famous contemporary as the intellectual Oxenby in *The Dresser*, there was some worry in theatrical circles that Pinter would be enraged. 'Oh, he found it very funny,' grins Harwood. 'Well,' he goes on modestly, 'he never told me that – but I'm told he was amused. … "Damn good play," he once told me after a production.'

What gave Harwood's evocation of Wolfit such power was his decision to set the play not at the time in which he had actually worked for him, but during the hard years of the Second World War. It was a fitting metaphor for both men's lifelong battle against what they have perceived to be the dark forces threatening them and their world. In one scene 'Sir' shakes his fist at the Luftwaffe overhead and cries: 'Bomb, bomb, bomb us into oblivion if you dare, but each word I speak will be a shield against your savagery, each line I utter protection from your terror.' The real Wolfit had, similarly, defied the authorities during the war to lay on special morale-boosting productions of Shakespeare at a time when the theatres were closed by government decree. 'Sir's' over-familiarity with some of the female members of his company might also be said to be art imitating life. It was by nurturing on-stage, to say nothing of backstage, chemistry with his leading lady, Rosalind Iden, that Wolfit wooed his third wife. She was to become a force in Wolfit's company second only to Sir himself.

That, however, is probably as far as the parallel can be stretched. For Harwood is adamant that he in no regard resented his servitude. Completely sharing his fictional self's desire for everything to be 'lovely and painless', he could never have subscribed to the play's most bitter line, delivered by Norman over his master's mortal remains:

> Speak well of that old sod? I wouldn't give him a good character, not in a court of law. Ungrateful bastard.

Nor was there even a hint of homosexual tension between Harwood and his idol. 'He loved me,' he explains unblinkingly, '… [but] his dislike of homosexuals was deep-rooted.' To highlight this point, Harwood recalls an occasion when a gay actor was brought into the company at short notice. Wolfit, waiting in the wings extravagantly made-up as Shylock, heard the young man speaking with a tell-tale lisp. 'Jo,' murmured the improbable merchant to an attendant, 'we've got a nancy in the company.' When it was later pointed out that another one of his actors, for whom he had great admiration, was also this way inclined, Wolfit replied simply: 'Yes, but he's quite harmless.'

As Sir's dresser, it was Harwood's role to perform all the little rituals to which the veteran actor-manager had become accustomed over the years. Besides putting on his costumes and attending to his make-up, the young man was also expected to carry about a silver salver upon which he placed a small bunch of peeled grapes, a glass or two of Guinness and a small leather strap with which Sir used to wipe his brow. The amount of Guinness always depended on the performance in question: 'Lear demanded most,' chuckles Harwood, 'Touchstone least.' Sometimes this habit could lead to embarrassment. Once, shortly after the King's season, when they were performing at the Church Hall, Edinburgh, the Father Superior paid a visit backstage to meet the famous actor. 'Hide the Guinness!' bellowed Wolfit. But it was no use. Although Harwood dutifully placed the offending receptacles beneath one of the loaded trestle tables, Father James Christie knew his drink. Upon entering the room he sniffed the air and declared cheerfully, 'Ah, Guinness!' Reluctantly, the introverted showman ordered his dresser to pour out two small measures of the beverage.

More often, however, Harwood's duties were not so agreeable. Bent over a basin for long periods of the day, washing Sir's underwear and other personal garments, the young man was something of a theatrical Cinderella. The sole benefit of this was that he had plenty of time for daydreaming. Still eager to make it upon the stage, he envisaged one day becoming an actor of comparable stature to Wolfit or his great adversary, Sir Laurence Olivier, whose *Hamlet* had so long ago kindled his enthusiasm. But to call these theatrical titans rivals would certainly be to flatter Wolfit: the actress Hermione Gingold jibed that 'Olivier is a *tour de force* and Wolfit is forced to tour.' It may be guessed, then, how Wolfit responded to hearing that his young dresser had arrived late for work one evening for no better reason than that he had been to see Olivier playing Macbeth at Stratford. 'Was it good?' the wounded diva huffed. 'It was…', stammered his awestruck assistant, '… *sublime*.' Wolfit's eyes narrowed: 'Clean my boots!' he snapped.

It was in other respects unfortunate that Harwood entered Wolfit's camp just as his career lurched towards its final curtain. This eventuality was hurried on by the older man's understandable, but undoubtedly ill-judged, decision to extend his season at the King's Theatre. His choice of plays proved inferior to his acting ability. The first flop was *The Wandering Jew*, in which the young Harold Pinter made a cameo in the final scene carrying a cross past a window. After a few weeks of this execrable production, the company reverted to the usual repertory. But Wolfit could not summon the ancient fire that Harwood so admired. Disastrous productions of *School for Scandal*, *Henry IV* and, finally, *The Clandestine Marriage*, sealed his fate. 'The days of the Shakespearean actor-manager,' sighs Harwood wistfully, 'were finally over.' On 31 October 1953 the tottering giant played Lear for the very last time. Two months later he was to reappear elsewhere – but this time as Captain Hook in *Peter Pan*.

The *coup de grace* for Wolfit's acting career was delivered by the influential young critic Kenneth Tynan. Writing in his weekly column in *The Observer*, this herald of the new theatrical age jibed that Wolfit's performance in *The Wandering Jew* was as threadbare as his costumes. These included, he alleged, 'a faded horse-blanket', 'a bath robe', 'a tea cosy', and 'an inverted galvanised iron bucket with two holes knocked in it.' But he reserved his most feline comments for the final scene, in which the Wandering Jew is burnt at the stake: it was, quipped Tynan, 'like the annual roasting of an ox on Shakespeare's birthday at Stratford.' When Wolfit attempted a comeback after his brief fling with pantomime, the Oxford-educated dramaturge delivered an even crueller blow. 'The play needs Olivier,' he wrote of a revival of two works by Henry de Montherlant. 'Mr Wolfit,' he concluded, 'is not really the actor for Malatesta, whose kaleidoscopic mind he reduces to a few bold and primary colours.'

That, to all intents and purposes, was that. Wolfit passed out the last few years of his working life in a state of semi-retirement. Although his acting style was generally deemed too intense for the cinema, he starred in a few British films, including *Becket, Svengali,* and *Blood of the Vampire,* in which he was perfectly cast – though not entirely to his liking – as a grotesque Dracula-figure. In between these well-remunerated diversions, he would occasionally hit the road again with the remnants of his company, appearing in off-beat productions such as *The Strong are Lonely* by Fritz Hochwälder at the newly-established Edinburgh Festival in 1956. Despite securing an unexpectedly sympathetic review in the *Sunday Times* from Harold Hobson – a rare accolade for a play yet to reach London – the comeback was tantalizingly short-lived. A few weeks after excitedly finding himself stationed in a dressing room with an en-suite bathroom at the Theatre Royal, Haymarket, Wolfit once again found himself gazing down at row upon row of upturned seats. With the production's failure, the outplayed old actor fittingly disappeared into manly obscurity.

Harwood experienced these disasters at first hand. As the wheels came off the Wolfit bandwagon, Sir was in need of a new business manager. 'When he found out that I was Jewish,' he recalls, 'he delegated this role to me.' This developement – which Harwood insists not to have betokened anti-Semitism – instigated an entirely new facet of the young actor's personality. To his delight, he discovered that whatever his older brother's doubts about his *savoir faire,* he could be remarkably organized and diligent. Under his direction, the company's decline was temporarily halted, but there were forces at work beyond the control of the untested twenty-year-old. One gets a picture of the financial difficulties besetting the company from Wolfit's insistence that fresh apples be omitted from a scene in which a character enjoys a picnic. 'Three and six a week on apples!' he thundered at Harwood over the ledgers:

call it four shillings – that's sixteen shillings a month – call it a
pound – that's three pounds a quarter – call it five: twenty pounds
a year on apples!

Other instances of Wolfit's rigorous economies included his preference for
only using the notepaper provided at his club, and the care with which he
steamed off unfranked stamps. Towards the end of his life, however, this
apparent miserliness would pay off. Complimented on the size of his estate
by his proud disciple, the great man remarked coolly: 'Yes, not bad for a
touring mummer.'

Harwood's financial position was not nearly so satisfactory. Paid well
below the Equity minimum wage as Wolfit's dresser, bookkeeper and map-
carrier, the aspiring actor found temporary lodgings all over West London
before finally settling in a damp set of rooms in Airlie Gardens, a stone's
throw from the flat where he had stayed on his arrival in the capital. He was
joined on this grimy odyssey by his old friend from South Africa, Gerald
Mosselson (now anglicized to Masters), who had come to London with hopes
of becoming a writer. Already something of a veteran, Harwood eagerly took
up the role of sage and mentor to his young compatriot, suggesting works
of literature and theatrical productions for his edification. Though this was
gratefully appreciated by the newcomer, Masters could be forgiven for finding
his friend's infectious enthusiasm a little enervating at times. 'Ronnie was
always completely certain that he would succeed as an actor,' recalls Masters:
'I, however, soon discovered that progress in the literary world was not quite
as easy as he seemed to suggest.' Determind that he would not become the
familiar pessimist formed through prolonged association with an optimist,
Masters remained convinced that his old companion would, somehow,
triumph in the end.

To tide them over during the off-season, the young bohemians took a
variety of low-paid jobs, including a stint in the kitchens of the long-defunct
St Charles' hospital in Ladbroke Grove. Did Harwood consider this work to

be beneath him? 'No,' he says after a slight pause, 'I accepted the work as part of being a young actor – it was only the other people I couldn't stand.' Most offensive of all to his refined sensibilities was an Irishman whose method of buttering bread was to bring each slice into rough contact with the contents of the packet. So desperate was Harwood to escape from this man's company that he had himself transferred to the 'diet kitchen' where the staff were more genteel and the utensils more homely. Another little trick devised by the enterprising potato-peelers was to appear for work each day dressed in suits rather than the grubby overalls of the other kitchen staff. Assumed by the security guards to be doctors, they found that they could easily leave in the evening with their briefcases loaded with whatever delicacies they could purloin. This, as well as their liberal supply of lightly-taxed cigarettes, helped them through even the bleakest of winters.

All that Harwood wanted for was a girlfriend. He eventually found one in the person of a young actress named Gillian Raine. Considerably wealthier than most of the other members of Wolfit's company, she lived in a small flat in Nell Gwyn House, Sloane Street. The liaison did not, however, please Harwood's mother, who was shortly to appear in the capital styled, touchingly, as Bella Harwood. As well as being 'out' (non-Jewish), Gillian was also nearly a decade older than her infatuated young boyfriend. 'I was mad about her,' he recalls with some regret, 'and we had a very happy time together.' Alas, it soon turned out that Gillian had met another young man while touring the provinces with a different theatre company. 'It was crushing,' laments the octogenarian, 'as it was the first time in my life I had ever experienced rejection.'

Harwood responded with a full-scale nervous breakdown. Worsened by the monumental strain of work to which he had subjected himself, he spent several weeks delirious with grief. Even sixty years later he remembers his feelings of anger and emptiness as he stood on the rain-splattered pavement gazing up at Gillian's flat, alive with gaiety and buzz – but without him. So serious was the crisis that it was not long before it came to Wolfit's attention.

Act Two:

A STAR IS BORN

4

Early Magic

Never, never despairing. Well. Perhaps. Sometimes. At night. Or at Christmas
when you can't get a panto.
The Dresser, *Act Two*

It was during the filming of his 2001 adaptation of his play *Taking Sides* that Harwood first dreamt of leading a full orchestra. 'What could be better,' he muses, 'than commanding a hundred or so people with a little wooden baton?' Not for a moment did the seasoned playwright worry that his addiction to classical music might not avail him in this untried specialism. After being promised temporary control of a famous ensemble a few years later, he began taking lessons. 'I wasn't too bad,' he says with feigned surprise, 'but sadly never got the chance to have a go with a professional orchestra.'

Such forwardness was hardly a new departure for Harwood: for over sixty years it has been the hallmark of his career. Whatever the task, whatever the challenge, whatever the situation, he has always been more than willing to 'have a go'. And never more spectacularly than the famous occasion at the Grand Theatre, Blackpool, when he volunteered to dance the role of von Rothbart at a Saturday matinee of *Swan Lake*.

'I realize this memorable performance of mine may require some further explanation,' sighs Harwood in reverie. 'It was off-season in 1954; I was flat broke, and needed to come up with something fast to avoid being made homeless.' The man he turned to was Wolfit's administrator, Llewellyn Rees, who had proved to be far gentler and more affable than his stern demeanour at Harwood's first interview had portended. 'Lulu and I saw a lot of each other,' continues Harwood happily, 'and whenever he could he helped me to find work.' After initially securing him a job as delivery-driver for the Carl

Rosa Opera Company, Rees mentioned that a friend of his named George Kirsta was in the process of setting up a touring ballet company to which he was to serve as administrator. He suggested that the struggling actor apply to become its stage manager.

Harwood scraped together the necessary Tube fare to meet Kirsta at his rented studio near the Tottenham Court Road. Although his sister Evvy had given the young man some exposure to the ballet as a child, this was the first time that Harwood had been allowed into the ballerinas' inner sanctum. Through a door marked 'BALLET COMIQUE – NO ADMITTANCE', he was confronted by the sight of twenty or so lithe young women performing their *battements frappés* to the accompaniment of Schubert's *Rosamunde*. 'I gaped and gaped,' recalls the dramatist, '– Oh, God, those legs!' But before the visitor could fully drink in this wondrous vision, their gatekeeper, Mr Kirsta, demanded a quiet word in his paper-strewn office. 'So you wish to be stage manager of Ballet Comique,' he said in heavily accented Slavic tones. 'I have just two questions. What star sign are you?' The supplicant cautiously offered, 'Scorpio.' 'Good, good,' the old man nodded. There was an interminable silence, and then: 'Are you a homosexual?' There was another deafening pause – 'I wanted the job badly,' recollects Harwood dryly, 'but decided the price might be too high.' 'No,' he said, meeting his companion's gaze manfully. Kirsta closed his eyes and replied, 'That is good.' 'You see all those girls,' he said pointing in the direction of the dancers, '– I wish you to fuck them all.'

The unexpected command had, so Kirsta believed, some logic. 'Unhappy company make good company,' he laconically explained. Whether or not this notion was any crazier than the Russian impresario's fantasy that the great cities of northern England were crying out for a touring ballet company (compete with full orchestra) in the early months of 1954, cannot easily be determined. Yet Harwood was delighted to be among so many talented and beautiful dancers hailing from infinitely more stylish and refined environs than the grimy surroundings of the Tottenham Court Road.

The only trouble was that the international reputations of Irene Skorik and the other ballerinas conscripted by Kirsta had not yet reached Liverpool, where the company was to begin its tour. The town was shortly to be swept away not by the endeavours of the Ballet Comique, but the music of four young men with the ability to transform simple three chord ditties into masterpieces of soulfulness and longing. It may be an exaggeration to say that herein may be traced the origins of Harwood's lifelong disdain for popular music, but it contains a grain of truth.

Still, Harwood remained as ignorant as ever that he was shortly to be confronted by disaster. 'Hope characterized the atmosphere of the train journey to Liverpool,' he remembers of the troupe's first outing. But there was soon evidence enough that the Ballet Comique was not going to fulfil the eclectic companions' heady aspirations. After arranging a flea-market of fabrics and furniture on the stage of the city's alarmingly spacious Empire Theatre, Harwood was ordered by Kirsta to disappear into Scotland Road to find an expensive roll-top desk needed for one of the short ballets to be performed that evening, *Junior Clerk*. By the time that the young stage manager had returned with this cumbersome item, the dress-rehearsal was already in full-swing. Feigning outrage, Kirsta launched into a violent denunciation of his young assistant – 'like a frustrated ballerina who knows she is past her prime,' surmises Harwood knowingly. 'Understanding more about the theatre now than I did then,' he continues, 'I suspect the advance booking was bad if not non-existent, and the poor man had to take his distress out on someone.'

Harwood tried to console himself by making himself useful backstage. 'I had so far neglected the duty to which Kirsta appeared to attach so much importance,' he says with a roguish leer. But Harwood soon discovered that the conversation of his ballerinas was as limited as their practice schedules were gruelling. 'I could not contribute much to talk of *pirouettes* and *plies*, tendons and *tutus*, blisters and bunions,' he regrets: 'but I lived in hope.' Whenever possible he would scamper into their dressing room on an imaginary errand, only to find the ballerinas tired and sullen. He particularly recalls one of them thumbing through a Merseyside journal. 'I do not like it,' she lisped sulkily: 'On ze night I am to dance *Swan Lake*, ze man 'e call me "ducky". Is not nice, you know.' Not long afterwards another unfortunate ballerina was dropped from shoulder height by two butch hussars. Kirsta's response was only to yell: 'In the name of God, wipe blood from chin.' No wonder these young things were not, as Harwood puts it, 'gasping for any extra-balletic activity.'

The opportunity to play von Rothbart arose at the company's next staging post: Blackpool. The ballet master, who also doubled up as Tchaikovsky's wicked magician, asked Harwood if he would go on for him so that he could watch the afternoon production from the stalls. 'I said no,' he recounts defiantly. 'He pleaded,' the veteran continues: 'There was nothing to it, he assured me.' All he would have to do, apparently, was wear the ballet master's leotard and head-dress, and, at the appropriate moment in the music, step on stage into a green spotlight in order to draw the Swan Queen to her doom using magical gestures. 'I said no,' repeats Harwood. But then the ballet master had a fiendish insight – 'or perhaps I was more transparent than I thought,' adds Harwood unselfconsciously. He promised to put in a good word with one of the ballerinas. Ronnie said yes.

Word quickly spread through the company that the 'devastating' young stage manager had assumed the role of understudy. 'Everyone cheered up,' recalls Harwood with reference to the money problems which had plagued the troupe's brief existence. Whatever the Swan Queen's view of the matter – 'Do little; I do much,' she curtly explained – the other members of the cast were brimming with delight. Particularly Harwood remembers the uxorious attentions of a gay huntsman. 'I was fussed over as if I were to play Prince Siegfried himself,' he laughs. Smeared with thick eye-liner and equipped with a jock-strap stuffed with four handkerchiefs ('Five would be boasting,' his mentor counselled), Harwood felt as ready as he ever would to dance with the cygnets. With an indulgent kiss on the younger man's forehead, the loving huntsman declared: 'A star is born.'

All that now remained was to lure the Swan Queen from the embrace of her prince charming at the right moment in the score. Harwood says that he knew exactly when this was to take place, but nerves played tricks with his mind. 'The orchestra that afternoon could have been playing The Teddy Bears' Picnic as far as I was concerned,' he explains boyishly. Thankfully, right on cue, a sympathetic hand shoved him into his garish spotlight. Then the real terror began. 'Skorik, like all good ballerinas,' recalls Harwood of his Swan Queen, 'gave the impression of gossamer to the audience: light, noiseless and graceful – but on stage it was a different matter.' In response to his awkward gestures, this world-class ballerina assumed another form. Harwood shudders as he remembers her spiralling towards him on pointed toes from the opposite corner of the stage. 'I shall never forget the lightning speed of that short journey or the pounding noise of her blocked ballet shoes or the glistening sweat on her face and body or the crazed look in her eye,' he gasps. Terrified, he took fright and fled.

Yet Harwood had done it. 'I experienced a modest elation,' he explains without exaggeration. He felt, for the first time, an accepted member of the company: 'I saw before me a tour of Britain, a regular wage and my delightful duties still to be performed,' he exults. But then he pauses; his smile temporarily overcast by a frown: 'I was sacked the next week in Leeds.'

The reason for this setback has always been mysterious to Harwood, but he supposes that he was the victim of a falling out which shortly afterwards took place between Llewellyn Rees and the company's financial backers. 'Kirsta talked of Diaghilev and how money debases dreams,' he laments. The remaining cast subsequently had to pay their own train fares from Edinburgh to Oxford, where their beautiful scenery was impounded. Several years later the former stage manager would find the huge canvasses propped up against the back wall of the New Theatre gathering mould and decay.

Asked why this brief dalliance with ballet clearly had such a profound effect on him, Harwood smiles with a mixture of pity and disbelief. He explains:

I have been in and around theatres for a great many years. I have witnessed or been involved with memorable performances. I have seen all the leading actors of my time demonstrate their extraordinary gifts. I have been moved and exhilarated by revivals of old plays and by performances of new ones. I have myself known success and failure. But when life in the theatre becomes oppressive, or when I take it or myself too seriously, a joyful image of that matinee of *Swan Lake* bursts into my mind. I see myself in that obscene leotard, my arms waving meaninglessly in the air, Skorik frightening the magic out of me, and I know all is again well with the world.

The story does, however, have a postscript. With his modest two-weeks' pay in lieu of notice, Harwood removed himself to Paris. Here he enjoyed for the first time the delights of the Latin Quarter, the Left Bank and the heights of Montmartre. He also fell in love with 'a gloriously voluptuous belly-dancer called Yasmin who turned out to be a man.'

It was as if Kirsta was having the last strangled laugh.

For those born without Harwood's domineering self-confidence, it seems incredible to believe that the mid-1950s were among the happiest and most productive of his entire life. He had no permanent home, no regular income and few influential friends; yet he was rich in spirit. Whether he was manfully assisting in another Wolfit revival; dossing down opposite a provincial playhouse, or hungrily thumbing through the unfamiliar masterpieces of Western literature, the young actor bounced from adventure to adventure cocooned in a protective bubble of puckish mirth and naïve self-satisfaction.

This was all to the good. Many a lesser character would have long since abandoned ship to find contentment in calmer waters. Not Ronnie Harwood. 'I am not certain I have ever really grown up,' he beams, '... and at no point did I ever – even for a minute – consider the possibility of throwing it all in. The theatre was everything to me.' Pressed a little about why, then, he soon decided to slip from the stage into the writer's study, Harwood confesses with a light chuckle: 'Well, I didn't have the egomania for acting. ... And when I saw that Pinter had gone off and become a successful writer, I thought: "Well, if he can: I can."'

Harwood's West End debut does not entirely live up to the first of these intriguing assertions. It was a production of one of Oscar Wilde's less frequently performed plays, *Salome*. 'I was out of work again and very short of funds,' recalls Harwood of the period following his return from Paris. 'I do not now remember how I managed to pay my rent or buy cigarettes or feed myself – I was finding the going hard.' No sooner had he heard that *Salome* was in the process of being partially recast and moved from the suburban Q Theatre to the West End than Harwood put himself forward for audition. Once again Lady Luck delivered: 'I was to be the Second Jew,' he says flatly.

The play opened on 20 July 1954 before a scattered audience at the St Martin's Theatre in Covent Garden. The venue had been made famous a generation earlier by productions of new plays by John Galsworthy, Arnold Bennett and W. Somerset Maugham; later it was to become the beloved home of the longest running play in theatre history, *The Mousetrap*. Despite numbering some minor future stars in the cast, this production of *Salome* was not destined to be quite so remarkable. Fronted by an Australian actor named Frank Thring (shortly to appear as Pontius Pilot in *Ben Hur*), there were supporting roles for the future film director John Schlesinger and the Trinidad-born actor and playwright, Errol John, who was soon to be bestowed with the award of the *Observer* Play of the Year for his debut, *Moon on a Rainbow*. Also walking the boards at the St Martin's on opening night was the future hero of daytime horror and whodunit films, Maurice Kaufmann, as well as Noel Davis, who went on to appear in a number of B-movies before becoming a successful casting director. Beneath this small constellation of distant stars was a medley of enthusiastic wannabes, including Harwood and the leading man's young boyfriend – a fellow Australian known simply as 'Thring's Thing'.

'The three of us,' reminisces Harwood, ' – Maurice, Errol and I – were, I think, the only heterosexuals in the company and were teased and flirted with mercilessly by the other actors led by John Schlesinger and Noel Davis.' Many a frenetic rehearsal during the broiling summer of 1954 was followed by a visit by Harwood to the couple's flat to admire Noel's amateur photography over a glass of whatever could be found – 'they saw life through bubbles of champagne,' chuckles Harwood. On stage the unlikely trio were equally mischievous; most especially during Salome's 'Dance of the Seven Veils'. 'We were obliged,' explains Harwood gravely, 'to grovel at her feet, to pass our hands as close to her body as was decent, to feign lecherous facial expressions and to make noises that were supposed to convey unbridled lust.' The only trouble was that their particular Salome, played by Agnes Bernelle, was not quite up to the standard of physical beauty apparently enjoyed by the 'real' one that Harwood had so recently fallen for in Paris.

'Miss Bernelle was a fine figure of a woman,' relates Harwood baldly, 'but on the voluptuous side of svelte.' Looking back, he supposes that she was embarrassed at having to strip off down to her g-string for the sake of Oscar Wilde. So unsexy were her gyrations in the eyes of her co-stars that Schlesinger was able to transform Harwood's grunts of simulated carnal desire into stifled laughter with an array of thinly disguised retching noises. 'Poor Miss Bernelle,' concludes Harwood with an attempt at gallantry, 'probably thought she was making John uncontrollably randy.'

Not surprisingly *Salome* did not last long at the St Martin's. In a breezy review for the *Illustrated London News*, the influential critic J. C. Trewin regretted that he was unable to say that 'the present revival endears the piece to me.' The play, no less than this particular production, he explained, 'for all its gaudiness... is repulsively decadent, sometimes just silly.' Only Thring's performance stood out in his opinion; yet even this faint praise was diminished by the rider that his abilities should not be 'wasted upon verbal reeling and writhing.' As for the rest of the cast – Trewin found there to be 'not much to note'. In those four seemingly insignificant words Ronnie Harwood received his first, shattering putdown at the hands of a Major Critic. 'Ah, critics,' he breaks in, before casting his mind back to Blackpool: 'It's worth noting that in Moscow at its first performance in 1877, *Swan Lake* was dismissed and reviled.'

As ever, the closing of one door led swiftly to the opening of another one for young Harwood. This came in the form of a postcard from Dicky Scott, who had followed his former protégé's progress with paternal satisfaction since his graduation from PARADA. Now in charge of a repertory company in Salisbury, he invited the veteran of his student production of *Present Laughter* to join him for a 'special week' of one-off plays. Harwood snatched at the lifeline.

So began an incredible series of developments for the young actor. The week in Salisbury became a year; that year melded into a season at the Chesterfield repertory company; that season in turn led him to his wife, Natasha, who shortly afterwards gave birth to their first child, Antony. All in the space of six crowded years.

It all began at the Playhouse on Fisherton Street, Salisbury. 'It was not a pre-possessing building,' recalls Harwood of his arrival at the theatre in the late summer of 1954. A tired and anonymous hulk, it had undergone several transformations since its construction in the late 1800s as a Nonconformist chapel. Successively a cinema and a store-house, no one had known what to do with it until the Entertainments National Service Association turned it into a makeshift garrison theatre during the Second World War. A 'seasonally permanent' repertory company had been formed there in 1951, producing works that have been aptly described as 'not low, ill-written and vulgar, and not too *avant-garde* either.' A more suitable academy for Ronnie Harwood to hone his craft could scarcely be imagined.[7]

Not that the work was easy. In the vanished world of repertory theatre, every member of the company was required, during any particular week, to step effortlessly out of an Agatha Christie murder mystery and into a new West End hit; from a slapstick farce and into a provincial favourite, or from a jolly musical and into a work by Shakespeare. 'I was known as a "good study,"' says Harwood proudly, 'as I could in those days learn a long part quickly and fairly accurately.'

The working week would begin on Tuesday morning, when Scott would distribute ragged scripts to the cast and block out the stage directions for the production. In the evening they would perform last week's piece before retiring to the pub. 'Then we would all hurry back to our digs,' explains Harwood, 'to have supper and learn our roles in Act One.' Over the course of the ensuing days the troupe would rehearse each act in turn until Saturday, when the first run-through of the play would take place. Sundays were devoted to revising lines and polishing the delivery. At lunchtime on Monday the dress-rehearsal was launched and that night the play opened to the public. In this way, Harwood took his first deep draught of repertory drama. 'It was hard, exhilarating labour,' he concludes with a triumphant grin.

Yet even amid this happy toil, Harwood was already gliding into the orbit of the world to which he had for so long aspired: High Society. While his fellow actors took lodgings above down-at-heel taverns and lice-infested boarding houses, Harwood landed himself a room at one of Salisbury's most impressive residencies, Crane Lodge. Boasting both a Georgian and an Elizabethan wing, this palatial building was owned by an eccentric socialite named Vivian Macan, who took in paying guests from the theatre as a kind of hobby. 'He was,' recalls Harwood fondly, 'a queenly gentleman – tall, thin and willowy with white hair and sad blue eyes.' All domestic negotiations with his lodgers were conducted through the medium of his enormous tabby cat, Poozey. 'Holding the animal close to his face,' relates Harwood, 'he would purr, "Poozey says you owe her two pounds for last week and she does so want to buy a new pair of gloves."' Late night assignations, of which there were many, were a particular bugbear of hers: 'Poozey heard someone leaving the house very noisily last night,' declared the old man brandishing his feline companion, 'and wonders if your lovers could be a little more quiet – hers always are.'

Although Harwood regrets that this effete Englishman was 'a breathtaking snob', the young man was more than a little impressed by the armies of grandees who journeyed to Crane Lodge for his famous garden parties. Contentedly Harwood recalls espying Sir Anthony Eden's wife, Clarissa, 'elegant and serene'; Cecil Beaton, 'effortlessly superior'; Greta Garbo, 'who never removed her dark glasses'; Augustus John, 'an elderly satyr fallen on hard times' – and a Lord Vivian, 'who had been shot in a sensitive part of his anatomy at a range of three inches by his paramour, Mrs Wheeler, then on trial at Salisbury Assizes.'

This was the stuff of which many of Harwood's future plays and novels would be loosely based; yet, at the time, the young actor remained painfully conscious of his position as an outsider. Practically the only time that he was invited to make up the numbers at the lunch table, he found himself seated next to a lady who exhibited the worst traits of her class and time. 'Hoping, as always,' recounts Harwood of this Yuletide encounter, 'to avoid embarrassment, I replied to her question about midnight mass that I would be unlikely to be attending since I was a Jew.' This attempt to circumvent fuss, however, could not have been responded to more boorishly. 'A Jew!' exclaimed his wide-eyed companion. 'Arthur!' she called across the table, 'did you hear that? Mr Harwood's a Jew! But how absolutely fascinating! A Jew! Really? How exotic, how thrilling...' At this moment Harwood ceases his mimicry and looks terribly serious. 'She may have indulged her astonishment in similar vein for a little longer,' he continues, 'I cannot now remember.' After the meal, their host apologized on her behalf, but the damage was done.

'Sufferance is the badge of all our tribe,' he reflects philosophically, before adding rather unconvincingly: 'And anyway – I am certain she meant well.'

It was this sense of alienation that pushed Harwood to new heights as an actor. 'Long before he had achieved even a modest amount of success,' recalls a veteran companion, 'he radiated a kind of star quality.' When Wolfit came up to visit – itself a sign of Harwood's growing status – the young man experienced the elation of the celebrated actor agreeing then and there to stage Ibsen's *The Master Builder* in order to boost the Playhouse's stricken finances. Everyone in the company, from Dicky Scott to the most junior technician, was amazed by the youth's impressive coup. Some, however, evidently found him a little too slavish in his tactical obsequiousness. When the daughter of the 16th Earl of Huntingdon, Lady Moorea Plantagenet Hastings, came up shortly afterwards to take part in another 'special week', disparaging remarks were made about the rising starlet's attempts to cosy up to the titled visitor and her distinguished fiancé, the Labour MP Woodrow Wyatt. Yet Harwood was either unaware or unconcerned by these sniping comments. After the last performance, Wyatt and Lady Moorea gave their new friend a lift back to London, stopping en route for a picnic at Stonehenge. 'There,' sighs Harwood dreamily, 'around midnight on a warm summer's night under a radiant moon, we drank champagne and ate our delicious sandwiches in the dark mysterious shadows of the great stones.' 'And there,' he continues with a flourish worthy of the patriotic writer H. V. Morton, 'my romantic image of England was cemented.'

Yet Harwood's love of England was soon to be eclipsed by a far more visceral kind of passion. Having returned to Wolfit's company with a year's experience in Salisbury to his name and subsequently going on to enjoy a degree of success playing six small parts in a new play at the Edinburgh Festival called *The Hidden King*, the versatile apprentice unexpectedly took up residence in a rather luxurious flat off the Fulham Road. This windfall came following the gift of a prayer card of St Thérèse of Lisieux from a Roman Catholic fellow cast member in Edinburgh named Robert Bernal.

'On the day I was leaving the city,' states the unsuperstitious playwright, 'I received a telephone call from an acquaintance who explained that a friend of a friend was going away for a couple of months and wanted someone to look after his flat in Chelsea, let in the cleaner, take messages and generally care for the place.' Harwood replied that he might manage to oblige. It was from here that he was invited to pay another visit to Dicky Scott, who was now setting up a repertory company in Chesterfield. Harwood went over to discuss 'a good run of parts' and the position of stage manager with the touring impresario at his London home. At the end of the meeting, Scott mentioned that there was one more job to fill: assistant stage manager. 'I've seen two young women,' explained Scott anxiously, 'one very experienced; the other very beautiful. I can't make up my mind between them.' His man-of-the-world friend, however, saw no dilemma: 'Oh, take the beautiful one,' he said as he threw on his jacket and stepped out into the night.

A few weeks later Harwood caught the train up to Chesterfield and made his way to the Stephenson Memorial Hall. 'The theatre seemed deserted,' he recalls, 'but I wandered into the wings and found my way onto the stage.' There he found himself in the presence of a young woman making a bed. 'Dark, exquisite, with a wondrous figure,' recalls Harwood, 'she was unquestionably the most beautiful woman I had ever beheld.' She looked up and smiled, then continued to make the bed.

A new phase had begun. Enter Natasha.

5

'Mine for the Asking'

How has it happened... that I should be the one to complete this circle, the cog to give history such an apparently graceful symmetry?
Home, *'Prologue'*

Of all the redeeming features of Sir Ronald Harwood's self-confessed egoism, his inability to keep anything secret about himself is perhaps the greatest. 'I do not like discussing my late wife with people who did not know her personally,' he gravely intones on meeting strangers. Yet, with a little prompting, he will speak at length about his courtship – 'to use a delicate or not so delicate euphemism' – of the glamorous assistant stage manager at the Chesterfield Playhouse, Natasha Riehle (pronounced 'Reely').

Admittedly Harwood's hand was somewhat forced in this matter by another veteran of that notable Chesterfield season, Dame Diana Rigg, who announced in a public broadcast in 2008 that she had seen rather too much of the future Sir Ronald and Lady Natasha when wandering into the theatre early one morning. 'This was 1957,' explains Harwood curtly, 'Natasha was not allowed to bring men into her digs and I shared a room with two other male members of the repertory company on the first floor of the Red Lion public house.' The young lovers' only hope of consummating their mutual attraction came in the form of a broken-down chaise longue in the prop room – or the stage beds used in the company's productions. It was this latter course which suggested itself most forcibly to the wily young stage manager, who wielded his modest powers with Machiavellian insight. 'I suggested,' he resumes, 'among other suitable productions, *The Diary of Anne Frank* (at least two beds), *Desperate Hours* (the same), *High Temperature* (a farce with a bedroom scene), and several more which required at the very least large sofas.' 'It was a very happy arrangement,' he reminisces, before sweeping on briskly – 'Mind you, it would have been better if we could have stayed at Chatsworth.'

The idea of carrying on his illicit romance at Derbyshire's most famous stately home came, albeit several decades later, from none other than the Duchess of Devonshire, 'Debo' Devonshire, herself. *I can never go into Chesterfield again,*' she once berated her distinguished friend, *'without thinking of you and Natasha on the stage of that awful little theatre! Why couldn't you have stayed here?*'

That the pearly gates of Chatsworth House would ever be unbarred to Ronnie Harwood owed a great deal to Natasha Riehle. A descendant of the illegitimate child of Catherine the Great and her impetuous lover, Count Grigory Orlov, she belonged to a grand Russian family known to history as the Bobrinskys. The family name, derived from the Russian word for beaver, purportedly originated from the fact that Catherine's new-born baby, Alexei, was wrapped in the skin of that animal. 'Another interpretation,' interjects Harwood professorially, 'has it that the baby was spirited away to a small town near Tula called Bobrinki, which is the more probable source of the title.' In any case, generations of Bobrinskys were born and raised at the neoclassical palace of Bogoroditsk, two hundred miles south of Moscow, before the birth, in 1914, of Natasha's mother, Elyena, who was to be the last member of the family born under the auspices of the *ancien régime.*

Helen, as she later became known, would one day relate her family's fall from grandeur to her improbable son-in-law. 'I stirred her memories,' remembers Harwood sadly, 'and she wrote a brief but fascinating account of her life at the time of the revolution.' This was to become one of the cornerstones of Harwood's scarcely veiled loathing of socialism in all its forms. After years of feigned deference to their social superiors, the people of Russia were given licence to denounce, rob and slay their former masters with impunity. Mighty scions of the old aristocracy were overnight turned out of their palaces and reduced to a state of near-beggary: one princess sold homemade pies; another reinvented herself as an undergarment maker, while a widow of one of the late Tsar's generals was reduced to selling matches. In one village, a poor and hitherto popular noblewoman was compelled to take her own life when the new Soviet aristocracy, having confiscated or destroyed her every worldly possession, left her pet dog dead on her doorstep in an act of pure spite. 'As is the way with revolutions,' laments Harwood, 'these new rulers became more powerful and ruthless than their predecessors, Lenin more vicious and terrible than any Tsar that had preceded him, his secret police, the Cheka under Felix Dzerzhinsky, more effective and therefore more vile.'[8]

The destruction of the house of Bobrinsky was all the more awful for its agonizing delay. Protected by its remoteness and the general good-will of the surrounding population, the count and countess, Lev and Vera, continued to lead the same charmed life as their ancestors right up until the spring of 1919. Then, late one evening, a game of cards was interrupted by the sound of boots marching across the ice. 'They're here!' someone choked. Proceeding up the driveway, with the confidence of a thousand bloody executions, was a gang of torch-bearing ruffians led by a sailor wielding a gleaming sword. Upon their forced entry into the chateau, the family were herded into the music room and informed that their property now belonged 'to the Russian people'. During the course of an all-night search of the premises (allegedly for firearms, but in reality for jewellery and vodka), the crying baby Elyena was soothed by the macabre sound of her mother playing a final rendition of Chopin's 'Raindrop' prelude on her ornate grand piano. At sunrise, the count was arrested and sent to die a lonely prisoner in a Moscow gaol. The rest of the family, meanwhile, were pointed in the direction of the village and wished 'bon voyage'.[9]

For several desperate months, Vera and her three young daughters found sanctuary in the home of a peasant family in Bogoroditsk, where they earned their keep by working in the fields. It was an experience that strengthened the character of these noble fugitives from the Soviet terror. Even towards the end of her life Vera was known to spend entire days happily performing heavy agricultural labour in her Surrey garden – 'The first time I met her,' recalls Harwood rather loftily, 'I actually could have mistaken her for a Russian peasant, so preoccupied was she by her furrowing and weeding.' Yet the remnants of the Bobinskys were not to remain in the new Russia for long. After moving to Moscow to eke out a living as a jewellery saleswoman and musical accompanist, Vera was given the opportunity to emigrate to London (via a brief stint in Paris) due to the happy coincidence of Lenin's liberalizing New Economic Policy and the marriage of her two eldest daughters, Alexandra and Sonia, to men with international connections: a volunteer on Herbert Hoover's famine relief project named Philip Baldwin, and an Englishman from the Moscow office of the Cunard Line named Reginald Witte respectively.

Like so many Russian exiles, the Bobrinskys took up residence in the borderland between Baron's Court and Chiswick (always mispronounced 'Chyesick') in West London. It was here that Helen Bobrinsky, at the time working as a child's nurse, was awoken late one night by a knock at the door. The visit was to be scarcely less momentous than that of the commissars fifteen years previously. Before her the elegant young woman saw a prematurely bald compatriot whose breath smelt heavily of alcohol. Haltingly, he explained that he and a group of fellow Russians over the road were having a party and had run out of glasses – could she assist? Within a year the strangers would be man and wife.

The visitor's provenance was no less extraordinary than that of the fair Helen. Born in 1904 to Lev and Olga Riehle, he was known in the years before the Revolution as Vassily. As a boy he had sat dumbfounded in a dentist's waiting room having seen one of the chief architects of the Russian tragedy, Leon Trotsky, rushed in before him to have a tooth removed. When it became clear that Trotsky and his confreres intended to uproot the Russian bourgeoisie in similar fashion, Vassily and his family escaped to Germany, where the boy became known as Wilhelm and, after completing his education, went on to enter the workaday world as a tea merchant. It was as though the family had fled Hiroshima for Nagasaki, for no sooner had Wilhelm established himself in his profession than the political barometer again pointed towards stormy. Decades later, he would furnish his son-in-law with a first-hand account of the triumphant Nazis marching in procession before the Reich Chancellery singing their swaggering anthem, the *Horst Wessel Lied*. Instinctively he knew that Nazi Germany would be as brutal and unpleasant as Soviet Russia: 'Lenin, Stalin and Hitler were moulded from the same piece of shit,' a thinly disguised character philosophizes in Harwood's 1993 novel, *Home*: 'a turd passed by the devil when he had constipation.' Shortly after Hitler's seizure of power in January 1933, Wilhelm fled to England where he reinvented himself once again: this time as a typewriter salesman named Bill.

A multiplicity of forenames was to become a feature of the Riehle family even in their adopted homeland. Two years after the birth of Bill and Helen's first daughter, Marina (Marishka, Pishka, Marie), in 1936 came Natalya, 'known always,' expounds Harwood, 'as Natasha, but to her family for impenetrable reasons as Tu or Tutska, Natty to some of her English friends, Nathan (to Albert Finney alone) and Tash, Tashy or Tasha to me.' Encouraged by her mother to become a professional ballerina, she attended Elmhurst School of Dance, at that time near Camberley in Surrey, where she rose to become head girl, only to be told in the lead up to her final examinations that she was 'too tall' to pursue her vocation any further. Yet this setback was not entirely lamented by the graceful young woman. 'Although she loved the theatre in general and ballet in particular,' relates Harwood, 'she was averse to performing.' 'She had no need to show off,' he continues merrily, 'and always detested unnecessary self-assertion – in this respect her influence on me may not be immediately apparent.'

What dwarfed these minor temperamental differences between Ronnie and Natasha was not only their strong attraction, but their fundamentally similar heritage. 'Her family,' explains Harwood, 'were called émigrés; mine were called immigrants … the Riehle household was somehow familiar to me.' Both he and his future wife knew what it was to have nothing and yet to be happy. Nor did their similarities end there. 'To find a career in the theatre was her aim,' empathizes the playwright. Practical and dexterous, she found her way into the repertory company of Dicky Scott following her graduation from what was at the time the only training academy for theatre management in the country: the Bristol Old Vic School. And so, Harwood believes, Destiny delivered him his Natasha, adored wife for over fifty years.

Yet securing Natasha's hand was not quite as easy as Harwood's fairy-tale version of events would suggest. Firstly, he was not alone in trying to woo the attractive young woman: 'All the boys were after her,' he bashfully recalls, 'and I played a very cool waiting game, unusually cautious for me.' Whether this unwonted reserve stemmed from an experiment in self-control or the high-handed manner with which Natasha beat off his competitors can only be imagined. Certainly, the nineteen-year-old assistant stage manager was no easy catch. 'She was blessed with natural dignity,' explains Harwood, 'that was sometimes interpreted by others as aristocratic hauteur.' So formidable was this protective veneer that one admiring contemporary judged her deportment to 'verge on the regal'. It is a testament both to Harwood's native charm as well as to his dogged determination that this born princess accepted his marriage proposal before the Chesterfield season was out.

Natasha's acquiescence, however, still left one step in Harwood's way. This was his prospective father-in-law. Liberal and Nazi-hating though he was, Bill Riehle was not without the stain of anti-Semitism which pervaded so many Russians of his class and generation. 'When he found out that his daughter was in love with a Jew,' explains Harwood, 'he confessed to having nightmares.' The reason for this, he generously allows, was that he shared the widespread misconception that the Russian Revolution had been inspired and orchestrated by Jews: 'a not uncommon view,' he pleads, 'given that Karl Marx and so many of the first commissars were Jewish.' 'Moreover,' adds Harwood casually, 'and this is not supposed to echo the cliché, he had close

Jewish friends.' The motivations for Bill's misgivings about his daughter's overzealous Romeo were certainly deeper than crude racial prejudice. Without settled employment or clear prospects for the future, it was far from apparent how the young man would support his wife, let alone how he would provide for any future children. 'I was not the ideal son-in-law,' he shrugs impishly.

For more than a year Harwood played the role of deferential suitor, journeying down to Natasha's family home, Farways near Godalming in Surrey, whenever theatrical commitments allowed. With each visit, Harwood was made to feel a little more welcome. 'For the first time since arriving in England,' he explains, 'I felt at ease – or at least less self-conscious.' Eventually his prospective father-in-law began to warm to him in spite of himself. Then, on a summer's afternoon in 1959, Harwood retired with Bill into the study to ask for his daughter's hand in marriage. 'I do not remember much about our rambling conversation,' recalls Harwood, 'except that I nodded and said "yes" a lot.' Clearer in his memory was the presence of the family's beloved boxer, Brandy, who insisted on resting her jaws on his foot and slobbering all over his shoes. 'I was more frightened of the dog than of the interview,' he grimaces: 'I always was, and still am, terrified of most dogs.' When Brandy and the two men emerged from the study, the good news was delivered to the awaiting womenfolk. 'Vodka and tears flowed,' concludes Harwood with laconic satisfaction.

Now all that remained for Harwood was the difficulty of earning a living. Having relied upon his young wife and her family to pay not only for the wedding, Parisian honeymoon, and, shortly afterwards, for the deposit on a small flat in Barnes, the struggling actor also relied on his bride to find him gainful employment. 'After suffering a severe bout of influenza and exhausted by the unrelenting labour of stage management,' he recounts, 'Natasha was forced to leave Chesterfield before I did.' Within a few weeks she was called for interview by a young director called Michael Elliott, who was in the process of setting up a new outfit called the 59 Theatre Company at one of Donald Wolfit's old stomping grounds: the Lyric Theatre, Hammersmith.

'She had the gall to make two conditions,' smirks Harwood: they had to let her have a week off for her wedding and honeymoon, and they had to find a role for her out-of-work husband. 'To her astonishment,' he exults, 'Elliott agreed and a few weeks later I was interviewed by him and offered small parts which I gratefully accepted.' It was the start of something big.

Not that Harwood was yet aware of it. His first collaboration with the talented director who would go on to help launch his first six dramatic works was uncharacteristically modest. The company was staging a revival of Ibsen's *Brand* to follow on from a successful run of a play called *Danton's Death* by Georg Büchner. 'It was the vehicle that transported others to the forefront,' reminisces Harwood: 'Michael Meyer, the translator; Richard Negri, the set designer and Patrick McGoohan, whose performance in the title role was universally acclaimed.' But Harwood was not to be transported anywhere. At the behest of the authoritarian stage manager, the veteran of countless bit-parts was conscripted at the last minute to play a villager with the one line, 'Kill him!' 'Elliott later assured me,' adds Harwood, 'that I was rather effective.'

Working alongside Elliott at the Lyric was a delicate Finnish aristocrat named Casper Wrede. 'The first time I saw him,' recalls Harwood of the director, 'I thought him a woman.' He was to become another major influence in the life of the future playwright. It began when Wrede asked Ronnie and Natasha to join him and other members of the company on a tour of Ireland with a play by Alun Owen called *The Rough and Ready Lot*. The production was not a huge success, but it established Harwood as a prominent member of Elliott's theatre company. He played a Native American, Pablo, opposite one June Brown, later to become famous as the beloved grandmother character in *EastEnders*, Dot Cotton. The failure of the play is attributed by Harwood to the inadequacy of the text and its unsuitability for an Irish audience – though personal animus may well be an aggravating factor in this diagnosis. For Owen had, coincidentally, been a member of Wolfit's company, and the two men were not friendly. 'He and Pinter had been a few years my senior,' complains Harwood, 'and because I was Wolfit's dresser they treated me with suspicion.' Owen, who was a Welsh Liverpudlian by birth, gave a speech in 'lilting Irish' at the curtain call on opening night, but few punters were taken in either by his accent or his play. 'A year or so later,' continues Harwood acerbically, 'he had a hit with a television play called *No Trams to Lime Street* and was predictably hailed as "the Bard of Liverpool", or some such cheap journalistic codswallop.' Shortly thereafter Owen was asked to write the screenplay of *A Hard Day's Night* for The Beatles.

It was, as ever, off stage that Harwood made the greatest impact. Affable and eager to please, he became a personality in the touring company second only to Wrede himself. His connection with the beautiful Natasha was not negligible in this regard. During one break from rehearsals a member of the cast invited the couple to share a taxi with him to his stud farm outside Dublin. 'He crossed himself fervently each time we passed a church,' remembers Harwood, 'which was often and just as often we stopped at pubs and inns and so were somewhat unsteady by the time we reached our destination.' When they finally disembarked the meter in the cab had reset itself, but the companions were still able to find time to admire an exquisite filly, which the Irishman promised to name Natasheen in his guests' honour. 'For weeks afterwards,' laments Harwood, 'we scanned the racing pages but never found a mention of her.' It was, he later discovered, a form of Irish hospitality to rename a horse after a visitor, but only for a day. He also learnt that the trainers cheated his friend out of most of his money, leaving him penniless.

The Harwoods would soon learn the meaning of that unhappy word. Their return to London coincided with the close of the 59 Theatre Company's brief season and the couple once again had to fall back upon their own resources. 'The outlook for work was bleak,' recalls the playwright, 'but our high spirits could not be dampened.' Walled up in their small West London flat, the couple reluctantly signed on to the dole, and Harwood contemplated a future either building the Hammersmith flyover or joining a travelling circus – suggestions put to him by the officials at the Labour Exchange. Like his great contemporaries Michael Caine and Sean Connery, who briefly found themselves in similar circumstances at the outset of their careers, the young actor was not to be defeated by these experiences. 'There was great camaraderie among the dole-seekers,' he says gingerly, '… known and unknown actors mingled easily with the labourers and others seeking employment.' It was a fellowship encouraged by the belligerent attitude of the clerks, who treated their eclectic supplicants as virtually subhuman. Harwood recalls that he and his companions enjoyed puncturing the inflated egos of these self-important persons by highlighting their inefficiency whenever possible: ''Ere, Charlie,' he mimics, 'you kept us waiting! You been at the wankers' ball?'

Though he did not fully appreciate it at the time, life was changing for Harwood: he was reluctantly growing up. The process was hastened by the unexpected news that Natasha had fallen pregnant with their first child, Antony. It appeared as if the worst fears of Bill Riehle had been realized, but Harwood maintains that his father-in-law remained highly supportive. 'He used often to telephone unexpectedly and take us out to a slap-up lunch at his favourite restaurant, the Brompton Grill, opposite the Oratory,' chirps Harwood. 'And after lunch,' he continues excitedly, 'he would have his chauffeur, Boulter, drop us at the Labour Exchange, or rather just around the corner from the Labour Exchange, so that we could not be seen stepping out of a limousine to sign on and collect our money.' Even in those faraway days, Harwood enjoyed the good life.

But Bill Riehle did something of even greater importance for his ambitious son-in-law. For his twenty-fifth birthday present, he gave him a lightweight, portable typewriter made by a firm called Facit, whose interests he represented. 'In the small second bedroom that was to be the nursery,' recounts Harwood of the remainder of that momentous day, 'I sat down and began to type.' He typed and typed – and loved it. 'Natasha thought I was just teaching myself the mechanics of the keyboard,' he chuckles, 'but in fact, before long, I had started to type a story.' It was about a young Zulu houseboy, George Washington September, who is tricked by a brothel-keeper and his beautiful accomplice, Nancy ('a filled Coca-Cola bottle'), into revealing the whereabouts of his activist uncle, Kalanga. 'On the morning that I began the last section,' resumes Harwood, 'I had a sudden and unexpected realization. The adventures I had put my hero through were, it transpired in that final spasm, all part of a plot engineered by the South African police. ... My hero's victimisation encapsulated, without my being conscious of it, the viciousness of the totalitarian state South Africa had become.' The dreamy young writer began to hyperventilate. 'I knew with wonderful certainty,' he recalls, 'that I had tapped into some deep source within myself, a source of which I had never before been remotely aware.'

All the Same Shadows, as the novel was entitled, was published by Jonathan Cape in March 1961 – a mere ten years after *The Catcher in the Rye* and less than twelve months after *To Kill a Mockingbird*. The book was heavily indebted to both of these masterpieces. But Harwood's debut novel, it is fair to say, was not quite in the same league. Although it dealt with major issues affecting South Africa with as much frankness as any book since the publication, in 1948, of *Cry, the Beloved Country*, it is essentially a drama built around a week in the life of the only character in the book who really lives – the protagonist. Harwood confesses to the book being 'partly autobiographical', and there is certainly a character in the story who is supposed to mirror its author. This is Master Abel, the teenage son of the houseboy's European employers. Savvy and understanding, he is described by George Washington as:

> one big decent fellow and has nineteen years and is very clever and very educated and is now at university, and that, man, is educated. He's got one big brain like my uncle Kalanga. And this Master Abel he is teaching me about many things. ... [H]e says I'll be altogether educated native boy when I get educated about myself. And I don't believe all he says, because man, I don't understand it but I do like he say because he is himself so damn educated. And that boy is so nice because when his parents are away, like at the present time, he

is giving me many afternoons and evenings off and even letting me have a bath in his bathroom upstairs until mine is fixed, and I am telling you the truth when I say his parents would hang both me and him if they found out.

Yet careful readers of the book may find a truer portrait of the young Harwood in the person of the breathless, love-sick Zulu houseboy himself. A scene in which a stall-keeper attempts to dupe George and his monosyllabic friend Pete into buying under-the-counter contraceptive pills is particularly germane:

'You boys maybe having slip-slap, hey?' he ask.

'Sure thing. Sure are. I'm liking that slip-slap. My!' say Pete.

'You like that slip-slap, hey sonny?'

'Sure do. My!' say Pete. 'You got women, hey, maybe?'

'No, but boys, I got something for you. You have slip-slap, right?'

'Sure do. Yes, sir!' say Pete.

'And maybe after a few months that girl is coming to you and saying I'm going to have a baby. Hey?'

'No, sir. No, sir. No, sir,' say Pete.

'Listen, sonny. These things happen. Gotallah! Don't I know? Now you listen to me. I got pills, sonny. You just take one of these pills before you have the slip-slap, see? And man, it's impossible for that girl to get herself a baby.'

Crude and simplistic though the book at times is, the earthy power of the writing carries the reader along – many believed the unknown author to have actually been a semi-literate Zulu. It certainly impressed Wolfit's former administrator, Llewellyn Rees, who was largely responsible for persuading Harwood to submit the manuscript to an editor he knew at the publishing firm. 'With work on the Hammersmith flyover looming closer,' recollects Harwood, 'Lulu came to supper and asked what I'd been up to.' Harwood casually mentioned that he had written a novel, but added that 'everyone writes a novel' and that he did not really think his was good enough. After a little arm-twisting, however, the redundant actor was persuaded to make copies of his manuscript and submit it at once to Jonathan Cape. The novel appeared in bookshops shortly thereafter, and so Harwood became a published author. 'I thought the Nobel Prize was mine for the asking,' he adds with a sly grin.

This heady optimism was encouraged by a series of glowing reviews in the press. 'Mr Harwood's *All the Same Shadows*,' wrote the anonymous reviewer in the *Times Literary Supplement*, 'is astonishingly good.' Particularly, the reviewer was impressed by the central character, whose mixture of 'naivety and shrewdness ... frank sensuality and respect (instinctive) for higher values' he found to be delineated with great 'insight and understanding'. Likewise the reviewer in *The Guardian* marvelled at the quality of the 'naïve and candid chatter', which he believed to be well-employed for both serious and comic effect. In another complimentary notice, author Muriel Spark hailed the unknown young novelist as 'a moralist', which sounded to Harwood 'rather grim and too judgemental.' Yet it was also remarkably apt. Moral dilemmas were to prove to be the meat and drink of the future playwright: 'The great thing about being a moralist,' says Harwood in an undertone, 'is that one doesn't have to be moral.'

No reviewer, however, quite grasped the potential of the young author more than Diana and Meir Gillon in the *Sunday Times*. After praising his 'remarkably accomplished hand', this husband and wife literary team discerned that Harwood's greatest skill lay in 'translating apparently "documentary" evidence into artistic truth.' It was a talent, they believed, that 'should take him a very long way indeed.'[10]

The Hammersmith flyover would be constructed without the assistance of Ronnie Harwood after all.

Act Three:

BEYOND OLYMPIA

6

Show Business

I realize it's not Racine but there's no need to look quite so critical.
After the Lions, *Act One*

'Scribble, scribble, scribble,' was the Duke of Gloucester's famous dictum on the activities of the author of the *Decline and Fall of the Roman Empire*. His language would have needed little modification in order to anticipate the recreations of the obscure young author who would one day be known to the world as Sir Ronald Harwood. For while the Sixties swung and a new era in British life and politics was begun, there was just one sound emanating from the solitary spare room of this impecunious young man: 'tap, tap, tap'. So busy was Harwood's weary Facit typewriter that by the end of the decade it had produced a body of work comparable – at least in length – to a volume of Gibbon's unrelenting masterpiece.

'I just wanted to go on writing and writing,' recalls Harwood of the exciting period after the acceptance of his first novel. Like the cataracts and hurricanoes that assailed Lear, ideas threw themselves upon the young author with a ferocity which terrified him and those around him. He had no clue from whence they came. 'I have few if any insights,' remarks Harwood, 'into where or how my ideas are born or why suddenly I should have had the compulsion to write about the subjects that plague me and have continued to plague me for more than fifty years.' 'My instincts,' he sighs dreamily, 'tell me that to examine my creative process too closely would be calamitous.'

The natural course of action at this point might have been for Harwood to begin another novel. But this was not – and never has been – his preferred creative vehicle. He wanted first and foremost to be a playwright. The only difficulty was that theatreland was just then being swept by a new wave of subversive 'kitchen sink' dramas written by talented firebrands such as Arnold Wesker and John Osborne. It shows Harwood's tenacity and ingenuity that he was able to adapt his preferences to chime with the moment. Rather than embarking on a script in the tradition of Coward and Rattigan, he chose to compose a three act play about a struggling Jewish barber from Stamford Hill. And, crucially, he would write it not for the overcrowded theatrical scene, but to quell the insatiable maw of television instead.

It is curious to note that Harwood felt no compulsion to visit Stamford Hill before beginning this ambitious project. Nor did he make even the most preliminary enquiries about the technicalities of hairdressing. 'It was *my* Stamford Hill,' he explains curtly. Somehow he felt able to create an imaginary world that rang truer than life itself.

His confidence was not entirely misplaced. Knowing personally about the patient strivings of many immigrants, there was little need for him to investigate the lives of the hardworking Jewish barbers, clerks and tailors who had settled in the North London district of Stamford Hill during the final years of the nineteenth century. It was a community, he believed, that largely shared his own wish to integrate into British society, though at the same time retain a degree of spiritual identity. Into the character of Mr Figg, the barber of the story, he poured the damned-up torrent of his hopes, anxieties and secret miseries.

The Barber of Stamford Hill is a simple, yet infinitely touching tale. Mr Figg is a popular and respectably bawdy barber, who dominates his modest hair salon like a music hall entertainer: 'Listen,' he chirps to a customer in the opening scene, 'what did the chorus girl sing who was going to have a baby? ... She sang, "I *should* have danced all night!" Hey? How about that? Good, ain't it?' But when his client asks him if he has become a grandfather yet, Figg's face loses its mirthful vitality. 'Not yet,' he says rather unctuously: 'I mean... (a long pause) ... my kids are a bit young yet, you know. Two I got. Wish I could have had more.' The suspicion that he has invented many of the details of his private life is confirmed absolutely when he returns home at the end of the day not to the imagined semi-detached family home, but to a cramped studio flat decorated only by a pair of Sabbath candles.[11]

Figg is soon visited by his only friend in the world: a mute called Dober. The two men enjoy a watery broth between laborious exchanges about their mutual interests of stamp collecting and chess. The story, however, comes to life when Dober produces a photograph of the two of them with a widow who lives across the street, Mrs Werner. 'Always so neat and tidy,' says Figg happily; 'always cheerful too, is Mrs Werner, always cheerful – I bet her house is cheerful too, eh? Cheerful and tidy. Typical, typical, lovely, yes….' Comparing her situation with his miserable surroundings, he launches into a fierce attack on everything he and Dober have unwittingly come to represent: 'This ain't a home, Dober,' he protests,

> It ain't warm. It ain't – (searching) it ain't – homely. I was talking today with this customer, this customer that looked at me in the mirror. I was thinking, what's the use? This customer, Mr O., as I call him, tells me he's going to be a grandfather soon, for the first time. And then he asks me if I'm a grandfather yet? … He doesn't want to think, 'Poor Figg. He's all alone.' … And then I think to myself: You're mad Figg, all these lies. You're mad. Then and there I should have said, 'I ain't got a family at all, Mr O. I'm a bachelor.' Well, is it such a terrible thing to be a bachelor?

In his desperate state of mind, Figg decides at that moment to leave Dober – whose own feelings are scarcely considered – in order to march across the road and make a bold romantic proposition to Mrs Werner. But when he arrives, the adventurer is quickly made aware of the futility of his efforts. Not only does Mrs Werner accidentally rebuff his feeble intimations; it is also clear that she shares neither his values nor his religious convictions. He returns at the end of the play to Dober, who has loyally waited for him. 'You can't teach an old dog new tricks,' says Figg resignedly. He is doomed to continue with his life as it was before – and is all the happier for it.

The finished manuscript was lovingly enshrined by the author's wife in a homemade cardboard binding and sent off to a producer at Associated Television, Stella Richman, who was then in the process of commissioning a series of half-hour evening plays. A few days later Harwood was unexpectedly invited to meet the influential television impresario herself. He was not, however, terribly impressed. 'She was a busy little woman,' he recalls of his would-be patron. While simultaneously drafting letters and despatching messengers all over London, she said that she liked his play and would produce it – but only if he cut it by half. 'I declined,' says Harwood as humbly as he can muster, 'and to this day I do not know why.'

Once again, it was Natasha who came to the rescue. She suggested that Harwood send his play to their former colleague, Casper Wrede. Despite the budding playwright's initial scepticism – 'What would a bollock-eyed Finn know about a Jewish barber from Stamford Hill?' he mused – Harwood duly sent the director a copy. Chance would have it that Wrede had recently signed a contract to direct two plays a year for Associated Television: specifically for Donald Wolfit's old adversary, Hugh 'Binkie' Beaumont. The producer at the helm of this somewhat unholy alliance between television and theatre – quickly dubbed 'Binkievision' – might not have been any less brusque than the unfortunate Miss Richman, but he demanded no cuts. After a cursory reading of the script, Cecil Clarke made arrangements for it to be recorded in little more than a single take.

The play was broadcast on ITV at 9.40 p.m. on Thursday 28 July 1960. Had it not been for the good fortune that Wrede enlisted the brilliant television actor Lee Montague to play the barber, this production may well have gone the way of such Binkievision offerings as *The Balance of Her Mind* and *There's No Room for You Here for a Start* – that is to say, it might have been instantly forgotten. Thankfully for Harwood, however, a gratifying chorus of thumbnail reviews in the press encouraged a small production company recently founded by Ben Arbeid to turn his television play into a feature film. 'I have no idea how he raised the money from the distributors, British Lion,' recalls Harwood, 'but he did.' Suddenly, almost without being conscious of it, the young man was now 'writing for the movies'.

It was an altogether heady time for Harwood. Socially, he and Natasha were invited to cocktail parties where they rubbed shoulders with well-known writers, politicians, actors and professional socialites. Particularly Harwood remembers the soirees of the veteran Hollywood actress Luise Rainer, whose husband, Robert Knittel, had been the editorial director at Jonathan Cape who accepted *All the Same Shadows*. In their elegant muse house off Eaton Square, this formidable pair introduced Harwood to the likes of the film director Jean Renoir, the movie star Leslie Caron, and the aged paramour Baroness Moura Budberg, whose extensive career in seduction had brought her into close association with gentlemen as diverse as the diplomat Bruce Lockhart, the Russian author Maxim Gorky and the polymath H. G. Wells. (Recently, her name re-entered the news when her great-nephew, Nick Clegg, was appointed Deputy Prime Minister in 2010). To be even a dwarf planet in this bright constellation was sheer ecstasy for the awestruck young writer.

Yet there was still much to learn. When Knittel invited Harwood into his offices in Bedford Square to deliver a speech to the 'drummers' (sales agents) assigned to promote his debut novel, the enthusiast made the first of several endearing blunders. Having been advised by Llewellyn Rees to 'start with something funny', Harwood began cheerfully. 'As you can see,' he said with a jaunty smile, 'I am not a Zulu.' But the gag was met only by a deathly silence. 'A sea of stony faces gazed at me stonily,' recalls the playwright. 'Well,' he continues unapologetically, 'I knew it wasn't a great joke, but I thought it might have gone down rather better or at least have evinced an affectionate titter.' Whatever Harwood had planned to say evaporated into the clammy stillness. After what seemed like an eternity, a sympathetic hand tugged at his sleeve: 'They haven't read the book,' whispered Knittel. Several minutes later Harwood had concluded a rambling and largely inaccurate summary of the plot and characters. The outlook was not good. 'Books about coloureds,' said one of the drummers over coffee, 'don't usually sell well.'

And yet, Harwood was blessed once again with good fortune. With the Civil Rights movement exploding in the United States of America, and international outrage sweeping the developed world in the aftermath of the Sharpeville Massacre in South Africa, his tale of a young black man's struggle against oppression had a certain topicality. This undoubtedly helped the book to sell a respectable 3,500 copies in the United Kingdom, and an even greater number in the United States, where it was cleverly retitled *George Washington September, Sir!* So impeccable were the novel's political credentials that its author was invited by the reformist Canon of St Paul's Cathedral, John Collins, to write a monthly column for *Christian Action*, and it was not long before his name became known to a small collection of readers as far away as Selma and Montgomery, Alabama. 'On my first visit to the United States,' contends Harwood, 'a man fell to his knees and said: "You made me into a Civil Rights activist."' Although he sadly did not catch the name of this admirer, one is left with an abiding sense that if it was not Martin Luther King himself, it was at least a figure of comparable significance.

New suits, better seats at the theatre and more spacious accommodation followed quickly upon Harwood's early success. He had become a man of importance – and was quietly aware of the fact. With his television play now being made into a film, he had the exhilarating experience of strutting around a real-life studio in the guise of 'the screenwriter'. For a former actor who had never been fortunate enough to get near such a place, he was doubly satisfied. Never has Harwood forgotten the morning that he purposefully bowled up to the great portal of Shepperton Studios, Pinewood, to show his credentials to a stern-faced guard at the barrier. In a few moments he was drifting through a sea of runners and technicians, actors and directors, make-up artists and hair stylists. 'There was a tangible atmosphere,' reminisces Harwood, 'of permanence and contentment, and even a kind of serenity which is common to all closed communities.' Past the huge hangars in which the majority of the filming was carried out, he proceeded along the tarmac driveway to 'a hideous pseudo-Tudor construction' inhabited by the Olympian producers. Arbeid greeted Harwood warmly before taking him to see the filming of one of the early scenes.

But before Harwood's exalted head could knock against the stars, he received a devastating little blow. After the sixteenth take of the leading actor, John Bennett, opening a door, one of the prop men swung round with a raised eyebrow. ''Ere, Ron,' he enquired, 'when does this film break into a gallop?' The extent of Harwood's displeasure can be gauged by the fact that, to this day, he will only grudgingly step foot on a film set.

The Barber of Stamford Hill was premiered on a drizzly evening in April 1963 at the Gala Royal cinema: an unmodernized 'flea-pit' on the Edgware Road famous to locals for its Monday evening blue movies. From such unprepossessing surroundings, a generations-spanning career in motion pictures was born. Perhaps the very fact that the film was at odds with the new breed of racy, frivolous and violent cinema which was to dominate the field in the 1960s contributed to its unlikely success. This was certainly the impression of *The Guardian*'s anonymous film critic, who lavished two columns on the low-budget production. 'What a relief it is,' he wrote, 'after the brutal buffetings received this week from the "new cinema" ... to encounter the timeless humanity of *The Barber of Stamford Hill*.' He saw the film as a 'brave, small, significant proclamation that kindness, too, and gentleness are human attributes and are, accordingly, worth a place, as well as gore and misery and meanness, in the realist cinema.' Other than a friendly barb about the slow pace of the film – 'an hour ... is the right time for it' – there was not an unsympathetic word about actor, director or author. Such an accolade was not to become routine for the young writer: but he could not have wished for a better welcome from the discerning masters of Fleet Street.

Contracts for films, plays and novels now came to Harwood almost faster than he could accept them. 'If I had thought about the future realistically,' he says with a gentle chuckle, 'or managed a remotely objective view, I might have taken fright and decided the labour gang on the Hammersmith flyover was the more sensible option.' All day and every day – and often all night too – he wrote furiously. It was a cruel, self-inflicted punishment for a man of unbounded gregariousness and sociability; but he had the stamina to keep at it. 'I did not for a moment contemplate,' explains Harwood, 'the loneliness of the long distance writer.' What little he saw of his wife and young child he barely recalls, but never did he feel family life impeded his labour. 'I could not have pulled through it without Natasha,' he says with retrospective gratitude: 'Every time I had to leave the house she would make sure I had my wallet, keys and so forth.' It was a partnership built on the foundation of a writer's unquenchable longing and debilitating outward disorganization.

Harwood was not, however, so green as to say 'yes' to everything that came his way. When Cecil Clarke of 'Binkievision' offered him a contract to write three television plays a year, Harwood demurred. This was largely thanks to the intervention of Casper Wrede, who sensed that his young friend was in danger of writing himself out before he was even thirty. 'Three plays a year,' he counselled, 'is to become – you know – a hack. Maximum – you know – two.' Harwood did not argue. 'His eyes burned into me,' he remembers, 'and I was hooked.' A revised contract was swiftly drawn up by the lawyers at Binkievision and by the end of 1960 Harwood was earning £1,000 per annum as a playwright, albeit for television. 'It may seem trivial now,' he smiles, 'but it was my first important lesson in disciplining my creative energy.' As well as giving him a much-needed comfort blanket of a regular income, he was now free to pursue other writing opportunities to the full.

And he was about to hit on something even bigger than *The Barber of Stamford Hill*. 'The confusion of the dream continues,' explains Harwood. 'I am unable to recall the events in strict chronology; the precise sequence eludes me and dawdles in my mind like a rough-cut of a film that needs work.' Lying on a bed of discarded foolscap paper on his study floor, Harwood suddenly had the idea for a television play about a soldier who involuntarily calls out during a covert patrol. The reason, decided Harwood, was that the young man had seen God. He entitled the script *Private Potter*.

Hot with inspiration, Harwood rushed over to see Wrede, who instantly saw the play's wide appeal. Having already shared a degree of Harwood's glory through their first collaboration, he ensured that their second project would be even better. Yet the two men by no means shared the same approach to their work. Even today, Harwood thinks nothing of throwing down a few thousand words on a page, only meticulously to revise them at a later date. By contrast, Wrede liked to weigh up each line and was known to suffer from agonizing bouts of mental paralysis. 'I was intolerant of his working process,' recalls Harwood contemptuously, 'which was painfully slow and laboured. His creativity would grind to a halt for hours on end and he would sit staring into space or playing games of patience. ... Our sessions together often filled me with resentment and anger.' Yet Wrede also taught Harwood something important. 'He made me value my new profession,' he explains, 'and set me standards to which, he insisted, I must aspire no matter how short I may fall.' Before *The Barber of Stamford Hill* even hit cinema screens, they had completed the script of *Private Potter* and Wrede immediately set about finding a suitable actor for the lead part.

It was with considerable enthusiasm, then, that Wrede telephoned Harwood early one morning with news that he had interested an exciting young actor in the role. Although completely unknown at the time, the youth was shortly to appear in a film for Woodfall Film Productions called *The Loneliness of the Long Distance Runner*. The Finnish director had booked a table for the three of them at the Savile Club in Mayfair that afternoon. Nonchalantly, Harwood donned a raffish suit and a loud tie and made his way to the elegant gentlemen's club. When he arrived, he found Wrede talking with the actor in a secluded corner of the bar. Harwood inwardly sighed as the proposed candidate came into view. 'Slight, shoulders hunched, tongue-tied and agonized,' he recalls of the young man, 'he made me feel as awkward as he looked.' For an hour or so, Harwood attempted to make polite conversation with his lunch companions, before the obscure student-actor departed – 'to visit,' he correctly supposes, 'his dentist.' At last free to speak his mind, the young dramatist drained his coffee cup, and, with a broad smile to his friend, declared: 'That boy cannot act at all.'

The history of British cinema may well have worked out differently had Wrede not rounded on his protégé. 'If you don't want him,' he said calmly, 'I won't do the play.' Without a blink, Harwood shot back: 'No – I think he'll be very good in the part.' And so the role of Private Potter fell into the grateful lap of the future Sir Tom Courtenay.

From the first rehearsal, Harwood realized that he was in the presence of a new breed of actor: original, unmannered and arresting. With a winning combination of sullen modesty and vulnerable piety, Courtenay persuaded audiences that Private Potter was the only sane man in a mad, cruel world. The reviews were rapturous. The critic in the *Daily Mirror* foresaw that this was a television debut of a man 'who seems destined to go places': an actor 'being talked about as another Albert Finney, brilliant star of the film *Saturday Night and Sunday Morning*.' Even more gratifying were the notices following the release of the feature film – again produced by Arbeid – a mere six months later. Writing in the *Daily Express*, the doyen of breakfast-table journalism, Godfrey Winn, implored his readers to go and hear 'The Scream that made me Search my Soul.' 'Supposing you met someone like Private Potter,' he asked in his Saturday column,

> would you throw scorn on him, automatically assuming that he was an hysterical exhibitionist, a coward in the face of the enemy, or had hit on the perfect excuse for a long, soft rest in a psychiatric ward? Myself, I came out into the daylight and bustle of St James' Street utterly convinced the other way... For are we not all searching in our different ways for oneness with the universe? Are we not all pilgrims seeking a way home?[12]

It was a hit – a palpable hit. Vast crowds flocked to experience the moral dilemma of the film. As well as contributing to Courtenay's rapid rise to fame, it established Harwood as one of the foremost young screenplay writers in Britain. That the two men would remain friends and colleagues for the rest of their lives stands as testament to the camaraderie born of their mutual struggle to the top. 'If it was hard for working-class lads like me and Albert,' reflects Sir Tom today, 'I can only imagine how hard it must have been for a South African like Ronnie, who literally knew no one at all.'

The secret was his relentlessness. Even amid the bustle and excitement of his early television plays and film scripts, Harwood was still able to rattle off a 60,000 word novel about a former concentration-camp commandant living in disguise in South America. This book, entitled *The Guilt Merchants*, was loosely based on the story of Adolf Eichmann, the Nazi colonel who had recently been sentenced to death in Israel for his role in organizing the Holocaust. As if such a compelling story needed embellishment, Harwood added several details calculated variously to delight and appal his readers. Firstly, he invented a novel camouflage for the former Nazi: that of an Orthodox Jew, 'Señor Anido', working in the offices of the Cordonez Cattle Company in the fictional two-horse town of El Pueblo. Early in the story, the reader is made to feel considerable sympathy for this lonely exile. Abused for his feigned identity by his colleagues in the office – 'Damn Jew!' bleats one – he looks back with regret and sadness at his allegedly cruel treatment in his homeland. 'Oh, God,' he thinks while gazing at a map of Germany. 'Despite what she had done,' waxes the narrator, 'despite everything, he could not help loving her.' Even his kindly Jewish boss, Señor Cordonez, objects to his overt piety. 'People forget I'm Jewish,' he tells Mr Sidnitz, the Nazi-hunting protagonist of the story. 'Not that I'm ashamed of being a Jew…' he quickly goes on. 'But, with Anido … I mean that beard. In this day and age? It's all right in a Rabbi but – you know what I mean?'

When Anido refuses to bare his arms in the office, even in the hottest weather, it is intimated that he does not wish to expose the dehumanizing number branded into his flesh by his Nazi captors. However, as the story progresses, the reader learns the truth: what he conceals is his SS identity number. It is this that sets up the real twist in the plot. Having devoted years of his life to hunting down the renegade Nazi, it is impossible for Sidnitz to go through with arresting him. In the tale's denouement, the would-be hero explains that he was only assigned to his solitary mission as a punishment for refusing to force Arabs from their land in Israel. 'We have no right to take him,' agrees another character: 'We are all the same!' The reader is left to decide for himself whether Sidnitz is correct to leave vengeance to the Lord, or to side with Cordonez, who indignantly hurls abuse at his erstwhile companion for shirking his responsibility so spectacularly. In short, the novel was vintage Harwood.

The success of the book owed something to its commissioning editor, Tom Maschler. Although at the time a relative newcomer to the book trade, this literary visionary was already on his way to becoming one of the most important names in British publishing. Born in Berlin in the same year that Hitler came to power, he lost his father and all of his grandparents to the Nazis, and only avoided the same fate thanks to the fearless determination of his mother, who smuggled him to England after accepting a job as a lady's maid. Like Harwood, the young man's awareness of the sickening crimes committed against his people gave him a sense that his life had been spared for some greater purpose. Worshipped by his mother and unencumbered by formal education, he launched himself into the publishing world with a combination of bravura and elbow-grease which shook the established order. By the time that he succeeded Robert Knittel as editorial director at Jonathan Cape in 1960 he was only twenty-seven, but already had some justification in considering himself to be one of the biggest players in the industry. The editor of the memoirs of Ernest Hemingway and also of a seminal volume of essays devoted to the New Wave in British theatre entitled *Declaration*, he was more than qualified to act as handmaiden to the aspirations of Ronnie Harwood – colossal though those remained.[13]

Not least among Maschler's many gifts was his ability to keep Harwood's feet firmly planted on the ground. At one of their first meetings the young publisher took his excitable friend into his office and calmly told him that the bound proofs of his latest novel had just arrived. Seated opposite the visitor, Maschler gravely continued: 'I am now going to place in your hands the proofs of the best novel I will publish this year.' He then proceeded to pass over the proofs of a book by another writer. Harwood's brow knotted into a sulky frown. 'And when are you going to deliver the great Jewish showbiz novel?' he proceeded, unperturbed by his companion's mounting anger. 'I did not write another novel for five years,' recollects Harwood with a trace of lingering resentment. For the first time in his life, he had been told by an editor of great repute that his undoubted talents were … circumscribed.

Still, Maschler knew his business well enough to insist that Harwood pursue his suggested course. 'I feel that you have a greater understanding of the Jewish soul than any other writer in England,' he wrote in a letter to the author shortly before the book's release. '… It is not as a Jew,' he elaborated, 'that I would like to see you write this Jewish novel, but simply as someone who loves that kind of writing and regrets its absence.' This, as time would bear out, was indeed the area in which Harwood would soar to the greatest artistic heights.[14]

But for now, Maschler's wise, if unwelcome, advice sent Harwood deeper into the world of cinema. Largely pioneered from its inception in the 1920s and 1930s by Jews – denied entry into more established professions by tacit racism – there was high demand for writers combining Harwood's talents and cultural understanding. Even before Arbeid's production of *The Barber of Stamford Hill*, Harwood had been summoned to Pinewood about a proposed film concerning the Zionist British Army officer, Major General Orde Wingate. Harwood's recollections remain vivid. 'The first time I set foot in a film studio', he has written,

> was to meet a producer who said he wanted to employ me. He had seen [the television version of] *The Barber of Stamford Hill* and thought I would be ideal to write a screenplay about Major General Orde Wingate, the Chindit leader. His reasoning was never explained. I duly presented myself at Shepperton Studios and was directed to the door of an office on which was pinned a printed card:

S. Benjamin Fisz

On The Fiddle

On The Fiddle was the title of a film and in no way a slur on Mr
Fisz, a Polish air ace who fought for the RAF during the Second
World War. I knocked and a gruff voice ordered me to enter.
Standing behind his desk, a telephone receiver jammed between
his ear and shoulder, was a tanned, well-built man, who looked as
though he was wearing a toupee. He gestured for me to sit while he
went on talking into the telephone. I gathered from the one-sided
conversation that he was in the midst of negotiating an important
deal. There was much talk of gross and net profits. When at last he
replaced the receiver he turned on me and without any warning
asked in a thick Polish accent, 'What do you know about Wingate?'

I told him of the little I had read about the general. Mr Fisz seemed
pleased that my knowledge was so scanty. 'This is good,' he said.
'You are going to write me a great screenplay about a great man.'

Timidly I tried to explain that my experience was somewhat limited
and that I had only written one television play which was about a
Jewish barber in Stamford Hill.

'That is good also,' Mr Fisz declared, beaming. 'I am now going to
give you the opening sequence of our great film.'

Striding around his small office and in between taking several
telephone calls, he described with a great many sweeping and
dramatic gestures a series of images that centred around a man
seated on a rock on the hills overlooking Jerusalem. 'Now,' he
continued in a hoarse whisper, 'we hear a voice singing in Hebrew

from Psalm 99, "Great is the Lord in Zion!" Cut! Go in closer! The man is in the uniform of an English General. And he is the one who is doing the singing. Credits, title, *Wingate*!' He paused, studied me through narrowed eyes. 'Intriguing, no?'

'Very,' I said.

'Great! You start immediately. Next week comes to London international film director of *Peyton Place*, Mark Robson, ideal also for the movie. You will work with him. Goodbye.'

At the close of this dramatic, exhilarating meeting, Fisz shook Harwood by the hand and showed him the door.

The young man would never hear from him again.

Harwood's major break in movies stemmed from an encounter of a far more humdrum nature. During the filming of *Private Potter*, he was approached by a representative from Pan Books who wanted to know if he would be willing to adapt his screenplay into a novel. 'Believing I was too grand for such mundane work,' says Harwood dryly, 'I declined.' It was to prove a fortuitous decision, for the writer eventually assigned to undertake this thankless task was a script editor at 20th Century Fox, John Burke. Impressed by the style and economy of Harwood's writing, he invited him to compose the screenplay for a film recently commissioned by his studio: an adaptation of Richard Hughes' 1929 novel *A High Wind in Jamaica*.

Now this was a production of substance. Directed by Alexander ('Sandy') Mackendrick and starring Anthony Quinn, the film was intended for a worldwide audience, not merely the discerning 'arthouse' clientele of Ben

Arbeid Productions. It was also a radical and daring story; one which would have been almost unthinkable for a blockbuster in later years. Hughes' book revolves around the ordeal of a group of children kidnapped by pirates on their way back to England from the Caribbean. In one of the first fictional examples of 'Stockholm Syndrome', the children become enamoured with their ruggedly humane captors, who treat them in some respects better than their dominating and intolerant parents. Yet when the ship is captured by the British Navy and the men are subsequently put on trial in London, the pirates are sentenced to death on the evidence of one of the girls, Emily Thornton – for a murder that she committed herself. In the agony of the courtroom, this child becomes a lightning rod for the assumptions and prejudices of the Victorian society in which she exists. Harwood could not have wished for a more complex and intriguing storyline to open his account with a major studio.

He was also in good hands editorially. 'From the outset of our time together,' recalls the Oscar-winner, 'Sandy made his directorial intentions clear not by explaining but by drawing what he wanted to see and I in turn did my best to describe his ideas.' He taught Harwood to construct sequences so that the narrative could be expressed first and foremost visually. 'To aid this process,' continues the veteran, 'he introduced me to the use of a series of postcards on which one wrote the headlines of the scenes, pinned them to a cork board or laid them out on the floor, so that one could look at them, shuffle them around, construct sequences and imagine in "filmic" terms the story's progression.' Like his early encounter with *Hamlet*, this was a crucial lesson for the burgeoning dramatist.

Almost inevitably, however, Harwood's desire to impress the revered director of *The Man in the White Suit* and *The Ladykillers* blew him stylistically off course. Unmoved by the two existing screenplays of the novel – one by the legendary Hollywood writer Nunnally Johnson; the other by Peter Ustinov, whom Harwood recalls turning the story into a 'Disney-like romp for children' – the novice set to work in the manner of a twentieth-century

Charles Dickens. 'My first stab at the screenplay,' grimaces Harwood, ' – for Sandy's eyes only – began, as the novel begins, with a two or three page description of the wind starting to rise, using much of Hughes' descriptive language from the book.' After proudly delivering this picturesque account to Mackendrick, the director stared at the document blankly. 'What's this?' he spluttered. Harwood suddenly felt naked. 'The sea becoming rough and the wind beginning to rise,' he replied meekly, '– from the book.' Mackendrick cleared his throat noisily. 'Cut it,' he said: 'Put what you've just said – I'll do the rest.' It was Harwood's first instruction in keeping description to a minimum and avoiding literary pretensions in a screenplay.

When Harwood submitted the completed manuscript several weeks later, he was called in for a celebratory meeting at 20th Century Fox with Mackendrick and the head of the British division of the company, Elmo Williams. 'They seemed for the most part pleased with what I had done,' recalls Harwood modestly, 'but while we were discussing details and changes, a secretary rushed in with a three page cable from Daryl F. Zanuck, the head of 20th Century Fox.' In two days' time, the message informed them, there was to be a shareholders' meeting in New York and Zanuck needed something to impress his well-endowed audience. No one was quite prepared for what followed. Zanuck wanted Lila Kedrova, who had just won an Oscar for her performance as Madame Hortense in *Zorba the Greek*, shoe-horned into the film at the last minute. Harwood's orders were to change the gender of one of the minor characters in the script – a tough barman from one of the pirates' hideouts – and create a compelling scene involving her and Quinn, who had also received an Academy Award nomination for his performance in *Zorba*. All this, the rookie was told, had to be done in the next twenty-four hours so that Zanuck could announce the coup at his meeting.

Panic seized the young author. 'I knew that to rewrite about ten pages,' shudders Harwood today, '– let alone create a new character – in a day was not possible.' But Williams and Mackendrick batted away his reservations. 'Don't worry,' said Elmo, 'here's what we do.'

The plan was alluringly simple. Harwood was to go home and sleep for three hours. Then, at eight-thirty, a car would be dispatched to bring him back to Soho Square, where a special office, staffed by a relay of sleepless secretaries, would be put at his disposal. Although he said little, the scriptwriter could not disguise his anxiety. 'I'll come in and help,' said Mackendrick as if to settle the matter: 'We'll do it together.'

At nine o'clock Harwood was back at the offices of 20th Century Fox feeling neither rested nor remotely optimistic about the task that lay before him. The pressure of having a typist ready to preserve whatever came into his head did little to quell his nerves. Worse, there was no sign of Sandy. 'I said that we should wait for Mr Mackendrick,' relates Harwood, 'which is what we did.' They waited and waited, but in vain. 'I tried his home telephone number,' squirms the author, '– no reply.' Finally, around ten-thirty, 'the panic rising like nausea', the young man decided to begin without him and started dictating.

The rewrite was not going terribly well when, just after midnight, a woman burst into the office. She was wearing a full-length mink coat, which the young man supposed to be her only item of clothing. 'Where's Sandy?!' she screamed. Harwood replied that he had no idea and was actually wondering the same thing himself. Unconvinced, the stranger launched into a tirade against the hapless writer in full view of his dumbstruck secretary. 'You lying bastard!' the woman bellowed, '… You're a bastard! He's a bastard! You're all bastards!' A few moments later she vanished. To this day, the playwright has no clue as to her identity.

'I tried to go on with my dictation,' resumes Harwood, 'but the ideas that formed were lumps of clay.' As one secretary was replaced by another, the situation went from desperate to terminal. 'At about three in the morning,' he continues, 'Sandy himself suddenly made an entrance.' The esteemed film director made no apology for his lateness, but swayed in a manner that suggested the reason for his delay. 'He just stared at me as though he couldn't quite remember who I was,' says Harwood wryly, 'which, I suspect, he couldn't.' As casually as he could, the perplexed author made reference to the lady in the mink coat – but before he could go into details, Mackendrick turned on his heels and staggered out of the room. It was their last face-to-face meeting.

Nevertheless, the next day the revised passages were sent via a primitive fax machine to New York. This had the desired result: Kedrova accepted Zanuck's offer. Not for the last time, however, Harwood had silently to endure his handiwork being meddled with by other hands. When he proudly attended the film's premiere in Leicester Square in the spring of 1965, he observed with some disquiet that he shared the screenplay credits with two other writers. 'The most annoying thing,' snorts the veteran, 'was that I could not detect their contributions.' Even so, for the thirty-year-old former Lyon's Corner House assistant, the thrill of seeing his name blazoned across the silver screen was titanic. Unusually, however, his abiding memory of the whole affair is tinged with disappointment. 'The film was not well-received,' he says sulkily, 'but now, all these years later, has a cult following – but that is of no comfort to anyone.'

This judgement, however, does not entirely do justice to the historical record. Many prominent critics actually hailed the film as a minor classic. One of these enthusiasts was Philip French, whose booming voice in the columns of *The Observer* was considered by many to be gospel right up until his death in 2015. After declaring that Richard Hughes could 'count himself lucky' that his tale had fallen into such capable hands as those of Alexander Mackendrick and his 'three screenwriters', he went on to praise the 'ability and insight' with which they had explored the complex theme of 'innocence as a destructive force rather than a simple virtue…'[15]

Similarly generous in her praise was Dilys Powell of the *Sunday Times* who recognized the skill with which the 'disturbing quality' of the book had been preserved in Harwood's screenplay. Particularly she admired the mesmeric intensity of the real star of the film, Deborah Baxter, who played the young murderess. 'I am convinced by her behaviour,' wrote the critic, 'as I was not for a moment convinced by the well-drilled cavorting of the schoolboys in "Lord of the Flies."' No one, however, noticed the acting talents of the young Martin Amis, who played Emily's taciturn older brother. 'Whenever I see Martin,' chirps Harwood with a proprietorial grin, 'I always say: "I could have made an actor of you!"'[16]

Insignificant though *A High Wind in Jamaica* proved to be for the future writer of gritty 'state of the nation' novels, it set Harwood on his way to Hollywood. 'Mr Zanuck seemed pleased with my efforts,' he explains, 'and offered me more well-paid work, this time to rewrite scenes for Melvyn Douglas in a film called *Rapture* which, by the time I came on board, had been retitled by the crew *Rupture*.' Fraught with linguistic and cultural barriers from the outset, the shooting of this sad tale of a teenage girl who falls in love with a convict took place in Brittany. It was here, on a cloudless afternoon in the summer of 1965, that Harwood met the great Zanuck for the first and only time in his life. During the filming of an intimate scene on a headland, a large rotary contraption appeared on the horizon. 'Without warning,' smiles Harwood, 'the sound man snatched the headphones from his ears and looked towards the sky.' 'One by one,' he continues, 'all turned to him wondering what the hell was going on.' Barely audible, the man hissed: 'C'est Zanuck!' As the helicopter approached his words were passed around the set in awed whispers: 'C'est Zanuck! C'est Zanuck!'

Within a few moments the helicopter had landed on the headland. From the cabin emerged a long cigar closely followed by a short, grizzled man. Using his arms like a traffic policeman, Mr Zanuck directed people to follow him into a Nissen hut. Led by the film's director, John Guillermin, the unknown scriptwriter boldly joined in the procession. 'Guillermin introduced me,' recalls Harwood, 'but he barely acknowledged me.' 'Let's see the rewrites,' the great man muttered impatiently. Trembling pages were hurriedly thrust before him. 'He leafed through them at speed,' continues the playwright, 'made a few marks with a pencil, said, "Great!" and marched out again with all of us following him.' In a few seconds his helicopter had taken to the air and disappeared in the direction from whence it had come. One day, the young writer dreamt, he too would be such a man. And that day, he hoped, would be soon – very soon.

Such fantasies were encouraged by Harwood's increasing proximity to the great and the good. During the filming of *Rapture*, for instance, he had the honour of spending several hours each day working on the script with the film's leading actor, Melvyn Douglas. 'As is the way with these sessions,' confides Harwood, 'our work was interspersed with gossip and anecdotes.' One of these concerned Greta Garbo, who had played opposite Douglas in the 1939 classic, *Ninotchka*. 'The day they came to shoot the famous scene,' chuckles the octogenarian, 'in which Garbo [who played a stern Soviet commissar] is supposed to laugh, the director came to Douglas' dressing room and explained they had a problem: Garbo couldn't simulate laughter.' In desperation, it was resolved that the celebrated actress would just open her mouth, throw back her head and shake a little. The sound of laughter would be added later. 'For Melvyn,' continues Harwood, 'the several days spent on the scene were purgatorial. He was expected to laugh and chuckle enjoyably while Garbo sat slack-jawed and trembling silently as though suffering from severe ague.' The memory of this experience was powerfully brought back to Douglas when, shortly after the film's release, he saw a huge billboard advertising the movie on Sunset Boulevard. 'Garbo Laughs!' read the tag line. Seething with rage, the actor wound down the window of his chauffeur-driven limousine and yelled: 'No, she fucking well doesn't!'

Over the course of the next four years, Harwood's name became known to the studios of Europe as a writer capable of adapting screenplays quickly and, by industry standards, cheaply. 'He was always a good workman,' recalls someone who knew him throughout these years, 'and I cannot recall him ever complaining or missing a deadline.' One of the most bizarre features of this conscientiousness was the young author's enthusiastic acceptance of an unlikely offer to translate several scripts into English for the Italian producer Gianni Hecht. It was an altogether surreal experience for the monolingual writer, though he never questioned his suitability for the task. 'I was flown back and forth from Rome,' he recalls happily: 'And they paid me – for the first and only time in my career – in cash.'

This much-needed commodity was delivered to Harwood in the most Sicilian of fashions. 'During the course of our first meeting,' he explains, 'Hecht shouted "Fausto!" and out of what looked like a cupboard in the corner of his office crept a small man with bloodshot eyes.' After receiving a volley of instructions in Italian, this tragic figure disappeared into his confined quarters and moments later returned clutching lire notes. These were then counted out into Harwood's outstretched hand.

Harwood later discovered that Hecht's method of recruiting secretaries was just as random as his selection of writers. 'While waiting for a meeting,' he recalls, 'his secretary told me that when she applied for the job she was warned she must be fluent in French and expect a demanding test in the language. In due course she was interviewed by Signor Hecht.'

'Parlez-vous Français?' he asked.

'Oui,' she replied.

'Okay,' he said, 'you get the job.'

In this insane and somewhat sleazy world, Harwood was at once a baffled onlooker and an eager participant. By day he mooned around the city's bustling piazzas, sampling such innocent delicacies as pistachio ice-cream, while staggering his way through hackneyed Italian scripts with a dictionary. By night he met with fellow screenplay writers and a bevy of producers to discuss his progress. Even at this early stage, Harwood realized the utility of never raising doubts or daring to contradict his paymasters – regardless of how much he inwardly abhorred their crassness. On one occasion he sat passively while one of these individuals outlined a scene for him to flesh out. 'We cut all the bullshit,' the man explained, 'and start on a black cat. We pan her across a dark street, into a doorway. She brushes up against a man's leg. Miaow! Miaow!' he continued excitedly. 'We pan up slowly, and I mean slowly, and – ba-bahm! – it's Charlie! What d'you think of it?' Harwood politely suggested that this sounded rather like a film called *The Third Man*. 'Right! Great! Terrifico!' his companion boomed: 'I always say: if you're gonna steal, steal from the best! … *Ciao!*' The film, like so many other Harwood scripts over the years, was never even made.[17]

One memory, however, stands out in the aged playwright's mind from these heady Roman days. On one visit to the city, he was invited to the villa of the producer Franco Cristaldi to celebrate the birthday of the chisel-jawed, secretly gay, actor Rock Hudson, who happened to be in town. 'It was a grand do,' remembers Harwood contentedly. At one stage, the impressed young man found himself sitting on a sofa with the screenplay-writer Larry Gelbart, who later achieved fame as the creator of *M*A*S*H*. During the course of their conversation – heavily spiced with boyish humour – the pair became aware that the well-known Italian actresses Claudia Cardinale and Monica Vitti were dancing with one another. 'Larry said to me,' recounts Harwood, '"Nobody'll believe this. Two of the best looking dames in movies are dancing with each other and we're sitting here like *klutzes*… C'mon, let's ask them to dance!"' Harwood's smile instantly vanished. 'I'm not a good dancer,' he tried. Neither was Larry. 'Okay,' continued the American, 'let's sit here like *klutzes*.' And so they did.

At one point during the evening, the music temporarily went silent and Rock Hudson's sonorous voice became dangerously audible. Locked in conversation with a group of young male admirers, he was apparently describing fixtures and fittings. 'And in my bathroom,' he said, 'I have the walls lined with pink mirrors and I have chandeliers with cute little shades in ruched silk of a darker pink.' One of the boys expressed a desire to see it. 'I'd love for you to see it, too,' returned Hudson with a flirtatious smile: 'There's room in the tub for two…'

By this time Harwood and Gelbart were exchanging concerned glances. As the party began to break up, they were approached by Hudson, who asked if they would care to come with him and some others to a nightclub. 'Larry suddenly lowered his voice an octave,' chuckles the playwright, '"That's very kind of you," he said, "but I have to get back to my hotel – I'm expecting a call from my wife."' Harwood thought this a good ruse: 'So am I,' he squeezed in. Hudson looked amused. 'You're also expecting a call from *his* wife?' he said with a smile to his ribald band: 'Dear, oh dear, what have we stumbled upon?' The two *klutzes* tried to join in the merriment, but not too convincingly. 'We returned to our respective hotels,' concludes the dramatist, 'in separate cars, and alone.'

Harwood's other major escapade into the fringes of show business came about by means of his association with Ken Hughes, whose films included such classics as *The Trials of Oscar Wilde* and *Chitty Chitty Bang Bang*. When Harwood met him in 1966 it was in order to co-write a screenplay for the unfortunately entitled comedy *Drop Dead Darling* starring Tony Curtis and the glamorous Hungarian actress Zsa Zsa Gabor. No less than with his Italian confrères, the young screenwriter did not sit easily with the crazed but talented director. 'Small, with dyed blonde hair,' recalls Harwood, 'he suffered from twitchy eyes and an obsession with sexual athletics.' 'Each morning,' continues Harwood, 'before we started work, he would recount his previous night's adventures – wild, outlandish and whether true or not I was never able to decide.' Although well into his fourth decade, this feverish character was desperate to be a part of the Age of Aquarius, and was known to frequent all the latest and most fashionable nightclubs.

On one occasion Hughes invited Harwood and his wife to accompany him to one of these trendy haunts. It was not a huge success. 'We felt awkward and alien, much to his disapproval,' remembers the evergreen fogey. While Natasha complained of a headache, her husband feared the onset of laryngitis as a result of needing to shout in order to be heard. Towards the end of this sorry adventure, Hughes drunkenly delivered his verdict on his colleague: 'You're so square, Ron – and so boring!' 'My disdain for popular culture,' sniffs the playwright, 'dates, I suspect, from that moment.'

At an early stage of their collaboration Hughes and Harwood went to meet the star of their proposed film in central London. 'Ken telephoned asking me to be at the Dorchester Hotel on a Sunday morning at 11 a.m.,' recalls Harwood, 'because Curtis wanted to have the inevitable chat about the script before he started filming at Pinewood.' Wafting past a large crowd of teenage girls camped outside the hotel, the unlikely companions made their way into the hotel's impressive lobby. Here they were spotted by Zsa Zsa, whose fifth husband, the oil-baron Joshua S. Cosden Jnr., was slumped in an armchair beside her. The great diva was apparently not pleased with her present surroundings. 'Darlink,' she lisped as she approached the screenwriters, 'this is the third hotel we have tried this morning, but I don't like it – we are trying to find anudda.' With a weary sigh, Mr Cosden explained that they would shortly be heading over to Claridges. The dumbstruck wordsmiths made sympathetic noises before quietly backing away. As they were doing so, however, Zsa Zsa took hold of the younger man's arm. 'Darlink,' she implored, 'give me more jokes in the script. I don't have enough jokes and I am famous for my jokes.' Flattered, Harwood wanly suggested that he would raise it with Curtis. 'He is Hungarian like me,' she said darkly, '– we will not get on.'

Upon reaching the Oliver Messel Suite on the top floor of the hotel, Harwood and Hughes were shown into a lavish drawing room by a male secretary who seemed to be suffering from acute anxiety. In a few moments his master breezed in full of good cheer. At first all seemed to be going well. 'Listen,' said Curtis at one stage, 'I don't need people to say' – putting his hand to his brow with a mock cringe – '"Good Morning, Mr Movie Star". I just like to get on with work.' Little work, however, was actually conducted during the course of their meeting. 'Curtis,' explains Harwood, 'just walked around his suite waving a Cuban cigar in the guise of a down-to-earth actor who had not been ruined by the sweet smell of success.' It may have been this impression which caused Hughes, during a lull in the conversation, to mention something that he would come to regret. 'We met Zsa Zsa in the lobby,' he said with a broad grin, 'she says she wants us to give her more jokes.' Chiming in excitedly, Harwood added: 'She said she was famous for her jokes.' But Curtis' response completely changed the mood. 'From kindly Dr Jekyll,' he recalls, 'he was now a snarling Mr Hyde.' 'She wanted *what!?*' yelled the actor. 'That Hungarian cow,' he went on, 'is not going to have more lines never mind more jokes!'

Unable to placate Curtis, the two screenwriters were told that they would shortly be following him on a visit to Zsa Zsa's suite at Claridges. 'We've got to get this thing settled,' he fumed, '… right now, this morning!' Hurling instructions over his shoulder at his trembling assistant, the great man rose to his feet, embraced his wife – 'a little more passionately than was seemly' – and marched towards the lift. But when he and his reluctant henchmen reached the lobby he suddenly froze. 'Shit!' he snarled upon seeing the crowd that had gathered to catch a glimpse of him. Without a moment's hesitation, the actor took hold of Harwood's jacket and pushed him through the revolving doors. Seconds later the dazzled young man found himself being used as a human battering ram as they carved their way through the melee. 'They tore the buttons off my jacket,' he said lamely after being bundled onto the floor of the awaiting limousine: 'It's my best suit.' Curtis was unmoved. 'Gee,' he said while relighting his cigar, 'that's a shame.'

When they arrived at Claridges, the posse made their way to Zsa Zsa's suite. Resting his cigar on a radiator case, Curtis knocked on the door and was swiftly admitted to the room. 'He did not bother with any social preliminaries,' winces Harwood, 'but launched into Hungarian.' From his tone and the way in which his upper lip curled, it was clear that he was being far from respectful. After a few minutes of this cruel onslaught, Zsa Zsa turned to Harwood with wide, terrified eyes. 'Darlink,' she said, 'he is saying terrible things about me. He is calling me a Hungarian whore – Vy does he do this?' To this protestation, neither screenplay writer had any plausible answer. Then, as abruptly as it had begun, Curtis' diatribe came to an end. Harwood and Hughes could only mumble polite farewells as they followed the star back into the corridor, where he nonchalantly resumed his cigar.

'We won't have any more trouble from her,' he bellowed triumphantly into a cloud of exhaled smoke.

Back at the Dorchester, however, the drama continued. As soon as they returned to Curtis' suite, the actor demanded that his assistant get the film's producer on the phone. He wanted to have it stated in writing that Zsa Zsa would make no changes to the script without his express permission. By the time that Curtis finally slammed down the phone, the two Englishmen were beside themselves with embarrassment. During a brief period when they were left on their own – 'Curtis wandered off at one stage,' recalls Harwood, 'to find his wife, and, I think, a baby, but I cannot be sure' – Hughes said what they were both thinking: 'Why the fuck did I tell him we'd met Zsa Zsa in the lobby?'

It was a question that Harwood would continue to ponder over the coming weeks. 'The next day,' he explains, 'I got a call from Zsa Zsa saying that she wanted me to make some changes to the script.' The newcomer tried to tell her that she should speak with the director. 'I did, darlink,' she replied: 'he told me to speak to you.' 'Thanks, Ken,' thought Harwood. Before long the young man had been cajoled into arranging a secret meeting for Hughes and Zsa Zsa behind Curtis' back. 'She arrived,' grimaces the unwilling conspirator, 'with several awful jokes which she had either used before or thought up overnight.' Both men pretended to laugh a great deal and promised that they would make use of them if they could. 'Nothing came of it,' sighs Harwood with relief. When he visited the set a few weeks later he enquired whether Curtis was behaving himself. 'You know what he likes?' snapped Hughes: 'He likes people to salute, bow and say, "Good Morning, Mr Movie Star."'

Yet, for all the pain of working alongside Curtis, the result was a commercial success beyond Harwood's dreams. Released in the United States (as *Arrivederci, Baby!*) in the autumn of 1966 and in the United Kingdom early the following year, the film delighted a newly affluent young audience in search of relaxation and amusement. As with all Harwood's work, however, there was also a serious and introspective element to the production. Curtis' character in the film is a penniless foundling, who claws his way to fame and fortune by marrying and then murdering a string of wealthy older women. In the opening sequence, during which Curtis ascends into an aeroplane after kissing farewell to a beautiful young woman, the actor's voice is heard giving a description of his *modus operandi*: 'The fundamental requirements of a high-class conman,' he explains, 'are that he should be personable, well-dressed, amiable, well-mannered, good-looking, attractive to women and utterly without conscience or scruple.' It was a personality type to which Harwood would be endlessly drawn.

By the close of the 1960s, Harwood's own journey to a state of material comfort and ease was complete. With tens of thousands of pounds now safely stored in his bank account, he could afford to buy a large country house in the village of Liss, Hampshire, near Bedales School, where he would soon be sending Antony and his two subsequent children, Deborah (b. 1963) and Alexandra (b. 1966). Greatest of all his financial windfalls, though, was the £10,000 delivered to him by Richard Burton for the film rights to *The Guilt Merchants*: a fortune undiminished by the fact that the film never went into production. Yet the debonair young man still wanted something more, something big: he wanted to be a respected literary figure. To fulfilling this aspiration, Harwood now turned his attentions.

7
Man of Letters

But wouldn't you say you were someone really who hankers
for a bygone age and that the modern world is not to your liking?
The Ordeal of Gilbert Pinfold, *Act One*

For the biographer in search of a turning point in the life of Sir Ronald Harwood, there are few junctures more definite than the death of his father. Not, however, that of his biological father, whose demise left no recognizable scar or blemish on the future playwright; but that of his spiritual father, Sir Donald Wolfit, whose awesome shadow he has never truly escaped. If there was one consolation for the junior party in this tragedy, it was the fact that his old master lived just long enough to see him emerge from the chrysalis stage and beat his wings expectantly towards the grassy uplands of literary greatness.

Harwood's first recognition in this regard came directly from Wolfit himself. On 22 August 1966 the world-weary actor proposed him for election to the Garrick Club. For Harwood, this was a transition second in importance only to his arrival in England sixteen years previously. Simultaneously satisfying his longing to belong to a community of like-minded individuals as well as providing him with a suitably bespoke environment to conduct his social engagements, membership of the Garrick conferred upon Harwood an ease and tranquillity not obtained even through his love of family, religion and country. Today, Ronnie Harwood is perhaps best known, at least to his closest friends, as a clubman.

Little has changed at the famous club since Harwood first swept up the grand oak staircase at Garrick Street, Covent Garden, half a century ago. Closed to female members, anathema to vulgarity in all its forms and inhabited solely by the brightest stars in the broad firmament of the law and the arts, it remains what it was to Trollope, Dickens and Thackeray: a gentlemen's club. At the time of Harwood's election, the membership was experiencing modest growth, as careers in Britain's booming legal and media industries proliferated. Continuity was maintained by the unwritten customs and conventions passed down from member to member in unbroken succession back to the days of its foundation in 1831.

Fondly does Harwood recall his own initiation at the hands of his aged mentor. 'He had ever had few close friends,' explains Harwood in words more applicable to himself than he would readily acknowledge, 'but in the Garrick he had countless acquaintances who held him in genuine affection.' Two incidents involving Wolfit particularly stand out in Harwood's memory from those faraway salmon and cucumber days. 'During one evening in the Garrick,' he smirks, '[Wolfit] suddenly broke off in mid-sentence, half rose in his chair, bowed to an elderly man who was leaving the room, then explained: "Lord Evershed, former Master of the Rolls", and continued his conversation.' Another time the pair bumped into the actor and biographer Robert Speaight, who had just received the MBE. 'Wolfit complained that his knighthood was costing him a good deal of additional expense,' resumes Harwood: 'He concluded, "I expect you find the same thing, don't you, Bobby, in your own small way?"'18

Harwood and his wife happen to have dined with Wolfit at the Garrick a mere three weeks before his unexpected demise on 17 February 1968. 'We were concerned,' he relates, 'because his usually impeccable diction sounded a little slurred and when he walked he leaned a little to one side.' Believing their companion to be endowed with an almost superhuman constitution, it never occurred to either Harwood or his wife that he was suffering anything more than the aftereffects of slightly too much claret. Even when the former dresser went to see Wolfit at the Royal Masonic Hospital three days before his death, it did not seem at all likely to him that the end was near: 'He was full of good cheer,' he remembers. Only after the black day did Harwood realize that his Lear had given him every possible indication of his impending final exit. 'After his death,' he whispers, 'we were shown a photograph, one of the last taken of him, in which he appears haggard and prematurely in decline.' Love and admiration had blinded the young man to what was only too plain to see.

It was doubtless this quality which inspired Wolfit to invite Harwood to undertake one of the utmost tasks that a great man can bestow upon a smaller one. At the reading of the deceased actor's will, the following clause was solemnly read out:

> To my good friend Ronald Harwood the sum of FIFTY POUNDS
> with the hope that he will undertake (with the aid of my press books
> and letters) some form of biography of my work in the theatre with
> the assistance of my said wife.

Although the bequest came as a shock and even a minor burden for the ebullient author – 'the notion of writing any form of non-fiction had never occurred to me,' he grins – it proved to be the first step to his future rise. Inexperienced as he was in this new field, Harwood simply followed his usual method of finding his way through an expensive process of trial and error. He had, for instance, no idea whether it would be best to begin writing immediately or to spend several years amassing a large archive from which to draw material for the book. 'At first,' explains Harwood, 'I decided on the latter course, but my memories of him were so alive in me, the urge to write about him so pressing, that it soon became clear I had no alternative but to begin at once.' In little over two years he had completed what was to prove a classic in the genre: *Sir Donald Wolfit CBE: his life and work in the unfashionable theatre*. It did not, however, entail great financial reward – the royalties he received did not quite cover the £250 needed for Harwood to purchase a memento of the celebrated actor: a study in oils by Michael Noakes. 'So life-like!' enthused a relation of Wolfit's when she saw it hanging outside Harwood's study in Liss. 'I was told later,' he chuckles, 'that she had never met Donald face-to-face.'

The finished biography was every bit as convincing. While Wolfit's many detractors questioned the young Boswell's determination to confront the actor's arrogance and bullying tendencies – 'Now why would anyone want to write a book about *him!*' gasped one contemporary – the book was a chapter in the history of the dramatic arts no less than a portrait of one of its most intriguing characters. Such was the unanimous verdict of the reviewers. 'It is a biography written with love and laughter,' glowed Caryl Brahms in *The Guardian*, 'and who better to write it than Mr Harwood, who worked with Wolfit for some years under almost as many hats behind the scenes as the variety of parts he played upon the boards...?' Likewise, Robert Speaight put aside personal rancour for Wolfit to note in the *Times Literary Supplement* that despite Harwood's 'clear affection' for his subject, he had not been party to a whitewash. 'His comment is candid, generous and shrewd,' he wrote. 'He brings out the simplicity,' he continued, 'the sensitivity, and also the contradictions of Wolfit's character; and the estimate of his sheer *size* will not lightly be questioned by anybody who saw him at his best.' Eric Porter joined this favourable chorus with a lengthy review for the *Sunday Times*. 'Fortunately,' he insightfully observed,

> Mr Harwood does not attempt to excuse the warts, he explains them. He doesn't explain them away but, almost in spite of them, his book leaves us with a feeling of richness and warmth towards the man. Donald may have appeared to have loved himself overmuch (is not egomania the tip of the iceberg called insecurity?) but he did love Shakespeare – and he loved the theatre. ... I think that Donald could well say, from the centre of whatever Elysian spotlight he may be standing in, 'I wish no other herald, no other speaker of my living actions.'[19]

Crowning all of these accolades was the encyclical pronouncement of Harold Hobson in his 'Choice of the Year' selection for the same newspaper. 'As a rule I do not enjoy reading theatrical biographies', he loftily explained.

... But Mr Harwood is not only capable of accurately assessing Donald Wolfit as an actor, but understands him as a man. Wolfit began as a poor boy in Nottingham. He ended as a rich man with a title, after giving some of the finest as well as the most disputable performances of our time, and when he died not a single one of his eminent contemporaries could be found who was willing to give even the briefest address at his memorial service. Frankly, affectionately, with clear but sympathetic eyes Mr Harwood movingly tells this triumphant, tragic story.[20]

Looking back on a career of similar dimensions, Harwood prizes these words as the most touching and germane ever delivered upon his manifold activities. 'Somehow I felt I had been promoted from the ranks,' he beams. No longer simply a catchpenny novelist, the enterprising young author had been translated into a proud, dignified Man of Letters.

This status was anticipated by Harwood's first major profile in a national newspaper. Written for *The Guardian* in the autumn of 1969 by the sharp-eyed theatre scout Robin Thornber, the piece gave as true a picture of Harwood as anything published about him either before or since. 'Ronald Harwood,' narrated Thornber, 'refused to talk about his work, saying that such talk only led to a lot of pseudo-intellectual pomposity.' 'Smartly emblazered and healthily tanned,' he continued, 'he looks more like a visiting cricket captain from the colonies ... [than] your hairy intellectual.' Above all Thornber discerned at once that Harwood's greatest talent lay in his adaptability. 'He sees nothing significant in this versatility,' he wrote. As Harwood had knowingly explained to him: 'It's just part of the writing process. The content comes first and the form follows; anybody can learn form.' Whatever Thornber's inner reservations about his young subject's towering self-confidence, he was certain of his sincerity. 'This is the voice of a professional,' he judged, 'a craftsman, rather than a compulsive, tortured genius.' In the closing section of the article, he concurred with Harwood's not entirely objective view that his career conclusively proved that 'no door is closed to talent.' 'Even,' ended Thornber, 'a penniless South African Jew can make it.'[21]

But in which direction would this daring young Mallory channel his almost limitless energy? Movies, novels, biography, the theatre – all of these peaks seemed to tremble before him. His unshakable dedication to the last mentioned of them is perhaps the most surprising aspect of Harwood's early career. He had, after all, experienced only a modest amount of success as an actor, and his writing career so far had showed promise in almost every genre besides straight drama. Even while busily writing Wolfit's biography, he had produced with apparent felicity two well-received novels: *The Girl in Melanie Klein*, about a sane woman trapped in a comfortable nursing home for lunatics, and *Articles of Faith*, a hugely ambitious South African saga about a clan of Dutch settlers blighted by the nefarious activities of one of their revered forebears. In addition to these monuments of industry and creativity, the thirty-five-year-old had also written a screenplay adaptation for Casper Wrede of Solzhenitsyn's bleak classic, *One Day in the Life of Ivan Denisovich*, which was reportedly praised by the Russian master as being 'true to truth' – an aside which invited a wry smile from the British author as much as the Nobel Laureate's supposed complaint that there was not enough humour in the script.

By contrast to these solid achievements, Harwood had only written two stage plays to date: *March Hares* and *Country Matters*. Both of these works owed their genesis to the enthusiasm of Casper Wrede and Michael Elliott, who had reunited, after a decade-long hiatus, to form a new theatrical enterprise in the North-east: the 69 Theatre Company. While Harwood would eventually bring this company the success that it had never known in London, it cannot be said that these early offerings worked any miracles.

March Hares was performed at the Royal Court, Liverpool, in 1964. It was, wrote one reviewer, a 'threadbare comedy' about a 'beatnik couple' who try to murder each other for reasons that are not entirely clear. The latter play, which concerned the sexual frustrations of a group of middle-class hipsters intent on buying a large country house, was produced at the Manchester University Theatre in 1969. Despite the play's seemingly racy storyline, it was considered to be 'very boring' by *The Guardian's* young critic, Simon Hoggart. '[T]he author seems to recognize this,' he jibed, 'by tossing in a selection of jokes at the end of any long-winded or emotional passage.' 'One senses,' concluded the reviewer, 'that the play is trying to work on a highly serious level, and that the author has realized his failure to engage us intellectually.'[22]

The miscarriage of these plays did nothing, however, to dampen Harwood's dramatic aspirations. With typical certainty, he surmised the problem to be simply that British theatre was not quite ready for a return of the entertaining, 'well-made' plays in which he had so revelled in his youth, and for which he would eventually win acclaim. Slowly, however, the sands began to shift. 'As the decade wore on,' he explains, 'it felt as though the prevailing attitudes that had dominated the theatre for the past fifteen years had begun to weaken.' No longer were the names Osborne and Wesker held in awe: the 'angry young men' of the 1950s had become prematurely grey – the latter of these playwrights virtually disappeared from public view after the failure of his 1972 play, *The Journalists*. The way was now open for Ronnie Harwood. And, as ever, he seized his chance with eager hands.

His vehicle was an adaptation of Evelyn Waugh's 1957 novel, *The Ordeal of Gilbert Pinfold*. Just as in his student days, Harwood fell upon this neglected masterpiece with no preconceptions and for no reason in particular. Only its inviting position on the bookcase of a friend he was staying with in Helsinki during the filming of *Ivan Denisovich* brought it into his ken. 'On the way up to the guest bedroom,' he recalls, 'I was obliged to pass bookshelves that lined the stairwell.' Recognizing the name on the spine of one of these volumes, Harwood decided to take it up with him. 'Once settled in bed,' he recounts, 'I began to read and before I was half-way through knew I had stumbled on an ideal subject to dramatize.'

The selection of *Gilbert Pinfold* was highly revealing of Harwood's self-perception as an author, even in this early phase. Inspired by Waugh's own titanic ego and contemptuous misanthropy, it is the story of a successful but deeply dissatisfied writer whose disgust for the modern world manifests itself in a bout of temporary madness. 'His strongest tastes were negative,' wrote Waugh in the original: 'He abhorred plastics, Picasso, sunbathing and jazz – everything in fact that had happened in his own lifetime …

> He was neither a scholar not a regular soldier; the part for which he cast himself was a combination of eccentric don and testy colonel and he acted it strenuously, before his children in Lychpole and his cronies in London, until it came to dominate his whole outward personality. When he ceased to be alone, when he swung into his club or stumped up the nursery stairs, he left half of himself behind and the other half swelled to fill its place. He offered the world a front of pomposity mitigated by indiscretion, that was as hard, bright and antiquated as a cuirass.[23]

Waugh's self-portrait fitted the novice playwright with haunting precision. Feared by his children for his habit of improvising gruesome tales while they pressed their ears to his study door, and proudly disdainful of most of the social and political developments of the twentieth century, Harwood delighted in recasting Pinfold in his own image. Yet, no less than in the case of Waugh himself, there was in the character – as Harwood fairly acknowledges – an element of 'self-hatred', which is not present in the rest of either man's work. It was perhaps this feature that gave both the novel and the play the saving grace of unconscious humility.

Of all Harwood's plays, *Gilbert Pinfold* took more years than any other to reach the stage. This was the result of a five-year battle to secure a suitable venue, cast and legal authorization for the production. Looking back on this achievement today, Harwood credits Michael Elliott in particular for finally bringing it to fruition. 'An intellectual, quintessentially English,' he recalls, 'and blessed with an innate sense of theatricality and drama… he was without doubt the outstanding director of his generation bar none.'

Almost single-handed he had heroically taken up the challenge of converting Manchester's derelict Cotton Exchange into an epicentre of dramatic talent. Even while still utilizing the draughty University Theatre and – briefly – a large tent on the former cotton-trading floor, he still managed to draw some of theatreland's brightest lights to the smoggy industrial town. 'When he persuaded Tom Courtenay to come and play Young Marlowe in the first season,' wrote one admiring journalist, 'a Manchester paper phoned up to ask if he was any relation of *the* Tom Courtenay.' Subsequent productions starring Albert Finney (*Uncle Vanya*), Vanessa Redgrave (*Daniel Deronda*) and, once again, Courtenay (*Peer Gynt*) established the company and its newly-opened 750-seat circular theatre as an institution of comparable stature to anything in London's West End.[24]

Harwood was at once a beneficiary and an instigator of this swelling theatrical tide. 'It fell to me,' he recalls grumpily, 'to liaise with the Waugh estate in the person of his son, Auberon, who seemed to behave in imitation of his difficult father.' Permission was absolutely withheld unless the role of Pinfold was played by a suitably gargantuan star. This is where Harwood's ability to ingratiate himself with theatrical knights came into its own. For it so happened that Sir Alec Guinness, whom Harwood had briefly crossed paths with while working on Ken Hughes' 1970 film *Cromwell*, lived in the vicinity of Liss. The temptation to ask the great actor to play Pinfold was too great; but Harwood realized that he would only succeed in this audacious task if he first won Guinness' friendship. A dinner party offensive was swiftly launched.

It did not, however, begin particularly well. 'We were visitors to his house on countless occasions,' explains Harwood, 'but we only managed to get him to dinner at Berrygrove about three times in all the years we lived near him.' Always prepared to unfurl the red carpet for important guests, the budding playwright once lured Guinness to his home by organizing a lunch party at which the actress Margaret Leighton – with whom Guinness was infatuated – would also be present. 'All went swimmingly,' recounts Harwood, 'until we had finished the first course.' Then the Oscar-winning actor suddenly rose from his seat, placed his napkin over his left arm and started to impersonate a doddery, elderly waiter. 'He cleared the plates from the table,' snarls Harwood, 'and carried them into the back kitchen where Natasha was preparing to serve the next course.' Harwood had to excuse himself to resolve the matter: 'He improvised dialogue as though toothless,' he goes on with rising anger: '*What a great pleasure to see Miss Leighton here again,*' he mimics; '*I think you'll agree the food's improved …*' Only following a gentle rebuke from Leighton – 'Alec, do sit down, there's a dear' – did Guinness at length return to his place. 'He looked around,' snorts Harwood, 'for approval, but none was forthcoming.'

Yet the forty-two-year-old playwright had done it: in the autumn of 1976 he secured Guinness' agreement to play the role of Pinfold. 'Sir Alec was at first agreeable,' he recalls, 'not to say enthusiastic.' For several weeks the giddy arriviste marvelled at his impressive catch: 'For Sir Alec to appear in Manchester,' he continues with undiminished self-satisfaction, 'was evidently an event; the press made much of it.' But only a few weeks later it became clear that the actor's goodwill was unlikely to be transformed into deeds. The first alarm bell sounded when Harwood received a rare lunch invitation from Sir Alec. 'I must remember,' he wrote in his diary, 'that every time Guinness invites us to his house it is a prelude to his doing something really nasty.' Harwood guessed from the presence of another playwright what this might be. 'The other guest was Alan Bennett,' continued the furious diarist – 'ladylike, languid, and aloof, with a plaintive, high-pitched voice and Lancashire accent.' Within days it was announced that Guinness was pulling out of *Gilbert Pinfold* – supposedly for a hernia operation. It was not long, however, until his appearance in Bennett's new play, *The Old Country*, was publically advertised.[25]

To say that Harwood was bitterly incensed by these developments would be a libellous understatement. Agents, secretaries, actors, directors, technicians, stage managers all felt the indiscriminate lash of his unrelenting tongue. Central to his outrage was the complaint that Guinness' oversized ego was the reason for his 'betrayal': 'Pinfold is the centre,' blustered Harwood in his diary, 'and AG doesn't want to be the centre – he's too falsely modest for that, would rather stand off-centre and be noticed all the same.' Friends of Guinness, however, found there to be a more prosaic reason for the actor's behaviour: he considered Harwood's play to be 'wretched'. Hearing this through the clubland grapevine, the playwright affected blithe indifference. 'We kissed gently,' wrote Harwood on seeing Guinness for the last time about the matter, 'as we always do.' With one hand still resting on the dramatist's generously-padded shoulder, the famous actor said: 'You must think this a Judas kiss?' 'No, no', murmured the younger man in kindly tones. Only in his diary did Harwood issue his real verdict: 'shits will be shits'. Although convinced that he had 'very little personal venom' for Guinness, Harwood resolved never to offer a part to the mercurial star again.

In the event, the loss of Guinness was not calamitous for the production. 'Everything happens for the best,' grins Harwood, 'as my mother would say.' The mantle of Pinfold was taken up by an actor who blended the eccentricity of a Wolfit with the finesse of a Gielgud. Known principally for playing Shakespearean roles upon the stage, but happiest of all playing loquacious barristers and crusty admirals upon the screen, Michael Hordern was the kind of actor who appealed directly to Harwood's acute sense of the tragic and the ridiculous. 'We were fortunate to have Michael Hordern,' he recounts, 'play Pinfold, and he did so magnificently.' When the curtain went up on first night, Harwood sat back contentedly in the stalls awaiting his arrival as a major dramatist.

The notices in the press did not disappoint this heady aspiration. In a week in which Ian McKellen appeared in a reputation-making production of *Macbeth* at Stratford, Harwood's adaptation was even given the honour of centre stage by many of the leading critics. Most notable of these was Bernard Levin in the *Sunday Times*. '[T]here is a very Behemoth to be seen at the Royal Exchange, Manchester,' he uncharacteristically enthused. '[T]he play works uncommonly well,' he went on, 'walking the book's line between absurdity and terror as Pinfold's accusing voices multiply and his imaginary tormentors grow more ingenious and more cruel.' While accepting that Harwood's task had been considerably lightened by the fact that much of Waugh's 'diamond prose' had been preserved, he recognized something unique and haunting about the production. This, he proposed, was the brilliance of the leading actor: 'Mr Hordern's the thing,' cried the reviewer in his crescendo.

> And what a thing! He is off the stage for no more than a few seconds in the play's 150 minutes, and this performance is surely the crown of an immensely distinguished career. ... [W]hat other actor could so shamble and groan and grimace like this, without ever hinting at exaggeration, let alone self-aggrandisement? (Only Guinness.) What other performer could so suggest a man fighting to keep from his consciousness the conviction that he is mad? (Only Scofield.) How many other actors could simultaneously – simultaneously, not alternately – have us shaking with laughter and transfixed with pity? (Only Olivier.) Who else combines such classical diction with such expressive intonation? (Only Gielgud.) Who can match this generosity of gesture ... ? Only Hordern, I think, who with this performance has made himself the peer of that illustrious company.[26]

Not since his cameo in Blackpool had Harwood's wagon been so spectacularly hitched to a blazing star. Even for a man with his insatiable appetite for fame, the repercussions of Hordern's masterly performance were simply too good to be entirely believed by the breakthrough playwright. Almost simultaneously he was invited to review books each week in the *Sunday Times*, to host the BBC 2 paperback-review show, *Read All About It*, and also to front a thirteen-part documentary for the public broadcaster about the history of the theatre, *All the World's a Stage*. Nor was this all: new offers to write Hollywood screenplays also proliferated. 'It got me out of a bit of a hole,' he chuckles. Only a few months prior to the success of *Gilbert Pinfold* the hard-pressed family man had been forced to ask his wife to negotiate a discount on the school-fees at Bedales. For some time his beloved Berrygrove even appeared in the window of a Petersfield estate agent. With the play's success, these mundane worries began steadily to recede.

Harwood's brief experiment as a TV pundit forced him to develop a hitherto untested aspect of his personality. Professedly 'servile' by nature, it was a jolt to his system now to be leading dialogue with well-known authors and intellectuals. He certainly did not follow the interviewing style of the beady-eyed, neatly-trimmed journalist satirised in the opening scene of *Gilbert Pinfold*. Far from hectoring or scientifically dissecting his subjects, he charmed them and put them at their ease. Yet Harwood was no Michael Parkinson: he did not coax his guests into lowering their guards. Nor did he, like John Freeman, withdraw himself so as to leave them to squirm uncomfortably beneath the penetrating gaze of the camera. He met his interviewees on level ground: the viewer is left in no doubt that the presenter regarded himself as every inch their equal.

Considering the eminence of some of the guests interviewed by Harwood on BBC television and radio during the 1970s, this self-assuredness could easily be mistaken for unwarranted arrogance. They included such household names as Graham Greene, Sir John Betjeman, Dame Rebecca West, Roald Dahl and Stephen Spender. There is no doubt, however, that these literary masters accepted Harwood as one of their own. 'Greene asked me about my working habits,' says the proud playwright. 'He gave me invaluable guidance,' he goes on: '"Always stop," he said, "when it's going well."' Only occasionally did Harwood's clubbable manner slip into the bog-land of overfamiliarity. After sitting respectfully through Roald Dahl's evocative description of how he came up with the idea for *Charlie and the Chocolate Factory* ('I heard of a chocolate factory near my school where there was a secret room in which grown men and women spent their entire time thinking up new chocolate bars') Harwood cut in brusquely: 'I don't believe a word of it,' he chortled, before turning his attentions to another one of his guests.

Nevertheless, in all of the episodes which Harwood hosted he displayed ample knowledge, tact and humour to justify his exalted position. Two factors alone prevented him from sustaining himself as a noted television personality. First of all, he evidently considered the format to be populist and intellectually lightweight – his superior demeanour when discussing poetry with Joanna Lumley or exploring Victorian literature with the England women's cricket captain cannot be watched today without respectful embarrassment. 'I considered the work to be beneath me,' reflects Harwood: 'Oh,' he continues with a mock cringe, 'so you've won a prize for your little novel?' Added to this lofty condescension, Harwood was crippled by the fact that he was often forced by the pressure of other projects to scrimp. One individual to find himself on the receiving end of this unfortunate necessity was George Orwell's former flatmate, Rayner Hemppenstall. 'I have just seen the reviews in the Sunday papers,' he minuted in his diary upon the publication of his 1977 novel *Two Moons*. '[B]oth are incredibly vicious,' he railed: 'They are by Lorna Sage and Ronald Harwood, whoever they may be.' What especially angered Hemppenstall was the latter's merry confession that he had not actually read the book: 'Harwood,' continued the disgusted novelist, 'says nothing whatever about the content, but simply makes clever remarks about the form.' A complaint was formally lodged with the newspaper's literary editor, John Whitley: '[A]s Mr Harwood has found himself unable to read the book,' wrote Hemppenstall, '[you] should not have let the non-review appear in print.'[27]

However, what really made Harwood unsuited to life in the public eye was his scarcely disguised hypersensitivity. Shortly after his first outing as host of *Read All About It* a lengthy article by Julian Barnes appeared in the *New Statesman* contrasting Harwood's approach unfavourably with that of his predecessor, Melvyn Bragg. 'I met him at a party,' explains Harwood of a subsequent encounter with the future Man Booker Prize winner, 'and told him he just wanted the job himself – he got very angry indeed!' Not long thereafter a series of jokey articles by Richard Ingrams appeared in the *Spectator* mocking Harwood's 'infuriating assurance' and tendency to use his programme to promote his own work. Rather than accepting such snipes as an unavoidable feature of being a writer in the limelight, Harwood immediately instructed his solicitor to commence proceedings against the famous satirist. Despite experiencing the satisfaction of a rare out-of-court victory over the scurrilous editor of *Private Eye* – Harwood was heard to joke that he 'wished he was libelled more often' – he did not emerge from the incident with his credibility entirely intact.

Nevertheless, the in-demand author was now a permanent feature in the highest circles. Having renewed his friendship with his old sparring-partner Harold Pinter, the two playwrights entered into an entirely new phase of their long association. When Pinter split up with his first wife to live with Lady Antonia Fraser, it fell to the younger man to help shield the famous pair from the scrutiny of the press. 'They came to stay at Berrygrove often,' declares Harwood, 'and Harold and I would play squash together at Lords most weeks.' Asked who usually won these contests, he mouths: 'I did'. Lady Antonia appears to have been particularly taken by her new husband's erstwhile companion. 'Ronnie Harwood was wonderful!' she enthused upon their first meeting: 'Clever, charming, high-spirited.' Later Pinter would honour Harwood by directing his 1995 play *Taking Sides* and – scarcely less importantly – selecting him for his scratch cricket team. 'Ronnie Harwood,' wrote Fraser after watching this theatrical cohort lose decisively to the *Guardian*'s XI, 'was ebullient and rather good.' Harwood's teammates included not only Pinter himself, but also Simon Gray and Tom Stoppard. The first two of these playwrights would later cement their friendship with Harwood by holidaying together in Greece and also collaborating as members of the writers' pressure-group PEN, which Harwood presided over, for the English branch, between 1989 and 1993, and, internationally, from 1993 to 1997.[28]

Yet amid these satisfying personal triumphs, Harwood did not take his eye off a far more significant ball: the theatre. 'All I have to say,' wrote Michael Elliott in a letter to him shortly after the success of *Gilbert Pinfold*, 'is that I hope desperately we shall work together again soon and often. Please go on writing for us when you can. We need you badly. We really might come to something splendid. *Stay with us.*'[29]

The result was *A Family*. 'The play just burst out of me,' explained Harwood in an interview conducted by Ion Trewin of *The Times*. Even more than *Gilbert Pinfold*, the play was a personal story. 'Encouraged by what I regarded as my first toe-hold on the theatrical ladder,' reminisces Harwood, 'I wrote a play about my cousin Harold Berman's experiences in Italy during the Second World War, and of how his father parachuted into the country in order to search for his son.' The difficulty was that Harwood insisted on combining this story of derring-do with the machinations of a large Jewish family meeting together for a Sunday gathering. The discordant themes did not entirely resolve, at least in the eyes of the majority of the critics. 'For most of its length,' wrote Michael Billington in *The Guardian*, 'I assumed the play was intended as a ritual put-down of the cloying horror of family life.' Witheringly, he went on to explain that those who deigned to 'stay after the interval' would be surprised to find that 'the latter stages (quite movingly) convinced me that Mr Harwood was making the more original point that we miss the grappling-hooks when they are torn from our flesh...' Alas, surmised Billington, 'what Harwood is saying gets obscured by the gauche and clumsy way he says it.'[30]

Although the play succeeded in moving from Manchester to the Theatre Royal, Haymarket, its days in the capital were brutally curtailed by a series of reviews echoing the sentiments of Billington – the one by Irving Wardle in *The Times* actually made the playwright cry. 'Perhaps,' reflects Harwood today, 'things hadn't changed after all!' Once again, however, the writer fell back on the rock of his indefatigable optimism. There was, after all, much to enjoy from his first major outing as a dramatist. 'The play had a starry cast,' he remarks, 'including Paul Scofield, Harry Andrews and Irene Handl.' As ever, the South African-born playwright basked in this august company – even if his efforts to charm and please were sometimes met with cool disdain. On one occasion, Harwood forced his way into Scofield's dressing room to bombard him with questions about his performance and get-up. 'Don't you have a hairdryer?' he interposed with real anxiety. 'Oh no,' came the calm reply, 'I dry with a towel.' Another time, Harwood insisted on taking the veteran Hollywood hardman Rod Steiger backstage to meet the acclaimed star of his show. 'There was a long flight of stairs to Scofield's dressing room,' recalls a member of the cast, 'and Ronnie took him up it very slowly.' As they approached the great man's boudoir, however, Scofield suddenly emerged clutching a heavy suitcase. Reverently, Harwood introduced his two distinguished friends, but Scofield was not in the giving vein. 'Oh excuse me,' he said as he slipped away, 'I've got to catch my train.'[31]

To these experiences were blended Harwood's lifelong love of risqué humour and rib-digging double entendre. His play was saturated with such badinage, from the delightful malapropisms of the drama's kindly grandmother to the crude prescription of the character (played by Scofield) who happens also to be a doctor: asked by his brother-in-law about a cure for impotence, he responds, 'Have you thought, perhaps, of going to a whore?' It was such 'gags' that particularly riled the critics, who supposed them to add nothing whatsoever to the plot or characterization. Yet Harwood was still mixing the colours of his creative palette; still contemplating the limitless possibilities that the theatre presented. As he recalls:

> During the technical rehearsal at the Haymarket, I was sitting in the third or fourth row of the stalls, lost in thought, when Paul sauntered down the aisle about to resume a scene on stage. He stopped, looked at me, then pointed his enormously long forefinger. 'You're thinking about writing a play about us, aren't you?'

By some magical insight or intuition, Scofield had accurately read Harwood's thoughts. For deep within the playwright's subconscious mind a drama based on his own theatrical experiences was beginning to take shape: a play about an actor-manager and his dresser.

INTERVAL

8

The Good Companion

I remember everything in clear detail but I remember it wrong.
The Ordeal of Gilbert Pinfold, *Act One*

I once asked Sir Ronald what he thought of the published diaries of a certain well-known author. 'All bullshit,' he casually replied. There was an awkward pause. 'Well,' he went on more gingerly, 'don't tell her I said that: I haven't actually found the time to read them yet.'

It is with these cautionary words in mind that the reader must judge the longest continuous diary of the acclaimed playwright. It was written at odd moments – early in the morning, late at night, in the back of taxis, behind the scenes at the theatre – between 1972 and 1974, during which time he worked closely with the greatest literary figure with whom he has ever been associated: J. B. Priestley.

Harwood's narrative needs little commentary other than to say that he first came into contact with Priestley in the late 1960s while working on an ultimately unmade film adaptation of the Yorkshireman's 1965 novel *Lost Empires*. Readers with shorter theatrical memories than Harwood's may also appreciate a brief reminder of some of the *dramatis personae* who appear in the text: André Previn, immortalized by his appearance on the *Morecambe and Wise Show*, was for twelve years the inimitable conductor of the London Symphony Orchestra; Johnny Mercer, the legendary Broadway lyricist, whose wife, Ginger, also features in the text, was known to the world as the brains behind such hits as 'Moon River' and 'Charade'; Bernard (later Lord) Delfont, Peter Rawley and Richard Pilbrow ranked among the most successful British theatre managers and producers of the post-war era; Braham Murray was a young director who worked alongside Michael Elliott and Casper Wrede at the 69 Theatre Company and would go on to become one of the most noted figures in twentieth century British theatre; Laurens van der Post was a South African intellectual who, having assumed the role of 'guru' to Prince Charles, stood as godfather to Prince William; Jacquetta Hawkes, a world-famous archaeologist in her own right, was Priestley's third wife, and Sir Frederick Ashton was the chief choreographer, and later director, of the Royal Ballet from 1935 until his retirement in 1970. The production featured in this diary opened in July 1974 and ran for a respectable but unspectacular 252 performances at a number of West End Theatres: one of its stars, Judi Dench, recalls it as 'the only touring show in London.'[32]

A final point. It is clear that Harwood originally intended this diary for publication (at one stage he even intimated the idea of a documentary based on its contents to his then-agent, Felix de Wolfe). Parts of the lengthy – 12,000 word – manuscript were accordingly typed up at the time, often with details and nuances not entirely consistent with the original draft. Several scenes involving Priestley (lunch at the Westbury Hotel, breakfast at Priestley's home at Alveston, the discussion about cigars and the fireside chat) appear only in an article, based on the diary, which Harwood published over twenty years later in *The Author* magazine. I have used the 'best' version of the text wherever possible. Sadly, however, Harwood's gossipy chronicle abruptly ends in the immediate aftermath of the opening night, when he learnt that his manuscript was of little interest to his friends in the publishing world.

Did not Dr Johnson observe that 'no man but a blockhead ever wrote except for money'?

1972

20 July

Message on my answering-machine from André Previn: 'Ronnie? André. I want to talk to you about work. Please call me.'

21 July

I telephone Previn. Tell him that if he wants me to conduct the LSO I only know 'Invitation to the Waltz', and that I can't keep time, but my interpretive gifts are without equal. He says, 'Forget it then. How about doing a musical with Johnny Mercer and me?' I swallow hard and agree. 'Have you a subject?' I ask. '*The Good Companions* by J. B. Priestley,' he replies. I agree again. I cable Tasha the good news in the Dordogne.

End of July

I go over to Leigh to meet Johnny and Ginger Mercer. He is bearded, reserved, courteous, polite. But what's he THINKING? He has had a passion for *The Good Companions* since the late 1920s when it was first published. Mercers are off to Italy, and Johnny is going to work on the songs there. We part enthusiastic.

8 September

Mercer is back from Italy and I from California. I go up to his suite in the Connaught Hotel to work with him. He presents me with a full outline of the whole musical in three acts, but really it's just a précis of Priestley. However, he takes me all the way through it, and I make polite noises knowing all the time that, at some point, I'm going to have to come up with an idea that solves the 'shape' of the musical for the *theatre*.

October

I tell André of my idea to start the musical with a performance of the Concert Party and then flashback to reveal how Miss Trant, Inigo and Jess all come together. Previn very enthusiastic. He suggests the musical open with the opening chorus of The Dinky-Doos done *badly*. Rather good.

1 November

I meet with Priestley at Albany. He and Mrs Priestley give me tea and are charming. He much mellower since we last met. He tells me he has been signing copies of a prologue which Ralph Richardson is to speak at Sybil [Thorndike]'s ninetieth birthday. Vintage Priestley: 'I've just read it to Peggy Ashcroft. Of course she burst into tears,' and he gives an endearing little look under his heavy brows, almost impish, as if to say, 'It's easy when you know how.' Other gems: 'There's nothing you can tell me about the English. After all, I've turned down a knighthood, a C.H. and a Life Peerage.' I ask, 'Would you accept an O.M.?' 'Aye, but they won't give it me.' He is writing, or has just finished writing, a book to be called *The English*. He is very anti-Common Market, not on Socialist grounds, but because of something he calls 'Englishness' which he doesn't want destroyed. He asks me what I'm doing besides the musical. I tell him I am contemplating a full-scale biography of Chekhov. 'Oh,' says he, 'I've done one of those.' Loveable. I tell him how far we have got with 'The Good Companions' and promise to keep him informed. As I rise to leave he says, 'Oh, you won't have a Scotch, then?' I decline and depart. I really did enjoy this hour with him very much.

1973

19 February

To Leigh for meeting with Previn and Braham Murray who is to direct. He is very efficient and comes armed with a schedule. Opening night to be 4 February 1974. Discuss choreography. Previn suggests Sir Frederick Ashton but doubts if he'd do it.

6 March

I tear down to Golden Square to find Rawley (representing the collaborators' joint business interest), Braham and André already with Bernard Delfont. ... He reminds me of his brother Lew [(later Lord) Grade, producer at ATV] in a great many ways, but with one important difference: Lew offers his cigars as though they were Polo mints; Bernie doesn't.

It is all alarmingly quick. Out in the corridor André looks at me bewildered, 'Did he say we have a deal?' I answer I believe he did. None of us quite used to such speedy decisions. Rawley joins us in the lobby twenty minutes later: we have a deal. Delfont is to finance the first draft, then decide whether or not to go on.

8-9 March

Braham down to Berrygrove to work. We discuss and hammer out a shape to Act One, based on my flashback idea. Work goes well and easily.

19 April

Meet Braham and Johnny at [the] Connaught [Hotel], thence by the longest limousine to Leigh. ... We take Johnny though the outline. He hates it. He feels we have turned the story into a showbiz epic instead of concentrating on the *characters*. It's no use telling him what my intentions are as regards character, because he seems only to see the bare bones as contained in the outline.

2 May

Braham and I invited to Leigh to hear twelve songs. ... Previn goes to piano, Johnny sits in an armchair placed in the bow of the piano, and they go through the songs. I feel as though I'm in an old Hollywood movie: each time I turn to Braham and we both nod and smile, it's like acting out a cliché. Braham says we should dissolve now to the opening night! ... I cannot help feeling terribly honoured to be there, listening to the two of them. (I whispered this to Previn later and he got terribly embarrassed).

5-6-7 May

... I arrange for the Mercers to come down on Wednesday 8th. On Tuesday, at 10 p.m., I begin to type a fair copy [of the libretto] when I have a blinding flash of inspiration and see the answer to all our problems. The idea is that Miss Trant, Inigo and Jess should tell EACH OTHER how they have come to be in Rawsley. This gives us a narrative device which I've been searching for. ... I telephone Braham and try it out on him. He declares it a stroke of genius. I work through till 3.30 a.m. rewriting the first two scenes and all the outline. Sleep knowing it is solved. Now for Johnny.

8 May

Johnny and Ginger arrive. I open champagne and sit Johnny down in the library and hand him the first two scenes to read. He chuckles all the way through and is ecstatic! Thank God. I now take him through [the] outline and explain narrative device. He is even more happy and I can see him visibly breathe a sigh of relief. We go over the lyrics of his songs to get English references right. ... He wants to fit in Peter Cook and Dudley Moore who he has just seen in *Behind the Fringe.** He also thinks Lulu is great. I try to disabuse him of all three but he's an obstinate man. ... The only worrying thing is that Delfont hasn't yet sent his cheque. We've all been waiting three months.

11 May

Talk to Rawley. Delfont has 'signed' the cheque (this must be his twelfth signature on that poor cheque). We should receive it on Monday.

---

*　A follow-up to *Beyond the Fringe*, *Behind the Fringe* was a comedy revue , starring Dudley Moore and Peter Cook, which ran from November 1972 until August 1973 at the Cambridge Theatre, Covent Garden.

13 May

Previn cannot be contacted just at the moment when Mercer wants to work on new lyrics, and just when we want to finalise the Delfont meeting. Priestley telephones me to arrange meeting with him. I risk it and say we'll come on Friday 18 May at 10.30 a.m. If Previn can make it so much the better.

18 May

Priestley receives us [Harwood and Mercer] and is in terrific form. I take him through the outline and he glows with approval. Mercer indicates the theme of some of the songs, and Priestley makes two good suggestions: one, that Inigo's adventures which I thought of as a ballet should be done in the style of a flickering late Twenties movie, with Inigo talking rapidly over it. Also that the ship's hooter should sound just as Jess opens his last letter from Lily. After the working bit of the session is over, we chat away, swop theatrical stories, imbibe an enormous Scotch and soda each.

29 May

Tasha drives me up [to London] – I couldn't see straight – and we all meet. Previn has the worst cold I've ever seen: puffy eyes, fevered brow, thick voice and the look of one who longs for a hospital bed, a nurse and oblivion. Nevertheless he is in fairly good form, and makes a lot of good jokes. ... Everyone fairly happy and confident in anticipation of auditioning for Delfont on Thursday at 3 p.m. in the bar of the Prince of Wales theatre. We part, I collect Tasha and she drives me home. We arrive at 1.45 a.m. I take two pills and sleep till 10 a.m.

31 May

I watch Previn and Mercer at work [in the Essex Music studio on Poland Street] which is fascinating. As men they do not have a lot in common but as collaborators they appear to have a *rapport* that is almost tangible. The need for an extra syllable to fit a musical line, or the need for an extra note to accommodate an unwieldy word are quickly realized without much discussion. ... We lunch at Isow's on salt beef, and afterwards wander down to the Prince of Wales stalls bar which is cavernous, dimly lit and horribly depressing. The piano is stuck away in a corner and André discovers that most of the notes sustain themselves long after he's played them. But he says he'll manage.

Peter Rawley arrives and shortly after 3.10 Delfont himself, smiling, tanned and cigarred. He sits, we chat a little tentatively. He tells us how much he loved the film made by Victor Saville in the early Thirties. He expresses doubt as to how I am able to solve the problem of bringing the three main characters together. I try to reassure him but he looks doubtful.

We begin. Rawley flicks glances in all directions, mostly at Delfont, trying to gauge his reaction. Delfont intent, listening to every word, watches me like a hawk while I tell the story, and then, when Mercer sings, switches his gaze. When I reach the point of the flashback, and this the solution to the difficulty Bernie envisaged, he nods happily, inclines his head politely as if to say 'that's clever' and then listens contentedly to the songs right through until the end. When it's over he says, 'Fine. We'll do it.'

6 June

At Chappell's the music publishers to take Priestley through songs. He arrives a little hot and bothered, but settles down soon and enjoys himself very much indeed. Ginger Mercer, Diane Ferguson and Tasha also present, and are dutifully all impressed. Afterwards we have photographs taken, Mercer like a schoolboy fan with Priestley. Previn says that Mercer views Priestley as he, Previn, regards von Karajan: with awe.

As we all walk towards the Westbury Hotel for lunch, Previn and I walk a bit behind and he tells me that when he, Priestley and Itzhak

Perlman were all in South America, they came out of their hotel and Priestley said, 'Do not go gentle into that dark night!' to which Itzhak P. replied quite seriously, 'Hey, that's a good title for a song!' Priestley turned on him and said, 'I can see you don't know your poetry!' As André says, what does he expect from an Israeli fiddler?

Lunch a jolly affair. Priestley flirts with Tasha, tells her an idea he has for a play, adds the injunction, 'But don't tell yer husband!'

Just as we are sipping coffee, Previn and his wife are told that their car has arrived and they depart. Mercer, who is a generous man and has just sold his share in a record company for many millions, calls for the bill. He then takes out his credit card holder and flicks it open. The cards are contained in plastic envelopes, concertina fashion, and a long string of them unfold. The elderly Italian waiter puts on his reading glasses and starts studying the cards, bowing lower and lower until eventually he reaches the last card on the level of Mercer's knees. He straightens up and says, 'Sorry, we don't take any of these.' Mercer is aghast and an awkward silence follows. Priestley keeps his eyes averted. Natasha and I have a rather frantic, whispered conversation about our overdraft. I pay the bill. It drastically increases our borrowing. Two days later I receive a letter from Priestley:

Dear Ronald,

I was aware of your embarrassment yesterday when it came to paying the bill. I hope you realize there was nothing I could do to help since I was the Guest of Honour.

However, I trust you noticed that I had Boiled Beef and Carrots for my main course which happened to be the cheapest dish on the menu and which also happens to be my favourite.

Yours, JB.

[Priestley's actual letter was less jovial. He simply wrote: 'Incidentally I ordered only one dish – and that the cheapest. I feel restaurants now are just too damned expensive.' JBP to RH, 24.6.73]

6 October

I arrive at Kissing Tree House about four, having seen Jacquetta [Hawkes] walking with her two other house guests, Laurens and Ingaret van der Post. Priestley meets me, shows me to my bedroom and then takes me for a peep into a sort of box room, piled with every kind of edition of his work. Everyone meets for tea. Laurens van der Post is handsome, elegant and steely under a dreamy exterior. His wife Ingaret, who won the gold medal at RADA is thin, bright and enthusiastic. Conversation very erudite ranging from pre-Egyptian history to the contemporary theatre.

At about six, Priestley and I work on [the] libretto. His objections are to do with Act One and fall mainly into three: a) flashbacks, b) too much incident – in direct contradiction to Mercer, c) not enough music. He makes his suggestions which mostly are very good. At 7.30 prompt he goes up for his bath and I do the same. The house is marvellously and efficiently run. Jacquetta is a kind of ideal of an Englishwoman: intellectually gifted, intelligent, energetic, superb manners and displays real care and affection for her guests. The atmosphere is tranquil and civilized: Priestley later claims this is due to the happiness of their marriage. Occasionally he calls me 'ducky'.

After dinner, when the other guests have retired to bed, Priestley says, 'Let's have a night-cap.' We sit either side of the fire, smoking cigars and sipping brandy. He is mellow and warm and affectionate. We talk mostly about his four great loves: Jacquetta, the theatre, literature and England. Of Jacquetta: 'We fell in love the moment we clapped eyes on each other. We went to bed. Didn't rise for a week. At it all the time. My God, but we were passionate.'

We soon moved on to his memories of the theatre. 'I remember Willy Maugham sitting behind me on one of my first nights in London. Just before the curtain rose, he leaned towards me and said, "I suppose that now, Jack, you're going to show us how it ought to be done?" "Yes," I said, "I am – and I did."'

He was hard on Graham Greene. 'He always avoids the obligatory scene,' he said, but the statement is a clue to Priestley's Victorian roots as a novelist, the careful, plodding narrative and an even greater clue to Greene's modernity. 'Waugh's a fine prose writer, probably the best in the language, but what does he write *about*? Upper-class twerps or nothing at all.'

The conversation turned to England. He was proud of his broadcasts during the Second World War. 'But Churchill was jealous of me and had me taken off,' he said. I knew he had served in France during the First World War. I asked him why he had never written about his experiences either in fact or in fiction. It was clumsy of me. A haunted, doomed look crossed his face. He waved a hand repeatedly to and fro, banishing the subject from our conversation. He stared into the fire as though seeing again the horror, repeatedly biting his bottom lip, fighting the memories that were too painful, too terrible to be allowed to surface.

7 October

I come down early to join Jacquetta and Laurens. I take two rashers of bacon and a slice of toast. Jacquetta thinks I am being rather modest. I explain I am on a diet … This interests Laurens who launches into a lecture in his gentle South African voice about the ideal of the Thin Man in West Civilization starting with pre-Minoan culture in Crete. During his discourse, Priestley enters in his plaid dressing gown which somehow makes him look plumper than usual, a scarf round his neck – he has a horror of drafts and catching cold – and wearing woolly socks and slippers. He helps himself to everything the sideboard has to offer. His plate piled high, he sits at the table and tucks in ferociously.

Laurens continues and by then has reached the statue of the charioteer in Delphi, describing in some detail his slender, muscular grace. Priestley now becomes aware of what Laurens is saying: 'The thin man was also much admired in Rome and as for the Italian Renaissance…' – Priestley can bear no more. He slams down his knife and fork, leans across the table and says, 'Laurens, tell me this: when have you ever seen a thin Buddha?' The lecture ended.

Priestley and I work all morning and are followed by the others for drinks.

After a truly splendid lunch Priestley goes round the table offering cigars from a humidor. He comes to me. I reach in and am surprised to find the cigars are unusually small. He sees my reaction, 'You may have had bigger; you'll not have had better,' he says. He was right. They are sweet and succulent, Partagás No 7, obtainable only at J & J Fox. 'These cigars,' he says, 'were rolled on the inside of a Cuban woman's thighs. That's the most beautiful part of a woman, the inside of her thighs. If I remember correctly.'

17 December

I fetch [the prospective cast member] John Mills and take him to Chappell's Band Room. Braham, fresh from Manchester success with [a revival of Priestley's play] *Time and The Conways*, joins us. We play songs, take Mills through the show. I talk to Murray during two of the numbers which Previn later tells me not to do again. Mercer sings dreadfully. Afterwards, we crowd into Previn's car and go to the Garrick for lunch. Very jokey chatty lunch, then over coffee I ask him [Mills] straight: 'What about dates?' He stalls. Says he wants autumn opening. We part promising to sort things out.

30 December

Long call from Braham. I express some of my resentment at any interference or threat of interference or suggested interference in matters artistic from [the executive producer, Richard] Pilbrow. We are all to meet on Tuesday.

1974

1 January

At the studio we meet Braham, Malcolm [Pride, the set designer], Jonathan [Taylor, the choreographer], Pilbrow, Pamela Hay [the assistant choreographer]. Everything is cold, bleak and miserable because of industrial crisis. We repair to studio and Johnny and André do their stuff. Johnny sings his new links for Act Two. The others leave for our crunch meeting. We wander off to find food. Hardly anywhere open, town like a morgue. At last we find a steak house called Gameio. Food almost inedible, but we go though each song in detail.

15 January

Auditions at Prince of Wales [Theatre] all day; very depressing as auditions always are.

16 January

More auditions. In the evening meet Judi Dench. We are considering her, though I do not think her right for the part. In the evening Pilbrow and I dine at Garrick, enjoy chat with [the judge Sir] Melford Stevenson and Lord Longford. Then pop across to studio for detailed work-through.

9 March

Apart from sitting through countless girls singing 'Pee-heople, pee-heople who love pee-heople!' the [casting] highlights for me were the look of bewilderment and pleasure when the man was told he could play Mr Joe, Michael Balfour's account of his early days on the halls, Judi Dench's voice's transformation when Previn accompanied her. … But the bore has been the search for [an actress to play] Susie. Hundreds of girls (120 in fact or more) have been seen. The bore has been trying to find someone who combines acting, singing and dancing gifts in equal proportions.

...

Johnny is proving not so much a problem as a burden. He is obstinate, persistent, single-minded and often destructive because he also suspects that others are not as keen or as competent at their jobs as he is at lyric writing. The basis of his behaviour is that he knows next to nothing about theatrical presentation in London in 1974. What he does know about is lyrics – and that is all.

29 April

First rehearsal. Full company, but André has LSO rehearsal so he & Mercer are coming in later. Braham welcomes us all then takes us through the set by Malcolm Pride scene by scene. Cast enraptured. I sit beside Johnny Mills who mutters 'marvellous, marvellous' from time to time...

15 May

Press conference at Savoy. Braham confides severe doubts about [the cast member playing Susie,] Celia [Bannerman,] to Richard Pilbrow. We decide to make final decision on Saturday.

18-19 May

First stagger-through. On the whole encouraging. At fault: swollen parts which are grotesquely overplayed (warned of this by John Mills last night who telephones). Pilbrow opens discussion with Celia. André very destructive. 'We're not running a clinic,' he says in reply to pleas that Celia has to be helped musically. Previn insists she will never, never be better: arrhythmic and atonal. However, it boils down to this: we have no alternative but to persevere with her. ... Previn is really hateful at this meeting: black, sour and nihilistic [?].

23 May

Take Priestley to lunch and then he and Jacquetta to run though of Act One in afternoon. He is highly delighted. She has tears running down her face at Miss Trant's 'I'm going to run the show'. Photographs are taken. He has encouraging word for the cast. Main criticism is the acting of small parts, especially Oakroyd & Apples scene. Mercer also there looking so awful as to make one really concerned. I doubt if we will get any more out of him.

25 May

Run through. It beings to feel like a show, and a good show. A Delfont man there, also George Hall & Malcolm [Pride]. All have good things to say (and good criticisms). The spectacular success of the day is Celia. But, of course André isn't there for the run-through, so he doesn't see it!!!

26-27 May

Late on Sunday evening Priestley phones to say *The Guardian* has stopped advertising!!! And to say he would welcome a programme note acknowledging his approval for what we've done. Also tells me he is bringing his 'two domestics' to [see the audience preview in] Manchester – 'Gives them an outing, y'know.'

4 June

André and I travel up to Manchester. Before I leave (last night in fact) I say to Tasha: 'Well, now begins the adventure. I hope we have a hit.' She says, 'Hit or miss it's still an adventure.'

7 June

Open [to a select audience] with [co-producer] Richard Mills. Not a very good show. Quite bewildering seeing it with an audience. Terrible areas of longueurs. I stand at back with André (we are stopped by an usher as we go in. André says, 'We wrote the show!') Afterwards, long meeting with Richard Mills. Celia a disaster. We decide to get rid of her.

8 June

The most depressing day I can ever remember. André goes back to London, leaving me more or less to cope. Delfont up tonight. After show long meeting in my suite. Present: Delfont, Mercer, Jonathan Taylor, Pilbrow, Braham & me. Delfont superb: a life-giver. Agrees to restructuring of Act One. i.e cutting flashbacks to minimum and bringing three stories together in 'Pleasure'. Delfont cheers me up no end.

10-16 June

The opening night seems a year away. The show, however, gets better & better but I predict bad notices – 'old-fashioned' etc. ... Johnny Mercer horrid and destructive at Saturday meeting (15 June). Unburdens on André who unburdens on me. Johnny goes to bed to write new song for Dinky Doos at beginning of show... André hardly even here. Goes to Iceland (Tue, Wed, Thu) and back home (Sun) promising to return WED!!! We spend a lot of time together but there is something hateful about him.

17-21 June

Priestley arrives with Jacquetta and sees the show that evening accompanied by [the Granada Television executive] Denis Foreman. (André of course doesn't appear). Priestley's reactions:

First scene worst he has seen in seventy years of play-going.

Johnny Mills too lightweight.

Judi's [Dench's] Helhenton scene not dramatic enough. Most of the show good.

Chris Gable [as Inigo Jollifant] terrific.

He tells the criticism directly to those concerned & of course causes crisis in Mills & Dench. Braham & I cut Redgauntlet lines in Judi's scene resulting in her hysterical after show; she cries for approx. two hours in Benni's steakhouse, wins, and we put back speech!

Priestley hates 'Susie for Everybody'. André confesses to me it is the only tune Mercer wrote.

André telephones from London trying to avoid coming up to Manchester immediately. When I try to pass the telephone over to Pilbrow, Previn screams down phone, 'Don't do that. I'm not going to kill myself for this show, you know!'

23 June

Dress rehearsal [at Her Majesty's Theatre, London], Sat; (Tasha comes up). ... Previn outrageous and hateful re design aspect of play, going on in the stalls in front of Malcolm [Pride], saying things like, 'Get rid of him, we all do *our* job why can't he do his' etc. in earshot.

1 July

First preview day. ... The performance in the evening is technically appalling ... The audience hardly react in any way whatsoever. Afterwards the inevitable meeting ... I get a cigar off Bernie – Delfont likes the show, really likes it and says wonderfully tactless things, eg. 'It's a lovely little show. I don't think this theatre gets a lot of coach parties, does it?'

2-5 July

Variety Club review on 2nd goes rather well, better than could have been expected. Priestley in with his niece Sadie Wykeham. Afterwards dinner at Stones Chop House. Priestley very nice and his niece enjoys it enormously. On Wednesday the 3rd (which would have been our opening night) the show goes so wonderfully well that everybody is terribly suspicious, superstitions (Delfont: 'It'll run three years ... if it's a success').

Ray [C.] Davis, the arch-cunt, attacks me (verbally) in wings for cutting his lines. He thinks only of himself and his effect. The show could be a dismal failure so long as he personally was successful. He is a vulgar, crass performer.

6-9 July

A strange, jumpy atmosphere prevails: people suspicious of the wonderful reception the show gets each night and all anticipating a bad press. Bernie also anticipates a bad press but intends to counteract it with heavy advertising. Feeling still runs high against Braham. Johnny Mills and Judi now joining the neurosis which is a symbol of the jumpiness I detect. On Sunday Johnny Mercer telephones with suggested changes at this late hour. ... The man is a drag of the first order.

11 July

Meet Priestley at 6.55 at stage door and take him up to back of circle. We begin to drink. He goes on about 1st scene and flashbacks! Marcus plays God Save the Queen. Overture (Quite exciting). Curtain up: NO SOUND! The piano doesn't come through. Ray C. Davis saves the day by counting out loud '1-2-3-4!' And then they go into 'Goodbye'. Ghastly moment. Braham turns grey. But we are on our way and with a very good performance. Priestley, Braham, Pilbrow and I in bar most of time nipping in and out to hear odd bits. First act applause good. Priestley and I hang about & see Jacquetta ... 2nd Act goes marvellously. Ray C. Davis stops show. So does 'Travelling Music' which gets almost continuous applause from last chorus to end. 'Ta, Luv' a sensation. Mills receives an ovation and cheers. Priestley and I return to bar. He tells me of his new *Time* play again, and about scene with Last Post. Also how Charles Evans (of Heinemann) purchased *Forsyte Saga* and turned it into Best Seller. ... Priestley, Pilbrow and I sit on stairs leading to pass door and wait. Chat about *Good Companions* being in theatre forty-three years before. Curtain calls ecstatic. I am curiously detached. John Mills brings Priestley on who makes a clever speech about the audience crying, not for Inigo or Miss Trant but for a lost England. Party afterwards.

Return to Savoy about 11.15. ... At 2a.m. Braham & I wander down Fleet Street. Manage to get *Express* (Kretzmer) which is bad. Taxi back to Savoy. Try to find ways of neutralising notice, but it is *bad* and no way round that. ... Tash & I on chaise-longue. Bed, to be disturbed by [cast member] Malcolm Rennie, his wife & loud-voiced, vulgar red-haired bird. Open bottle of champagne. Get rid of them. Try to sleep. Very disturbed. Suite terribly noisy.

7.30 get notices. Terrible. Irving Wardle the best!!! [Michael] Billington in *Guardian* awful. B.A. Young not bad. Make series of phone calls: John Mills (fine), Judi (fine), Braham (very depressed), André (very sore but 'chipper'). Mom very depressed. Tash et al. go home. ... Nothing to do in afternoon. Drop by theatre. All quiet. Buy tea and take away, see [the producer] David Deutsch & [his wife] Claire [in St James' Square] (feel like broken-down travelling salesman). Go back to theatre to drink tea, chat to Roy, stage-door keeper, then to Felix's, chat with Alun Owen... Do rounds backstage. Morale high. Johnny Mills makes speech over tannoy about [a revival of a] Seymour Hicks play [that had] ... bad notices, ran five years. Have drink with Pilbrow & Braham in Circle bar. As I hail taxi to leave for home see 'House Full' boards out!!

9 July *[sic. Final entry]*

A very good performance to a full house. Afterwards Bernie Delfont nit-picks about technical matters, especially the sound. Also wants a chorus cut from 'The Pools'. Talks to Johnny Mills who agrees if it is not to be too confusing. Afterwards Braham, Jonathan Taylor and

I have a drink in Savoy lounge and are joined momentarily by [the American actress and singer] Elaine Stritch who says, 'The theatre is all shit – but it's terrific shit!'

Act Four:

SARTOR RESARTUS

The Tailor Retailored

9

The Dresser

It'll be a chapter in the book...
The Dresser, *Act One*

Gyles Brandreth was once asked by a radio producer if there was anything that he had never done before. The writer and former MP for Chester stared heavenwards for a few moments and then replied: 'Taken a day off'. The same could well be said of Sir Ronald Harwood. 'What's my secret?' he has revealingly complained, '– writing is my life; I have no other life.' Not a man for sun-loungers, card games or country pursuits, Harwood has for over forty years listed only a single recreation in *Who's Who*: 'Watching cricket'. Yet even while engaging in this suitably genteel pastime, he is still very much 'on duty'.

An incident at Lords during the late 1990s perfectly illustrates this paradox. Harwood was leading a pair of distinguished guests from the Long Bar to their seats at the front of the famous Pavilion. As the trio solemnly proceeded down the gangway, their helmsman caught sight of a familiar streak of grey hair poking out from beneath a panama hat. 'Hey,' he said mischievously, 'let's go and say "hello."' In a few moments the three men were standing beside Britain's recently deposed premier. 'Mr Major,' chirped Harwood, 'may I introduce you to Tom Courtenay and Albert Finney – I taught them everything they know.'

As much as Harwood's reluctant protégés may have squirmed, the pleasantry had a kernel of truth. For seldom in their long careers have either of these acclaimed actors surpassed the heights they reached when performing in the film version of Harwood's most celebrated play: *The Dresser*. 'It's an outstanding piece of drama,' remarks Sir Tom today, 'and will be performed for as long as actors and theatres continue to exist.' '*The Dresser* is,' wrote another legendary actor to play the role of Norman, Sir Ian McKellen, 'with Pinero's *Trelawny of the "Wells"*, the most accurate portrayal of theatre life yet written by a playwright. It doesn't shy away from the [central] character's egotism and petty mindedness but it enfolds them in his love and admiration for theatre people onstage and backstage.'[33]

It is a play that has come to symbolize Harwood's life and legacy. 'No one thought it would get anywhere,' he chortles, '– when I told John Gielgud about the idea, he said, "Ah, backstage dramas never do well", and then hurried off!' Yet, just like Harwood himself, when the unexpected success finally came, it refused ever to go away again. 'Its appeal,' he continues with convincing incredulity, 'has been unbelievable – everyone from Mexican taxi-drivers to Soviet commissars have praised it. ... I don't think there's been a night since it first opened that it hasn't been performed somewhere in the world.'

Perhaps, however, the most striking feature of Harwood's most enduring 'hit' is that the story of its unlikely triumph was anticipated by a novel he wrote only two years before the play's opening night on 6 March 1980. The book came about when Harwood was sitting at home listening to a programme on Radio 3 about the composter César Franck. 'I had never even heard of him,' explains Harwood, 'but I listened with growing wonder ... Here was a man who for the first fifty years of his life was a complete mediocrity.' 'And then,' continues Harwood with arresting passion, 'he wrote one of the greatest pieces of music ever devised: the *Quintet* in F minor.' The reason, argued the programme's presenter, was that he had fallen in love with a young opera singer named Augusta Holmes. 'He was making love to her through his music,' explains Harwood gravely. Following a few months of research in London and Paris, Harwood set to work on *César and Augusta*, his most poignant and satisfying novel to date.

'Oh yes,' says the story's protagonist at one stage, 'that's the secret. My life is always just the same.' From his youthful experimentation with folk melodies to his years as the whiskered organ teacher at the Paris Conservatoire, Harwood's Franck takes himself with the utmost seriousness. 'What do people call you?' asks Augusta Holmes shortly after their first meeting. 'Mostly maître,' he pompously replies; 'Vincent d'Indy calls me *Pater seraphicus* and sometimes Father.' Yet as their friendship blossoms into an intense and platonic love affair, the eccentric and rather talentless composer gives birth to his masterpiece. Then he never speaks to his heart's desire again. 'The *Quintet*,' cries Augusta as an old woman at the end of the novel, '– my quintet ... all mine from the vein of gold I struck. And was he grateful? Bastard. ... He was only interested in himself. Self. Self. Self-preservation ... is what politicians, master-criminals and artists have in common.'

The parallels with Harwood's own masterpiece are manifold. 'It was very important to me to have recognition,' he expounds, 'and I was beginning to think I would never get it – I thought I'd perhaps be top of the second division, but never make it to the first.' Asked whether he, like Franck, was inspired finally to reach the summit of his lofty ambition by a powerful, sensuous influence, Harwood's eyes narrow. 'People talk about *The Dresser* being real life,' he snaps, 'but they don't give me credit for crafting it.' While he accepts that he could not have written the play without his experiences working for Sir Donald Wolfit, the play was above all else the fruit of his imagination and insight. 'There's a bit of everyone in the character of "Sir"', he goes on, '– Larry Olivier came up to me at a party and asked: "Is there anything of me in *The Dresser*?"' Harwood racked his brains, 'Oh, yes,' he replied: 'When "Sir" calls his wife Pussy.' 'He was pleased,' chuckles Harwood in the present-day, 'because that was what he called Vivien Leigh.'

There is no doubt, however, that *The Dresser* came from a deep and burning love every bit as overwhelming as César Franck's for Augusta Holmes. Not for a woman, however; nor even perhaps for Sir Donald Wolfit – but for the theatre itself. 'It is the theatrical equivalent,' smirks a long-time playgoer, 'of crack cocaine.' Each and every scene – from Norman's account of 'Sir's' striptease through the desolate northern town to the tragic shattering of the theatre company's hopes and dreams in the long-anticipated denouement – conveys an almost tangible passion for the sights, smells and sounds of everything theatrical. Among the mountains of congratulatory letters and telegrams that Harwood has received from actors over the years, none brings home this point more strongly than a missive he once received from John Abineri. '[A]bout twenty minutes in,' wrote this proudest of 'luvvies' after a celebrated production, 'I realized in a blinding flash how much I love you and how much you loves [sic] us and are part of us and I wanted a moment of sheer maudlin sentimentality such as is only allowed to drunkards to tell you, while you are still alive (I presume you are) that you've done something great and I love you for it (and for yourself).'[34]

As a tribute to the memory of Sir Donald Wolfit, *The Dresser* is more ambivalent. 'I know his family were unhappy about it,' growls Harwood, 'but I feel I've paid my dues to Donald.' In one sense, at least, the play presents the great actor in a favourable light. While 'Sir' may be broken down, self-obsessed and painfully insensitive, he also emits the ebbing brilliance of a cosmic supernova. That *such* a man should find himself clinging to his faded reputation in the grimy surroundings of an obscure provincial playhouse is as much a commentary on the banal cruelty of the modern world as it is a denigration of the eminent old actor himself. '[T]he book makes me sad,' wrote Paul Scofield upon reading Harwood's biography of Wolfit, '... there is a chill of loneliness & sustained misunderstanding & loss. If only courage & energy & talent could have been enough (& they are not – but why?)' Even more generous was the comment of Sir Ralph Richardson: 'Lucky fellow that Wolfit,' he told the playwright upon seeing the original production, '... when we're all dead and forgotten, he will be remembered because of your bloody play.'[35]

For all that, Harwood was undoubtedly aware of the upset his play would cause. 'I cannot remember precisely when or where I had the idea for the play,' he recalls, 'but I do remember being reluctant to write it.' Principally he was concerned that any play about an actor-manager and his dresser during a performance of *King Lear* would immediately and correctly be identified as Wolfit. For some weeks he agonized over this. Alternatives such as *Macbeth* and *The Tempest* flashed before his eyes. But the parallels between 'Sir' and Lear were already too overwhelming: 'the storm on the blasted heath,' says Harwood, 'and the Second World War air raid, Lear's depleted followers and "Sir's" depleted Shakespearean company, and other echoes too – but most important the echo of Lear and the Fool that were to be "Sir" and Norman.' At last he told Michael Elliott of his dilemma. Instantly the director shot back: 'It has to be Lear.' That decided the matter: Harwood set about writing the play in earnest.

It premiered at the Royal Exchange with Tom Courtenay playing the role of Norman and Freddie Jones as 'Sir'. For the first and perhaps only time in Harwood's career, there was a discernible sense in the theatre that evening that history was in the making. Mesmerized, the spectators encircling the stage laughed when they were invited to laugh and sat in dumbfounded admiration when the comedy transmuted into pathos. Only Harwood, it seems, refused to give in to the miracle of the production. 'I get nasty and aggressive when I'm nervous,' he explains. When an old friend ventured during the interval to say, 'It seems to be going rather well,' Harwood burst into a torrent of expletives and abruptly stormed out into the street. 'Oh,' consoled his wife, 'don't take any notice of him.'

To the playwright's abiding satisfaction, however, the critics did not heed his spouse's characteristically kindly and modest sentiment. Instantly hailed by *The Guardian* as 'one of the best things the Royal Exchange has ever done', it swiftly moved to London, where it continued to amass plaudits at The Queen's Theatre. 'Here is a stand-up comedy act', enthused James Fenton in the *Sunday Times*, 'which at the same time is a study of nervousness, viciousness, self-pity and real affection.' What Fenton particularly enjoyed was the dynamic the script created between the two leading characters: 'It is a battle', he wrote, 'which, for the play to work properly, Mr Courtenay must win. I think he does so, but only after Mr Jones has been physically eliminated.' Even the usually far from sanguine Michael Billington admitted to enjoying the play hugely. Describing it as a 'wonderfully affectionate and intelligent play', he explained that it was 'much more than a glimpse behind the curtain.' 'It is', he continued, '… about the ambiguous attitude of theatre people towards their art: a lament for its evanescence and the life-sacrifice it demands, combined with a love of its antique notions of service and loyalty.' The play was, echoed an old friend, J. C. Trewin of the *Illustrated London News*, 'Harwood's best play'.[36]

Like the city bus, fame came twice over for Ronnie Harwood. After five years of negotiating details, his series about the history of the theatre, *All the World's a Stage*, went into production just as *The Dresser* blast into the stratosphere. 'As far as I know,' says Harwood with reference to this dizzying prospect, 'there is no previous incidence of insanity in my family.' He was now simultaneously one of the most discussed dramatists of the moment and the connoisseur of every one of his predecessors from Ancient Greece to the present day. That he was too busy – or too ignorant – to undertake such a herculean task was a point of minor consideration for him. 'I remember meeting an American anthropologist,' sniggers Harwood, 'and telling him the unofficial subtitle of the series: "–but not China, India or Japan." He looked horrified! "But good God!" he said, "That's more than half the world's population!"' Harwood's history of the theatre was not to be an academic exercise. 'Secretly,' he says conspiratorially, 'I wanted to make thirteen hour long commercials for the theatre – for, in a way, there is no history of drama.'

To assist him in his audacious task Harwood had the assistance of two full-time researchers at the BBC's exuberant Music and Arts Department. These were Kit Hesketh-Harvey and Brent McGregor, who had both progressed from Oxbridge colleges to the hallowed precincts of the BBC with an ease which delighted the self-educated South African. 'He had a great respect for people with Oxford and Cambridge degrees,' recalls Hesketh-Harvey, 'and was always keen to ensure that his script met with the approval of the latest academic opinion.' 'Everybody envisaged it,' he continues wistfully, 'as a sequel to Kenneth Clark's *Civilisation*, and Ronnie worked very hard to live up to this high standard.' Others in the production team, however, saw little comparison between Harwood and his celebrated predecessor. 'I remember going out to do a shoot at his home in Liss,' remembers one of the directors. 'I was shocked,' he goes on. 'We were all ushered into the kitchen, where we were introduced to Harwood as he sat picking his toenails at the breakfast table, smoking heavily and swearing like a trooper – almost a stereotype of a *schmuck*.' Quickly dressed and tidied up by his stylish wife, Harwood was made presentable for the camera. 'In an instant he had transformed into a distinguished professional,' continues the witness, '... strolling around his large and well-manicured garden pontificating about Ibsen and Strindberg.'

This condescension was echoed by the critics when the series was finally transmitted in the spring of 1984. Of particular annoyance to these naysayers was the fact that Harwood chose to begin his 'personal journey' with a visit to the premiere of *The Dresser*, which happened to have moved to Broadway just as filming commenced. 'In the first episode', huffed Sean French in the *Sunday Times*,

> Harwood claimed plausibly that the reaction between performer
> and audience generates a magic that can be seen in no other art
> form. His immodest choice to illustrate this theory was the last five
> minutes of the Broadway opening night of his own play, *The Dresser*.
> 'Let's see if the magic works,' he murmured unendearingly.[37]

The same reviewer went on to take Harwood to task for the superficial nature of much of his theorizing. 'The best moment in the six episodes I've seen', continued French with mounting disdain, 'was when he demonstrated the near perfect acoustics of the ancient Epidaurus amphitheatre ... How does it work? Scientists don't know, he claimed. Couldn't he have done a bit better than that?' When Harwood went on to speculate airily that a 'vagrant secular theatre must have persisted' during the largely unchartered centuries of the Dark Ages, the journalist quipped: 'About half way through this sort of argument I start asking myself whether I care what Ronald Harwood believes.'

Reminded of these brickbats today, Harwood is unrepentant. 'My withers are unwrung!' he suggests with an impish shrug. 'At first I shied away from the idea [of featuring *The Dresser*],' he explains. 'The risks were too great – what if the play were a ghastly failure on Broadway? Wouldn't that make for a disastrous first episode?' Equally Harwood feared the consequences of the reverse. 'If the play was to turn out a success,' he continues, 'wouldn't that look like self-advertising on a monstrous scale?' Sincere though the dramatist undoubtedly was, there is little evidence from the archive footage that he was assailed by the slings and arrows of his outrageous good fortune. Strutting through the swing doors of Broadway's most garish theatre attired in a dinner jacket and the largest bow-tie in the house, Harwood looks every inch the showbiz dynamo. After the production he is seen mingling with the great and the good – or, in the less reverent words of Mr French, 'the ranks of tuxedoed fat-cats and yes-men who infest every Broadway first night.' Either way, Harwood was in his element.

This was the abiding impression of Kit Hesketh-Harvey, who happily found himself a witness to these events. The previous evening he had been invited by the acclaimed playwright to a dinner at 'a piss-elegant' restaurant in Greenwich Village hosted by none other than 'La Marquesa de Bogota' – 'Why she gave that party for Harwood,' recorded the merry courtier in his diary, 'none of us is really sure.' Rich, young and beautiful, this adornment to the minor aristocracy of the Americas explained to her distinguished guests that she had left the Marquis following his elopement with a chorus boy from the sexually-charged musical, *Oh! Calcutta!*, which he had just taken her to see. Seated around the dinner table with this bejewelled castoff were such tinselled grandees as Gina Lollobrigida ('dark, beautiful, old; a humourless has-been'); Paloma Picasso ('her black and gold heavy jewellery off-set by her father's famous flashing eyes'); La Marquesa's lover ('who looks like a TV heart-throb, but, we think, does nothing at all'); a 'riotous middle-aged lady swathed in sweeps of Irish tweed … [who boasted,] "I wear Dior, but travel in Chanel"', and the daughter of the owner of 20th Century Fox ('as spectacularly dim as she was pretty'). After gorging themselves on large quantities of the establishment's 'unspeakably filthy food', Harwood and his entourage tumbled into a taxi in the early hours 'screaming with laughter' and wondering, 'Why, in God's name, why?'[38]

It was only in the wake of the first night party later that evening that Harwood and his starry-eyed companions became aware of the hollowness of their Broadway adventure. Despite being greeted at the theatre by 'a blaze of anonymous trumpets and flashguns … the whole thing was over as quickly as it [had] begun,' lamented Hesketh-Harvey in his diary. After the performance and the champagne-fuelled after-party, the playwright, his wife, agent, director and several other members of his inseparable troupe 'sat post-coitally in JR's … lugubriously stirring our coffee and feeling oddly depressed.' 'Looking at Ronnie and Michael [Elliott],' concluded the sorrowful diarist, '… I was dumbfounded. I mean, it should have been their evening. But Broadway somehow egotistically had excluded them from their own party.'[39]

And yet the fizz would be following again before Harwood's hangover had even set in. A mere three hours after curtain down, the camera crew from *All the World's a Stage* descended upon the theatre's public relations team. '*Newsday* is excellent,' they captured an assistant nasally breathing into a telephone receiver, before reeling off a dozen or so other titles. Then the PR men and women are shown setting to work on the text for the advertisements in the morning's papers. 'Who wrote those copy lines?' asks the sour Brooklynite producer, Elizabeth I. McCann, '– they're all dreadful!' A young colleague swiftly suggests a new idea. 'Yeah,' the lady replies as though genuinely struck by its genius, 'What about, "Dressed and Ready to Go?"'

While this beacon of affability went on to declare the task of gutting the reviews to be 'the chicken-shit time', she could hardly have wished for fuller or more complimentary notices than her client received for *The Dresser*.

Foremost among these was the entire page laid on by the *New York Times*. 'To be sure,' the paper's theatre critic, Frank Rich, fairly declared, '*The Dresser* isn't *King Lear*, but the stars play it as if it were.' 'Mr Courtenay,' he expounded, 'never less than a brilliant actor, outdoes himself here.' Likewise, the critic marvelled at the performance of Paul Rogers, who had been preferred to Freddie Jones for the role on account of his greater Broadway experience. It was a display of acting brilliance that movingly showed 'Sir's' obvious frailties as well as his glories: '[H]e does', wrote Rich, 'achieve a star's grandeur once dressed in full Lear regalia.' Together, he concluded, '[Courtenay and Rogers] give their blood to prove that all the world can indeed be a stage.'

The play went on to run for a total of 200 performances on Broadway before closing abruptly in May 1982. One reason for its curtailment was simply that the plot and themes delineated in the play were alien to Americans. 'There is not the same tradition of touring repertory theatre in the States,' explains Harwood. Nor is Shakespeare as central to American culture as it has long been in Britain. ('We've got him back at last from the curriculum people,' he adds proudly). Nevertheless, there was much about *The Dresser* that was well-suited to Broadway audiences. 'The way they applaud when leading actors walk on stage,' says Harwood, 'is something that is simply not done in the West End, but was very much part of the repertory tradition.' 'Sir's' anti-Bolshevik, the-show-must-go-on attitude also chimed with the mood of Ronald Reagan's America. In lamenting the closure of the play, the actress playing Irene, Lisbeth Bartlett, expressed her bewilderment to the author. 'I truly feel the play was a *triumph* for you,' she wrote,

> ... I've never felt more proud, more overcome with joy and with sadness than I did on May 1st at curtain call. It was an extraordinary show for both Tom and Paul, and I just wish you could have been there to witness the stunning ovation ... All of NYC was buzzing about that final show and I've heard so much regret expressed by so

many about the closing. ... I wanted to let you know how much you were thought of that night.[40]

It was later reported that Harwood's play was similarly admired by Katharine Hepburn after a production in Connecticut. 'Last Sunday,' wrote an old friend of Harwood's from RADA days, Joan Shepard, 'Katharine Hepburn came to see your lovely play *The Dresser*...'. 'Miss Hepburn came back stage,' she continued, 'and heaped praise on us and on your play, which we all love doing.' Recalling their outing to see Hepburn in *The Millionairess* with fellow students in 1952, the actress hoped Harwood would be pleased by 'the artful circularity of these events.'[41]

Harwood derived even greater satisfaction from the news that, shortly after the end of the play's Broadway run, a British production company wanted to turn it into a film. Goldcrest Films might have only been in existence for three years, but it had already broken into fortress Hollywood with successes in the form of *Chariots of Fire* and *Gandhi*. Headed by a cultured and straight-dealing Canadian named Jake Eberts, it prided itself on doing business differently to its big-budget competitors. 'In Hollywood people don't cheat,' explained Eberts in later years, 'all they do is live up to the terms of the contract, line by line, detail by detail.' Eberts, by contrast, nurtured an almost uniquely congenial relationship between all parties. Having secured Harwood's verbal authorisation for the project, and also bringing on board Peter Yates as director, Eberts sent him a cheque for $60,000 to begin work on the screenplay without delay. '[W]hile it didn't mean a lot to us,' recalled Eberts magnanimously, 'it meant a lot to them, and the cheque that I sent to Ronnie more than anything else put Peter firmly into the Goldcrest camp.'[42]

Still, Yates required persuasion from Harwood that his play could be transposed for the cinema. 'We met at the house of a friend,' recalls Harwood. 'He was very anxious that so much of the action in the play occurs in a single room.' This is where Harwood's long experience 'opening out' scripts came in useful. Explaining that most of the action described in the first Act could be dramatized, Harwood made it clear that the film would not simply be a rehash of the play. But what sealed the deal was an idea that came to Harwood right on cue. 'I told him a story I had heard,' enthuses the octogenarian, '– I was not there personally – that Wolfit once used his powerful voice to stop a train as it rolled out of a station.' Yates beamed: 'It's a film.'

As well as writing the script, Harwood also assisted with the casting. 'Tom [Courtenay] was the first to agree,' he recalls, 'but finding a suitable actor for "Sir" proved more difficult.' His preference for Albert Finney did not initially meet with the approval of the acclaimed star. As well as recalling the experience of being asked by Harwood to direct a film that was never made, *The Girl in Melanie Klein*, Finney did not feel that he suited the part. 'He said he was too young,' reminisces Harwood, '– and he wasn't really wrong: "Sir" should be at least in his late fifties, and Albert was then only forty-five or so.' There was also the reality that an actor of his stature could have commanded a far larger fee than could ever be supplied by a small British production company. Nevertheless, cajoled by Courtenay, Eberts and Harwood, he agreed. 'It was decided that he would need to have his head shaved,' Harwood concludes proprietorially; '– Albert's got no vanity in that regard.'

Filming took place at Pinewood Studios and the Alhambra Theatre, Bradford. 'The budget was low,' recalls Harwood, 'and we didn't have a long time period to do our work.' Happily, however, this was ideal for *The Dresser*. From the cheap tin bath in which Norman washes his master to the tatty scenery and costumes used in the provincial playhouse, every prop and footlight radiated authenticity. Likewise the decision to cast, with the exception of Edward Fox as Oxenby, relatively unknown screen actors for the supporting roles perfectly captured the spirit of the Shakespearean company: cinema-goers could easily believe that Eileen Atkins (Madge) truly had spent twenty years thanklessly pressing buttons in the wings, or that Lockwood West really hoped for a late-blossoming of his modest talents after understudying as the Fool. Only when the production team attempted to economize in terms of technical personnel did this arrangement begin to go awry. 'Peter had to go to his daughter's graduation in California,' bubbles Harwood, 'so I got to have a go at directing for two days.' Sadly, however, this contribution to British cinema did not make the final cut. 'Both my shots,' he sighs, 'of Norman making up "Sir's" hands for Lear ended up on the cutting-room floor.'

Finney had first seen the play at the Royal Exchange and was determined to emphasize the steelier qualities of the grizzled old actor. He told the critic Michael Billington that he wanted to give the role 'flashes of greatness' and a 'touch of buried authority'. To achieve this, he was determined to learn everything he could about Sir Donald Wolfit. 'It's the old thing,' he told another journalist, 'of getting the details right and then the character, hopefully, follows from that.' Besides devouring Harwood's biography of the actor, Finney also spent many hours listening to recordings of Wolfit at the height of his powers, noting the strange emphasis on vowel sounds such as 'ou' in 'ground' and the clipped pronunciation of 'my' as 'me'. Useful though this was, in the final analysis Finney mastered the part of the threadbare, hammy actor by recalling the wisdom of Sir Laurence Olivier. Asked how he managed to sing, dance and tell jokes like a third-rater in *The Entertainer*, he replied: 'I did it as best I could.'[43]

The unselfconscious merriment of cast and crew was perfectly captured by the lens of Peter Yates. 'This proved to be the most pleasurable production with which I have ever been associated,' recalled Eberts of the movie, '… it was so lovingly made that it really didn't stand a chance of being a bad film.' Eschewing his usual practice of avoiding studios, Harwood was genuinely delighted to be on set almost every day of the filming. To Finney's Lear and Courtenay's Fool, the screenplay writer revelled in his role as courtier-in-chief. 'I'm a star-fucker,' he admits cheerfully. Whether or not this was entirely appreciated by the stars themselves is unclear. During an interview between Courtenay and a journalist some years later, the actor was prevented by Harwood from answering a question about the benefits of fame: 'The girls!' he cut in a little too eagerly. Finney's view of his would-be puppet-master is perhaps best indicated by his decision, after suggesting that he had some interesting tales to tell of his old friend, to 'keep his memories … private.'[44]

Yet at least from a financial perspective, no one involved with the film version of *The Dresser* had any cause for complaint. This was down to the weight that Jake Eberts now commanded in Hollywood. 'Normally,' he has explained,

> I would have expected to go back and forth, having maybe half a dozen short meetings spread over several months with Columbia, and then to repeat the process with three or four other studios, before getting a deal. This time there was only one meeting and it lasted fifteen minutes. … It was proof of one of the oldest and truest sayings in Hollywood: that when you're hot, you're hot.[45]

Columbia Pictures agreed to finance and distribute the film worldwide. Considering that the movie had only cost a modest $6 million to make, this was an almighty coup for Eberts, whose return on investment almost matched that of *Gandhi*. Harwood and the actors, too, came in for a share of the profits on a 'points' system that rewarded them for accepting low initial fees. The only irony was that Goldcrest folded within three years owing to the uncompetitiveness of the British film industry. Columbia, meanwhile, only ended up with a small financial gain in consequence of the vast commissions it needed to pay to cinema owners and the relatively modest takings of the film at the box-office outside of Britain.

Amply rewarded for his endeavours and swelled with self-satisfaction, Harwood now had the greatest prize in the movie business dangled before his eyes. Along with Yates, Courtenay and Finney, the film earned Harwood an Oscar nomination. It was, joked the compere of the 56th Academy Awards, Johnny Carson, 'the biggest British invasion since the Falkland Islands.' The evening, however, was a disappointment for Harwood and his fellow nominees. 'I never remember when I don't win,' replies Harwood to questions about his evening at the glitzy Dorothy Chandler Pavilion in Los Angeles. Seated somewhere at the back of the auditorium, the boom camera did not even do its customary close-up when Mel Gibson and Sissy Spacek announced his nomination. Harwood returned home frustrated, but hungry for more.

Recognition in Britain was only marginally better. While again facing disappointment at the BAFTA awards, *The Dresser* was chosen by Buckingham Palace for the annual Royal Film performance. It was an honour that was reportedly appreciated by the monarch herself. 'Good news for the Queen!' rejoiced the *Sunday Times* diarist, '... This year the committee have deemed she may be exposed to a hugely humorous dose of theatrical camp.' As well as celebrating the 'mincing and magnificent performance' of Tom Courtenay, the gossip-writer marvelled at a 'script of Cowardian proportions'.[46]

There was, however, one important person who was excluded from the glamour and the glory. 'I wasn't invited,' commented Lady Wolfit shortly after the screening with the Queen, '– but, anyway, wild horses wouldn't have dragged me there.' Regarding the play as a total betrayal and a 'wicked' calumny on the memory of her late husband, she explained to a journalist from the *Daily Mail* that she had only journeyed up to London to see the play after hearing rumours about its subject matter. 'Eventually,' she painfully recalled,

> I went to see it and it's awful! It isn't Donald – that failed actor being slightly dreadful with the young people ... When the actor burst through the front curtain, just as Donald used to do, that was it, I couldn't take it any more. I went backstage to see Tom Courtenay, who I'd never met before, and we just put our arms round each other; Tom wept, and I wept.[47]

Standing on the doorstep of her dilapidated old cottage, the former actress and erstwhile patron of her husband's young dresser said gently: 'But, whatever you write, please, please say how sweet and how kind Ronnie has been to me in the past. Our lives have separated – he has a great reputation ... I don't know what I'd do now if I saw him, but I'd try my best.'

10

With the Greats

... It's not such a bad idea. Critics give you bad reviews,
you send them to the Russian front.
Taking Sides, *Act Two*

Some years ago Sir Ronald paid a brief visit to a famous English public school. Attentive teachers and respectful students guided him around the Victorian cloisters and well-tended gardens. 'Yes,'Sir Ronald ... Of course, Sir Ronald ... Absolutely, Sir Ronald,' the headmaster purred. When it was all over a junior member of the staff body enquired what the visitor's claim to distinction happened to be. There was a lengthy silence before one of the English masters came to the rescue: 'Works in advertising, right?' he murmured lamely.

Aside from being something of an indictment of a system of education greatly admired by Harwood, the anecdote is revealing. Throughout his years of fame and success, beginning with the notable triumph of *The Dresser*, Harwood has regarded the theatre, at least to some extent, as a vehicle for self-aggrandisement. 'If he hadn't achieved what he wanted as a playwright,' an old acquaintance supposes, 'he'd have found some other route.'

That judgement may not stand up entirely to close scrutiny, but there is no doubt that Harwood has fully embraced the social and economic consequences of his manifold abilities. Painfully conscious of his lack of formal education, his first significant action after coming to major public notice was to put out feelers in the academic world he so revered. This was done via the conduit of Lady Antonia Fraser's son Damian, who was then an undergraduate at Oxford. Within a short space of time Harwood, aged fifty-one, was appointed Visitor in Theatre at Balliol. The boy from Sea Point had travelled far indeed.

Harwood's sojourn on Broad Street during the Trinity Term of 1986 was not, however, an unmitigated success. 'I found myself rather nervous', wrote Harwood in an exercise book he bought en route to Paddington station. 'I dozed on the train,' he continued, '[until] seeing the spires and domes of Oxford … caused a shudder of excitement.' He had a feeling that 'all would be well'. He was wrong.[48]

The first problem was his accommodation. 'The flat is at the top of the staircase,' he scrawled, ' – five or six flights – so, panting and pounding I reach it, open the door and find a filthy mess, smell of mustiness, old newspapers in the wardrobe, the bed unmade, no linen, no towels, filthy.' After remonstrating with the porter he was escorted to a new room, where he was invited to remain until his quarters were made more agreeable. But this, too, proved highly objectionable. 'The guest room is more appalling than the flat', thundered the diarist. But even these hardships were outdone by the droves of scruffy undergraduates roaming around the medieval quads. One of these individuals stood strumming an old guitar. 'Fuck you, England, I don't give a fuck about you,' he sang tunelessly. Harwood's first night at Oxford, he decided, would be spent at the Randolph Hotel.

Over the coming weeks, Harwood's romantic vision of the ancient university would be irrecoverably shattered. Although he enjoyed the company of young Damian Fraser ('astonishingly handsome, intelligent and possessed of great sweetness … he reminds me of his grandfather Frank [Lord] Longford') and was equally delighted by the 'adolescent' Professor Norman Stone ('he produces a stream of witty phrases which, one suspects, have been carefully prepared … We took to each other at once …'), Harwood could barely disguise his disappointment with High Table. 'Lunched in SCR,' he wrote after a typical feast in college, and there met Professor Lloyd-Roberts, an elderly schoolboy who is meant to be a great and distinguished classicist. His conversation was malicious, scatological, his diction deft and precise. His host was Jasper Griffin, also a classicist and (with Boardman and Murray) editor of the new *Oxford History of the Classical World*. I told Griffin I had just bought the book. The Prof. twinkled delightedly, praising it with enthusiasm, except for the essay by Robin Lane Fox. 'Shit, my dear,' he said, 'fucking shit.' He then went on to tell us that his wife had just written a review of a book about two lesbian nuns in America. 'One, I believe, was called Sylvia Manhandle, the other Dolly Cunt.' He proceeded to tell a Jewish Princess story. I topped him and made my exit.

There was little danger of Harwood abandoning playwriting for this. But his first plays after *The Dresser* were notable only for their lack of critical or commercial success. He began with *After the Lions*, a dramatisation of the twilight years of Sarah Bernhardt, who endured the trauma of a limb amputation after a bad fall from the stage. Intended as the second of a projected trilogy of 'Plays Theatrical', the play explores the relationship between the physically maimed actress and her devoted but unloved servant, Pitou. The critics, however, did not find the production as convincing as *The Dresser*. 'The first reason', explained Robert Hewison after its opening night at the Royal Exchange on 18 November 1982, 'is that while Harwood knew Wolfit, he only knows Bernhardt by report.' The second objection in the eyes of the *Sunday Times* critic was that Harwood had given the leading actress, Dorothy Tutin, the 'impossible task' of evoking 'the Bernhardt that was'. The result, he believed, was a melodrama that lapsed into farce while aspiring to poignancy.[49]

In Harwood's next play, *Tramway Road*, he returned to the more familiar territory of his youth. The work's title was the name of a street near his childhood home. 'It was a slum inhabited by Cape Coloured families,' recalls

Harwood, 'and we were warned that it was a dangerous enclave which, like a scar, dissected the white residential area.' The main character in the drama is a poor white South African, Emil Visser, who goes for elocution lessons with a secretly homosexual British émigré, Arthur Langley. The story comes to a head when the student is reclassified as 'coloured', making his projected journey to England impossible. When Arthur takes his former pupil to the Waldorf Hotel to inform him that he will no longer be able to provide him with lessons, the boy spits in his tea. 'I've done the right thing,' stammers the exile when he returns to tell his wife of his decision, '– haven't I, you agree with me, don't you, it would be impossible to continue as before –.' The play ends with the screech of tyres and the unmistakable suggestion that Emil has thrown himself beneath a car on Tramway Road.

Although the play opened at the Lyric Theatre with a stellar cast – Freddie Jones as Arthur Langley, Richard E. Grant as Emil and Annette Crosbie as Arthur's wife, Dora – the critics were reticent with their praise. 'As a South African émigré who has done very nicely for himself in the old country,' began Irving Wardle rather unpromisingly in *The Times*, 'Ronald Harwood may not be an ideal commentator on the present realities of apartheid ...' The critic went on to complain that the quality of the play was 'extremely uneven'. Whereas he considered Harwood to have used 'sledgehammer tactics' in Act One to contrast the enthusiastic pupil-teacher relationship with the 'wife's brutal and narcissistic interruptions', by the end of the play these dynamics are reversed with 'delicacy and emotional control'. This subtlety was not appreciated by Michael Billington in *The Guardian*. 'Where Fugard', he wrote, 'in *Master Harold and the Boys* provides a complex motivation for his hero's rejection of his friends, Mr Harwood offers a theatrical volt-farce.' The play did not survive long.[50]

Resilient as ever, Harwood remains unrepentant. 'Of all my plays that have not succeeded with audiences,' he sighs, '*Tramway Road* remains my favourite.' This is at least partly due to the fact that the play brought him back into close contact with his family in South Africa. Since his success as an author he had provided many of these near relations with generous financial support, but he seldom visited – he did not even fly to Cape Town to attend his mother's funeral in 1985 ('We had an agreement,' he explains, 'that I wouldn't waste money on a funeral'). Shortly before the announcement of the play's opening, he invited his sister, brother and mother to his Chelsea home for a family reunion. 'Before they left,' explains Harwood, 'I put a sealed package into my sister's hands and instructed her only to open it once she was on the plane.' Inside was the manuscript of *Tramway Road* and a dedication – to her. The gesture was not unappreciated. 'I read it ten times,' Evvy told a reporter from the *Cape Times*, 'I was so moved – I phoned him the minute I got in to say how proud I was that he'd dedicated the play to me.'[51]

Harwood's family were not, however, so unsubtle as to fail to detect that they were to some extent the inspiration for the play's unlovable characters. 'My sister was a teacher of ballet,' elucidates Harwood, 'and gave up many of her free nights to teach coloured children dancing.' 'Yet,' he continues, 'when a coloured man brushed against her on a bus, she was outraged … to the blacks and their misery we all turned a blind eye.' In her youth Evvy had even fallen in love with a young man from Tramway Road, but was forbidden from ever seeing him. Still, it was not deemed acceptable by Harwood's relations to discuss these matters before a gaping public, and Harwood would develop the theme of the parasitic playwright and his disapproving family in his 1992 play *Reflected Glory*. His siblings' real-life disapproval with much of what he wrote is indicated by a telephone call Evvy made to him after Harwood, in a newspaper interview, described their childhood neighbourhood as a 'kind of ghetto'. 'I reminded him,' explained Evvy to another reporter, 'that he always had enough to eat, was smartly dressed and was taken on Sunday evenings to hear the Cape Town Municipal Orchestra.' 'Some ghetto!' she bellowed.[52]

Over the coming years, Harwood would continue to dip his toes into the whirlpool of international politics, firstly with a play about the murdered Polish priest Jerzy Popieluszko and, then, a TV biopic of Nelson Mandela starring Danny Glover as the celebrated dissident. Current affairs, however, have never been Harwood's natural element. 'I wish I had had the courage,' says Harwood of his brief dalliance as a polemicist, 'to write [those kinds of narratives] as comedy – much as Chekhov considered his plays comedies. I wanted to, but then I backed off. I'm rather sorry about that.' Likewise, there was something that he came to regard as false about his obsession with racial politics. 'The moment apartheid fell in 1989,' he recalls,

> I began to feel guilty of what I had said and done. For the truth of the matter is that it was so easy for me to criticize at a distance of 6,000 miles. And it made me look like such a jolly good chap in the eyes of some of my fellow men. I was on the right side, no doubt about that, and I needed everyone to know it. But I risked nothing. Neither I nor my family were threatened in any way. And I wasn't even a very good witness because I did not live there. ... When I think of the real courage of writers like Athol Fugard and Nadine Gordimer, I shudder at my own arrogance, for I have come to understand that the one question I could not answer with any degree of honesty was, 'How would I have behaved?'

Answering this question would become Harwood's major theatrical task throughout the late 1980s and early 1990s. Like a process of evolution from a single-celled organism to a sentient creature, Harwood did so with a steady stream of plays that were forever getting closer to achieving his ideal. The long road to recovery began with *Interpreters*, which opened at the Queen's Theatre on 19 November 1985. A play about two translators from either side of the Iron Curtain, Viktor Belaev (Edward Fox) and Nadia Ogilvie-Smith (Maggie Smith), it succeeded in addressing the politics of the Cold War – but, crucially, on a personal level. In the opening scene, the main characters are facilitating a dialogue between their respective government representatives about an imminent visit to Britain by the Soviet premier. The greatest bone of contention is not ideological, but gastronomic – the Russian ambassador objects strongly to the plebeian menu proposed for the state banquet: 'If the Queen were to come to Moscow...' he snaps at the mention of vodka, 'you wouldn't expect us to serve her warm beer.' Later in the play it becomes clear that the two interpreters are lovers, and that Viktor plans to defect to be with his heart's desire. When he is found out, however, he is forced to renounce her: 'I admit I told her I wanted to defect,' he is compelled to tell both diplomats (painfully, through the medium of the distraught Nadia),

> But you know what women are. Some you have to tell you lust after their bodies, others that you are fascinated by their intellect [*Viktor shakes his head despairingly at her translation*]. In her case she wants stability, a future. All I wanted was to bed her. I tried lust, I tried love. In the end I told her what she wanted to hear –

Both diplomats accept this confession, and Nadia is eventually forced to resign on grounds of ill-health to avoid a scandal. She never receives Viktor's subsequent apology, nor his admission that he was '...not criminal but human ... not cruel but cowardly.' Instead she is visited by her former boss at the Foreign Office who, through stifled tears, promises that he and his colleagues will 'rally round' to find her translation work. It is a tale of the primacy of sordid self-interest over roseate romanticism; security over sentimentalism.

The reviewers regarded the play as a flawed diamond. John Peter in the *Sunday Times* considered some of the dialogue between Fox and Smith to have 'the forward drive of a thriller and the teasing ingenuity of a crossword puzzle.' The rub was the clunkiness of the final scene. 'This is like a dramatic exclamation mark,' continued Peter, 'overlong, overwritten and blood-curdlingly sentimental: the play needs a coda, but this improbable bit of tearjerking is not it.' For Michael Billington in *The Guardian*, however, it was Harwood's evident prejudice against Communism that robbed the production of ideological authenticity. 'Mr Harwood deserves credit for his dissection of emotional vulnerability,' he wrote schoolmasterishly, 'but it would be a vastly better play if it penetrated rather than stereotyped the Soviet mind.' Of particular offense to his predilections was the British diplomat's spirited defence of bourgeois values: 'If culture were left to the aristocrats and the working class,' explains the official to his Russian counterpart, 'we'd have nothing but horse-racing and homing-pigeons.' Billington was disgusted to find this 'downright lie' applauded by the audience 'as if it were a profound truth.'[53]

Such unpromising reviews contributed to the play's premature demise early in the new year. While Harwood did his level best to keep up the cast's morale, he was mentally already on his next project. This fact is clear from a conversation he had with Maggie Smith shortly after the play's opening night. Wandering into her dressing room unannounced, Harwood declared that he was terribly upset because he had just learnt that his mother had died – he felt guilty that he had still not cried. 'You will, dear,' assured the actress while removing her make-up ('I never did,' breaks in Harwood). Then, to lighten the mood, Smith asked what her visitor had been getting up to of late. 'Struggling with a new play, darling,' he grandly explained. Fed up with these lugubrious interruptions, Smith casually delivered a bracing douche of cold water: 'Aren't we all?' (Another version has the *grande dame* of British theatre declaring: 'Try finishing this one first').[54]

The new play gestating in Harwood's mind was without doubt his most ambitious piece of drama to date. It was simply entitled *J. J. Farr*. It tells the story of a distinguished atheist writer of the same name who, following a physical encounter with God, returns to his original vocation as a Catholic priest. This epiphany takes place while Farr is held prisoner in an Islamic country, where he has been taken hostage as retribution for his outspoken views. Told in the form of a flashback in the comfortable surroundings of a retreat for defrocked priests, the play comes to its dramatic climax when Farr relives the moment that he emerged from his confinement to drink a vial of 'white wine' consecrated by a priest who lay dying in the prison yard. Not even the fact that this impoverished minister had been forced to use an altogether less holy substance diminished the potency of his spiritual revelation. 'It was taking God,' explains Farr, 'or piss, into my mouth.'

When Harwood completed the first draft of the play, he took it excitedly to the Master of Balliol, Professor Antony Kenny, for approval. 'I took a dislike to it', recalls the distinguished author of *The Anatomy of the Soul*, *Aquinas on Mind* and two dozen or so kindred titles. The critics were no more enamoured by the play. 'Ignition is the problem with Ronald Harwood's *J. J. Farr*', sniffed Michael Ratcliffe in *The Observer*. 'It's like a car that will not start.' Likening Harwood's homespun philosophy to a 'series of theological lunges or judo falls', the critic delivered a sharp pen thrust at the familiar quire of 'faintly camp little jokes to assure the timorous that things are not so urgent after all.' ('She's – colossal,' declares one former priest of the unseen nurse: 'I mean, have you ever seen such bazonkers?'). Only the strong performance of Albert Finney as the lead character, continued Ratcliffe, 'lifts the play on to a higher plane of expectation'; but even this was ultimately not enough to salvage the production. 'Harwood loses interest in Farr completely,' he concluded, 'and transfers attention to his antagonist and bitter disciple Lowrie (Bob Peck), the kind of chap from Up North who crosses his legs at the very mention of Aristotle, attacks merely to conceal his own crisis and goes completely to pieces at the end.' In the more pithy words of Christopher Edwards of the *Spectator*, the trite philosophical arguments deployed in *J. J. Farr* were 'so sententious and banal that they could have come out of a Christmas cracker.'[55]

There is no doubt that Harwood was bruised by these salvos. 'I had put all my creative powers into those plays,' he sighs, 'and had been mocked and derided.' Yet his status as a major figure in the theatre remained intact. Alongside his dramatic works, he kept up a prolific flow of well-received books, lectures and articles about himself and his vocation. Of these titles a pair of collected essays celebrating the lives of Sir John Gielgud and Sir Alec Guinness were perhaps the most notable. 'He [Gielgud] has already written his memoirs several times,' explained Harwood's publisher, Ion Trewin, 'but it did occur to me that a collection of pieces by different people in the theatre about his own genius might make a rather terrific book with distinctly good commercial possibilities.' Harwood, who had already become well acquainted with the octogenarian star during the course of making *All the World's a Stage*, thrilled in orchestrating this editorial standing ovation. The only trouble was that many of Gielgud's friends and contemporaries were reluctant to divulge the juicy stories that would have made such a book really interesting. 'Flattery will get you almost anywhere', wrote the actor's near contemporary Major-General Sir Jeremy Moore, '– but not quite! I much regret that, whatever you may say about the non-necessity of competence, I do not have the ability to satisfy myself that I could do justice to so great a skill and professionalism as Sir John's in any published work on him.' Another problem was that both of Harwood's subjects were reluctant to offer him their full-blooded support. 'I must say I'd breathe more easily,' wrote Sir Alec, '[if the book were not published].' Touching lightly on a name that had a painful historical resonance for the playwright, he continued: 'Alan [Bennett] will be *conspicuously* absent. But I'd hate him or anyone to be pressurised. Why not wait until my (unlikely) eightieth? I would be ga-ga by then and not notice and no one who knew me in my twenties likely to be alive. So then you needn't do it at all.'[56]

Yet all these publications were dust in the balance when set against Harwood's real ambition: to be acclaimed as the most popular playwright of his generation. The greatest stumbling block in this regard was not, in Harwood's opinion, that his plays were not enjoyed by the public, but that they were looked down upon by the critics. 'I never write for critics,' he says brusquely, '– that would be fatal.' He did, however, decide to place the impersonal and often dysfunctional relationship between creator and commentator centre stage in his 1993 play, *Poison Pen*. Predictably this truly did prove fatal. Loosely based on the life of the music journalist Philip Heseltine, the play is about a critic, Eric Wells, who is besieged by death threats from a reclusive composer named Peter Godwin. The impetus for Godwin to write these vitriolic letters is that Wells has accused him not only of lapsing into mediocrity, but also plagiarising the music of Delius. When the brazen critic is visited by an irate representative from Godwin's publishing firm, Wells explains that he has turned against the composer at least in part because he loves him – it was he who launched his career. 'Young critics,' he tells the visitor, 'usually give anything new bad reviews.' 'That's because they're cautious,' he goes on, 'and because bad reviews are so much easier to write. But I threw caution to the winds and said that, after Delius, Peter Godwin was probably the most gifted composer of our time. ... However, in recent months, oh, it's well over a year now, there is no doubt in my mind that his music has deteriorated alarmingly ... I had no alternative but to make the matter public.'

During the course of the remainder of the play Wells' unloved boyfriend, a tragically untalented former dancer named Larry Rider, works in partnership with the disgruntled music publisher to find out more about Peter Godwin: he suspects that Wells is having an affair with Godwin's mistress. The denouement to all this is as unsettling as it is unexpected: Eric Wells *is* Peter Godwin.

The critics did not appreciate Harwood's thinly-veiled criticisms. 'The study in duality gets nowhere', scoffed Michael Coveney in *The Observer*, 'because Harwood is caught in a thriller trap, Wells keeping his "secret" from the go-between publisher who is trying to heal the breach between critic and artist.' Of greater interest – and historical accuracy – he continued with studied condescension, would have been an examination of Heseltine's 'friendship with D. H. Lawrence ... or his obsession with Celtic languages and the occult...' Nor were the reviewers much taken by Harwood's first attempt at directing – an experiment partly brought about by the unexpected death of Michael Elliott, aged fifty-four, in 1984. The result, in the words of *The Times*, was 'an egghead's Agatha Christie.'[57]

Winged, if not defeated, Harwood slumped back in the same stalls from which his career as a playwright had begun and contemplated his next move. He was fortunate in having some interesting reading material stowed in his knapsack. 'Towards the end of rehearsals in Manchester,' recalls Harwood, 'my wife joined me and brought with her a book she had just finished and strongly recommended.' This was *Berlin Days* by George Clare, the celebrated author of *The Last Waltz in Vienna*. Harwood now took up the book and was gripped. 'The moment I read the first few pages,' he continues, 'I knew at once that there was a play to be written on a moral issue that was of profound importance to me and my excitement was great.'

The drama to emerge from this Damascene revelation was closely based on Clare's own life and career. An assimilated Viennese Jew, he had fled Nazi persecution only to return to the conquered Third Reich in the uniform of a British intelligence officer. His role was to investigate the doings of prominent individuals who had been deprived of their positions under Control Council Directive No. 24, subheaded, 'Concerning the Removal from Office and Positions of Responsibility of Nazis and Persons Hostile to Allied Purposes.' His first assignment was to put together a file on the maestro of Hitler's Germany: Dr Wilhelm Furtwängler, Musical Director of the Berlin Philharmonic Orchestra. His findings were at once clear and ambiguous. While Furtwängler – who improbably doubled up as a Prussian Privy Councillor – had conducted beneath the swastika on the eve of Hitler's birthday and also before a Nuremberg rally, he had also helped save many Jewish musicians escape from persecution. Moreover, he had incurred the wrath of Joseph Goebbels by publicly criticizing the party's totalitarian 'cultural policy'. After completing his dossier for the denazification tribunal in Wiesbaden, Clare could not decide whose side to take: that of his aggressively vengeful superiors at the Control Council or the legions of music lovers who swore Furtwängler to be a good and honest man. 'When I had finished my work,' recalled Clare, 'and the file was ready to go to [his superior, Major] Sely I sat and looked at the closed folder for a long time. The Spruchkammer [Denazification tribunal] would have to give its verdict, but on what? That no one could live under a brutal dictatorship without becoming tainted? Compromising with evil to prevent worse, a defence I was to hear many times, is always futile, but to know this after the event was as easy as, except in a very few cases, it is difficult to recognize malignancy in its infancy.'[58]

This presented the central moral problem of Harwood's most successful play of the post-*Dresser* era: *Taking Sides*. Like all Harwood's historical works, it was researched with the enthusiasm of a zealot and the discernment of an inebriate. 'As soon as I returned to London,' recalls Harwood, 'I asked in a bookshop if they happened to have anything at all about a German conductor called Wilhelm Furtwängler.' By another one of those gifts of serendipity so typical of Harwood's career they had just taken stock of two books on the German conductor: *The Devil's Music Master* by Sam H. Shirakawa and *Trial of Strength* by Fred K. Prieberg. Harwood devoured these tomes, especially Shirakawa's, which despite being rubbished by Professor Richard J. Evans in the *Times Literary Supplement* ('his book is full of howlers that would be a disgrace in a first-year examination script'), was highly readable and eminently persuasive in exonerating the maligned musician. This was exactly what Harwood wanted. Of especial interest was a passage in which Shirakawa speculated about what took place in the crucial year between Clare compiling his dossier and Furtwängler's long-awaited hearing at Wiesbaden. 'If they could not induce him to be hoist by his own petard,' wrote Shirakawa, 'could the Americans have wanted to "frame" Furtwängler?' To assuage lingering academic qualms, Harwood discussed the matter with Professor Evans and subsequently paid an experienced researcher to comb the archives of the relevant institutions in Berlin, Fulton and London; but of the alleged conspiracy and its principal suspects he could find little hard evidence. 'I was pleased,' recounts Harwood, 'because that liberated me: I had no intention of writing a documentary or a docudrama. ... I knew that I now had the freedom to dramatize actual events without being hemmed in by a wall of ascertained facts.'

In Harwood's version, Furtwängler's file is taken up by a former insurance fraud investigator named Major Steve Arnold. A proud philistine, he sets out to 'nail' the legendary interpreter of Brahms and Beethoven with the same gusto that he evidently displayed when chasing bogus claimants in smallville. 'I knew another band leader once,' he boorishly explains at the outset of the play to his cultured German secretary, Emmi Straube.

> Name of Dix Dixon. Small time. Alto sax. Not bad, not good. But not bad. Played one night stands in Illinois and Michigan. A house he owned, where he and the band used to stay, burned down. Lost everything. Well, almost everything. But I got him. You know how? Because there's always one question the guilty can't answer. Get a sign writer, write it big: THERE'S ALWAYS ONE QUESTION THE GUILTY CAN'T ANSWER. In Dix's case, it was, 'How come, Dix, everybody lost everything except you? You've got your clothes, your sax, how come?' Couldn't answer. He was dumb, boy was he dumb. Owed the bookies. You understand, don't you Emmi? He burned down his house for the insurance money. We used to call that Jewish lightning.

Over the course of the remainder of the play, Major Arnold is able to put every piece of incriminating evidence before the deposed 'band leader': why did he accept the position of Prussian Privy Councillor and Vice-President of the Chamber of Music? Why did he conduct at one of the Nuremberg rallies and Hitler's fifty-third birthday celebration? Why did he not leave Germany after the rise of the Nazis? – and so on. In his staccato replies, Furtwängler tries to exonerate himself with a combination of haughty arrogance and genuine contrition: he tells Arnold that he believed in the separation of art and politics; that he was given no opportunity either to accept or refuse honours, and that he only ever performed on the evening *before* party events. Inevitably, the major is unmoved: 'That sounds like the small print in one of our insurance policies, Wilhelm,' he crows, '... I think you made a deal, you shook hands with the Devil and you became real close to him and his cohorts. You were so close you were in the same shithouse as them, you could wipe their asses for them –.'

Throughout these lacerating verbal onslaughts, Arnold's two colleagues – his secretary and a German-born liaison officer, Lieutenant Wills – vainly attempt to help the disgraced conductor, but to little avail. At the end of the last interrogation scene, the maestro finally breaks down: 'Yes, yes,' he stammers, 'it would have been better if I'd left in 1934, it would have been better if I'd left' – and then proceeds to vomit. 'Show your friend to the toilet,' yells Arnold at an on-looking second violinist, 'and then tell him to get the hell out of here.' The play ends with Wills placing Furtwängler's recording of Beethoven's Ninth Symphony onto a turntable just as Arnold telephones his superiors at Wiesbaden. 'Hey,' the major calls over the ensuing racket, 'turn that off, can't you see I'm on the phone?' But Wills just stares out of the window. In the bomb-damaged street below the trembling conductor hears the music but cannot fathom its source. 'Turn it off!' repeats Arnold as the lights fade to blackout.

The play opened at the Minerva Theatre, Chichester, on 18 May 1995, starring Michael Pennington as Major Arnold and Daniel Massey as Furtwängler. Harold Pinter directed. Such a combination of talents could not have failed to delight audiences and critics alike. 'It was a huge success,' recalls Pinter's widow, Lady Antonia Fraser, 'and I know that Harold loved working with Ronnie again after all those years – his admiration for him and his work was genuine and long-standing.' On the opening night the two veterans of Sir Donald Wolfit's theatre company stood at the back of the auditorium to savour the tangible connection between cast and audience. 'Listen to the silences,' murmured Pinter to his old sparring-partner. All were in agreement that Harwood's play was an instant classic.

Few critics dissented from this verdict. 'At the end of Ronald Harwood's new play,' wrote Charles Spencer in the *Daily Telegraph*, 'the audience didn't just clap, they stamped their feet with approval. … This is a tremendous play, tremendously performed.' Best of all was the consensus that, for the first time, Harwood had succeeded in combining the features of an entertaining 'well-made' play with the unresolved tension of a modern morality tale. Focusing on the moment in the drama when Arnold's secretary complains that he is behaving 'like them', the *Sunday Times* critic John Peter marvelled at Harwood's skill and control. 'A lesser writer', he wrote, 'might have made the major recoil in indignation. Harwood knows that things have gone too far: the major does not react because he does not understand.' Even Harwood's long-term critic Michael Billington was struck by the play's emotional power. 'It is fascinating to observe', he wrote in *The Guardian*, 'how the debate really takes off when Harwood downplays the American's crudity.' At moments, he conceded, 'the play achieves the force of dialectic.'[59]

These notices drew an incredible haul of distinguished visitors to the quiet market town. 'In brief,' wrote the legendary former editor of *The Mirror*, Hugh Cudlipp, in a letter to Harwood, '… Bloody Marvellous, and the audience knew it.' Likewise, veteran playwright Christopher Fry delighted in the production: 'I can't remember', he wrote on the back of a postcard, 'ever having come away from a production so at one with what I had seen: not by a hair's breadth would I have wanted anything different – six great performances of a measure with what they were playing. Thank you.' An equally delightful encomium came from a sedate mews house off Eaton Square. 'I am thrilled for you!' wrote Luise Rainer, '… When will you – it – be in London? I shall be there with *heart* and *soul!*' And towering above all these accolades, a generous card from the widow of Harwood's hero, Graham Greene: 'Last night', wrote Yvonne Cloetta shortly after the play's transfer to the capital, 'I had one of the best evenings in the theatre I can remember for a long time. *Taking Sides* should run and run. It is good to see a serious piece in the commercial theatre and be convinced that it will succeed. Congratulations.'[60]

There was, however, one potential fly in the ointment. When writing the play, Harwood had not realized that Furtwängler's widow, Elisabeth, was still alive. Fiercely protective of her late husband's reputation, she had only recently threatened to sue Bernard Levin for publically castigating the conductor as an 'exceptionally unpleasant anti-Semite' and a 'self-defeating weakling'. While Levin privately withdrew these statements – and also accepted Harwood's dedication of the play to him in thanks for a powerful dissenting judgement on *J. J. Farr* – the wrangling went on unabated. 'What you have done', wrote one of Frau Furtwängler's henchmen to the influential critic, 'is the act of a coward: to make an accusation and when asked to back it up with facts, to respond: "let's forget all about it". Bad enough, but you add something truly monstrous … You know something considerably worse than Furtwängler's being an exceptionally unpleasant anti-Semite – but you are not going to tell … an ugly threat: she runs the risk of your revealing that horrible fact (much worse than anti-Semitism, so it must be horrendous). I must borrow your description of Furtwängler to characterize a man who can act like you – a lamentable human being.'[61]

It fell to Harwood to reconcile the parties. In a letter to the conductor's widow, he asked her to forgive his 'old friend', Levin, for his hasty conclusions before moving on to the more central issue of the play itself. 'I have done my best to be fair to him,' he wrote, 'and, apart from one speech, I have only used his own words.' Yet this was merely the prelude to the real charm: 'I would be pleased,' continued Harwood, 'indeed, honoured to arrange seats for you at any performance you find convenient. Of course, you may want to have nothing to do with me either before or after the performance and I shall perfectly well understand if that is your wish. But do not hesitate to contact me if you desire so.' In due course the gentle old lady made her way to a production as the playwright's special guest. 'At the end,' recalls Harwood, 'she said that something was wrong. I was terrified! But she just said, "Wilhelm did not have so much hair."' Having promised to put the matter right with the wig maker, the pair went backstage to hobnob with Daniel Massey. 'She put her arm through his,' he grins, 'and just sat there with him silently contemplating times past.'[62]

The magic continued when the play transferred to the Criterion Theatre following a triumphant procession through the provinces. For the entire summer of 1995 audiences packed into the baroque auditorium to revel in the moral combat of Harwood's theatrical blockbuster. Among the many thousands of ordinary theatre-goers was an impressive constellation of big names, including cabinet ministers, distinguished judges, celebrated academics and members of the royal family. 'On Tuesday,' wrote one acquaintance, 'I was surrounded in the audience by friends from all over the world and I also was pleased to see Sir Claus Moser, Lord Montagu, Sir Isaiah Berlin and Lord (Max) Rayne. It had a tremendous reception of deep emotion and is undoubtedly one of the most mind-searing scripts I have heard for years.' The unmistakable inference that the play appealed strongly to the Anglo-Jewish community was not lost on another one of Frau Furtwängler's English acquaintances, who provided her with a vivid report of the same production. 'The audience in London,' he wrote,

> was, in my conservative estimate, seventy percent Jewish; my friends say ninety. Many octogenarian refugee ladies, still beautiful, came with their portly, sixtyish sons. I had the sense of being part of a historical continuum; an awareness of their presence as mourners, but also deep admirers, indeed representatives, of the great German culture of their youth; of their love for Furtwängler as part of their own identity. There were moments in the play when the audience seemed to stop breathing; and, unless I am mistaken, I heard some muffled sobs as the evidence of Furtwängler's intervention for Jews unfolded … But on this night it was the silence after the play, the sound of feet shuffling on carpet that spoke most eloquently both to our feelings for the victims and our respect for the artists who brought us the work.[63]

Having conquered Britain, Harwood now turned his attentions to Europe, where the play was similarly experienced by audiences in countries as various as Poland, Croatia, France, Austria and Germany itself. While an exhaustive account of these polyglot adventures would test the endurance of even Harwood's most unstinting admirers, they were highly significant for at least two reasons. Most crucially, they gave him a sense of genuine international stardom – an impression reinforced by István Szabó's offer to direct the 2001 film adaptation starring Harvey Keitel and Stellan Skarsgård. 'My expectation is of failure,' explains Harwood: 'Success is very rare, and … I'm slightly immobilized by it.' The widespread acclaim of *Taking Sides* allowed him to travel around the world in the guise of acclaimed public moralist. But he did not always like what he saw. During the course of one memorable night in Wiesbaden he was paralysed by an unexpected turn of phrase used by the actress playing Emmi Straube. 'I have no German,' explains Harwood, 'but I could tell she was speaking poetry because of the throb in her voice.' Later in the production, when the same character is supposed to scream that her father only joined in a plot against Hitler when the war was clearly lost, there was another awkward line alteration. 'She screamed alright,' huffs Harwood, 'but instead of my words she sprouted two lines of Goethe. I was not – how shall I put it? – pleased.'[64]

At the end of the production, the furious playwright made a beeline for the German director. 'Besides vandalizing the text,' he fumed in the middle of a crowded party, 'I told her she had completely distorted and sentimentalized the characters.' As the decibel count rose, the actress playing Emmi appeared to say a word in favour of the author of *The Sorrows of Young Werther* and *Faust*: 'But Goethe is a great writer,' she tried. It was no use: '*But he didn't write this play!*' replied Harwood in a tone somewhat redolent of Major Arnold. Still the drama continued. 'At that moment,' recalls Harwood, 'a handsome, smart middle-aged man intervened.' After asking in 'too-perfect English' if the playwright was prepared to negotiate, Harwood shot back: 'Who are you and what do you do?' When the intruder replied – with a 'self-satisfied smirk' – that he was a lawyer and also the former minister of culture for the state of Hesse, Harwood simply barked, 'Get lost!' The end result was that a new clause was inserted into all Harwood's contracts with artistic directors that no alterations could be made to his plays. Neither this, nor the playwright's subsequent decision to specify in his will that the character of 'Sir' can never be performed by a female actor, has particularly endeared him to the innumerable 'right on' members of the theatrical community. Not that Harwood appears to have taken their criticisms to heart: 'Fuck 'em,' he shrugs while slurping on a large whisky.

Yet there is one director for whom Harwood has always held the utmost respect and admiration. Attending a production of *Taking Sides* in Paris merely in the capacity of a private citizen, this individual realized by the interval that he had stumbled upon the masterhand to write the script of his next project: an adaption of a little-known memoir by Władysław Szpilman about his experiences in the Warsaw ghetto. The director's name was Roman Polanski; the project – *The Pianist*.

Before narrating Harwood's involvement in his most successful film to date, it is appropriate to outline his experiences working on a movie that won him neither exorbitant financial gain nor critical acclaim. For nothing would be falser than to imagine that Harwood's pathway from browbeaten playwright to acclaimed Hollywood wordsmith has been as straight as Sunset Boulevard. 'All the high points in my career,' says Harwood, 'have come late.' He might have added that they have been founded upon the wreckage of disaster, misery and adversity.

The journey began in the spring of 1988, when Harwood's agent, Judy Daish, relayed an invitation for him to meet the acclaimed Italian director Franco Zeffirelli. 'I flew out to meet him in L.A.,' reminisces Harwood, 'and spent several days with him discussing an autobiographical subject.' Although he was initially somewhat suspicious of the chubby, silver-tongued Florentine, Harwood quickly came to terms to write a screenplay about his early life. 'I was flattered,' he continues, 'because I had known and admired his work for many years – though I must say that I find his film adaptations much too visual for my liking.' Before parting it was arranged that Harwood would come and stay at the director's Roman villa for two weeks that summer to work on the script.

In the months prior to his visit, Harwood learnt what he could of his subject. The illegitimate son of a dressmaker, Zeffirelli was raised by a group of doting English ladies in Florence, where he was introduced to the same names that had sparked Harwood's own love of literature: W. Somerset Maugham, P. G. Wodehouse and the fountainhead itself – Shakespeare. Proudly Catholic, he and his unlikely minders spent much of the war attempting to save religious buildings and artefacts from Nazi destruction. Later the youth went on to read art and architecture at the University of Florence before abandoning his studies for directing. With his 1967 film adaptation of *The Taming of the Shrew*, starring Richard Burton and Elizabeth Taylor, his reputation was made: a long list of distinguished works including *Romeo and Juliet* and *Jesus of Nazareth* placed him incontrovertibly among the greats.

The Harwoods were met at Rome airport at the end of May by a feminine young man vaguely resembling the 1978 Wimbledon finalist Betty Stove. 'He was,' remarks Harwood, 'given that nickname by English actors, and served as Zeffirelli's chauffeur or adopted son.' This character deposited the couple at the aptly-named Villa Grande: a vast and garish mansion protected from the outside world by a series of automatic gates and CCTV cameras. 'Dogs and servants abounded,' recalls Harwood of his long walk from the car to his stately private suite. He was then ushered into the presence of the great man himself. 'He was on crutches after a hip operation,' recalls Harwood, 'but was buzzing with excitement because the previous evening he had seen Michael Jackson in concert.' This alone was enough to irritate Harwood, whose oeuvre includes an essay entitled 'The Pop Virus'. But things were soon to get even worse. 'I quickly discovered,' continues Harwood, 'that that very evening he was giving a party at the villa for the young singer himself.' Despite the telephone ringing off the hook – 'with people who did not know the meaning of the word pride' – the Harwoods refused to be swept away by the excitement. 'We went into the city,' explains the playwright haughtily, 'shopping in the via Condotti and lunching in the shade at La Rampa.'

Yet the Harwoods could not feign indifference forever. 'The atmosphere quickly communicated itself to Natasha and me,' recalls Harwood of their return to the villa later that afternoon. With an armed escort now stationed in the car park (not, it transpired, for 'M.J.', but rather for the US Ambassador to Italy, Maxwell M. Rabb) and wild rumours circulating about the guest list, Harwood ventured to enquire of one of the valets if Gore Vidal would be attending. 'Ssssh!' lisped the flunkey, 'don't mention that name. Franco 'e 'ates Gore Vidal! Gore Vidal 'e 'ates Franco!' The hard-to-impress playwright had to make do with a supporting cast that included the former Bond-girl Ursula Andress, the actors Marcello Mastroianni and Sophia Loren, the director Bernardo Bertolucci and the influential music producer Quincy Jones, who was bringing a personal entourage of fifteen.

'Neither Natasha nor I could decide what to wear,' recalls Harwood of the final moments before the arrival of the Pop King. After finally settling for a brand new pale fawn Giorgio Amani suit with navy linen shirt, navy shoes and navy socks, the famous author led his crimson-gowned damsel down a marble staircase. At its foot the couple found the other guests crowded into a large room watching football on an immense screen. Predictably displeased – 'I *loathe* football' – Harwood's mood was hardly improved by the sight of his host. 'Zeffirelli appeared,' continues Harwood, 'rather plainly dressed, I thought, admired Natasha (whom he elevated in introductions from Mrs Harwood to Princess Natasha before you could say "Positano") and raised his eyebrows, rather insultingly, I thought, at my Giorgio Amani.' Throughout the ensuing forty-five minutes, Harwood endured what he can only recall as the first half of a match that was 'like most football games … boring.' More interesting to his mind were the revealing little comments uttered by his host during the game: 'Cute kid,' he murmured every time an agreeable looking youth took possession of the ball.

With the party already in full swing, there was an announcement at about ten thirty that Jackson would shortly be entering the compound. Garbed in a bright red military tunic, he was greeted by a rehearsed round of applause. 'He smiled shyly,' recalls Harwood: 'We lined up and as he passed down the line like Royalty, he shook hands with each of us in turn.' Seemingly from nowhere a troupe of paparazzi appeared and began photographing the megastar with his arm around the woman known to film history as Honey Rider. 'Zeffirelli managed to push her out of the way,' chuckles Harwood, 'and be photographed instead.' A moment later the US Ambassador – looking 'like a jeans manufacturer whose business had been threatened by the Mafia' – was presented. 'And then! And then!' adds Harwood with a mock flourish, 'Micha' Ja'ssn was gone!' He had been at the party for no more than ten minutes. Harwood was later told the reason: ''E is madly in love with Sophia Loren's son,' murmured one of the attendants, '– capice? They kiss in public!'

Yet, whatever the reason for Jackson's premature departure, Harwood was pleased to be divested of his rival. 'Thank God he went,' he continues dryly, 'because that was the signal for food to be served. The Secretary General to the President of Italy beat me to the buffet, but I did all right.' Harwood spent the rest of the evening quietly chatting to Zeffirelli's taciturn English lawyer, John Stutter. Then, as the party was breaking up, a large black man – 'one of Quincy Jones' XV' – came and threw his arm around Harwood's neck in a tight headlock. Someone had told him that he was the intellect behind *The Dresser*: 'Man, I love that film,' the stranger slurred. 'It must be true,' recalls the playwright today, 'because there were no parts for big black men in the Zeffirelli movie.' Before staggering into the night, this nameless admirer whispered mysteriously into his ear: 'Just remember one thing, buddy. I don't care who you are or what you are so long as you've got a Yiddishe kop!'

Over the course of the coming weeks, the Harwoods followed the court of the movie emperor around his various Italian properties. 'High drama and subjects for several short stories proliferated like volcanic dust,' reminisces Harwood of this sybaritic interlude. Much of this involved Zeffirelli's 'wretched' favourite dog, Bambina, who contrived to torment her master's innumerable hangers-on. During one informal drinks party at Zeffirelli's getaway at Positano, a lady – at the time 'exuberantly admiring Betty Stove's Cartier wristwatch' – was bitten in the face within two minutes of her arrival and immediately rushed to a plastic surgeon in Naples. 'A terrible gloom descended,' recalls Harwood of the ensuing dinner. 'People talked in hushed whispers … Zeffirelli was very subdued but his appetite, like everyone else's, was in no way impaired.' Harwood, who had not yet seen the woman, was informed that she was extremely beautiful and obsessed with her appearance. When she eventually returned from hospital the next day he was somewhat disappointed. 'I did not think she was as beautiful as I had been led to believe,' he huffs, 'having rather less chin than the dog who bit her.'

Just two days later, Bambina struck again. This time the victim was Zeffirelli's devoted manservant, Ali. With blood pouring from his hand, this long-suffering member of the director's retinue disappeared into the kitchen only to return brandishing a broom: 'advancing on Bambina,' remembers Harwood, 'with what is best described as evil intent.' It later transpired that much of the man's anger was directed at Zeffirelli, who had shown total indifference to the incident. The nonchalant host did, however, take the opportunity of Ali's cursing to deliver a short lecture to his prospective Boswell. 'When Ali was berating the dog,' recounts Harwood, 'he repeated a word which sounded like "Catso" several times.' Loosely translated into English as 'prick', Zeffirelli explained that in *Romeo and Juliet* the warring factions cry 'Cats, ho!' at each other, which he believed to be irrefutable evidence that the Bard consorted with Italians. 'This proves not to be so,' concludes Harwood: 'There is no mention of "Cats, ho!" in *Romeo and Juliet* nor in any of the other plays set in Italy.' Ronnie 1, Franco 0.

It was almost a week before Harwood managed to raise the small matter of the screenplay he had come to write. 'I was getting anxious,' he recalls, 'not only about my figure, but also about starting work.' At last Harwood plucked up the courage to raise the matter with the maestro. He chose to do so at a rather inopportune moment. The celebrated director was just then frolicking with his inner circle in a bubbling cauldron situated at the rear of the mansion. 'What a lovely Jacuzzi, Franco,' was Harwood's innocuous icebreaker. But Zeffirelli merely smirked at his companions, before correcting his guest: 'It is not a Jacuzzi,' he replied with a wagging finger – 'It is a jet pool. Jacuzzis are for people in Swiss Cottage.' Crushed, Harwood had to wait until after dinner for his second attempt. 'When can we talk, Franco?' he resumed over coffee.

Zeffirelli: Very difficult.

Harwood: Why?

Zeffirelli: I have such trouble with *Young Toscanini*.

Harwood: We really must talk.

Zeffirelli: I know.

Harwood: When do you think we can go to Florence?

Zeffirelli: Is very difficult.

Harwood: Yes, but when, Franco?

Zeffirelli: I was hoping Wednesday, Thursday or Friday. Friday is good. But we need more than one day. We have to recharge our batteries.

Harwood: My batteries are fully charged.

Zeffirelli: Also I have TV chat show on Saturday night.

When Harwood did eventually get Zeffirelli to speak about his early days, things did not exactly go swimmingly. 'He waxed lyrical about his childhood,' recalls Harwood, 'but strayed into an account of his romance with Visconti to whom he owed so much and hinted at many affairs with some very celebrated names.' Harwood hoped that he might be able to make use of this. 'I suggested,' he goes on, 'a scene where the young Franco swims naked in a river and cavorts with other Florentine lads – a way, I thought, of establishing our hero's predilections.' The suggestion, however, was not appreciated.

Zeffirelli: Are you totally insane?

Harwood: I don't understand.

Zeffirelli: I advise the Vatican on television and film.

Harwood: I still don't understand.

Zeffirelli: I made *Jesus of Nazareth!*

Harwood: I know, but –

Zeffirelli: No buts. Maybe we have beautiful young virgin gazing at me while I swim. No boys!

With this instruction still ringing in his ears, Harwood sat down in the comfortable study laid on for his use and began his masterpiece. 'I decided that I must start writing,' explains the playwright, 'avoid his homosexuality and to hell with seeing the locations in Florence which, in any case, I knew well.' In under a week he had completed a first draft. After partaking in a victory dinner with the Princess Bernadotte and a small galaxy of fellow admirers, Harwood returned, first class, to London.

A few weeks later came the shattering fall: Zeffirelli rejected the screenplay. A replacement was later written by Sir John Mortimer. But Harwood would not join the throngs of cinemagoers to see *Tea with Mussolini* when it was finally released in 1999. 'I couldn't bring myself to watch it,' he murmurs at the mere mention of the title. Whether motivated by proud pique, sad submission or sheer jealousy, the thwarted screenplay-writer would not sulk for long: by the time of the film's release his star was already on the cusp of an altogether headier plane.

Act Five:

AUTUMN TRIUMPH

11

The Pianist

[O]nly virtuosi *can be indescribably bad one night,*
and indescribably magnificent on another.
Sir Donald Wolfit CBE: his life and work in the unfashionable theatre

During the making of his adaptation of *The Good Companions* in the early 1970s, it often fell to Harwood to drive André Previn to and from the rehearsal studio. On one occasion, he found himself awaiting his fare on a piano stool outside the great conductor's dressing room. 'He was taking so long,' recalls Harwood, 'that I decided to play something.' His repertoire, acquired years ago on a neighbour's unsteady upright piano, consisted of no more than the opening bars of Beethoven's vigorous First Sonata. At the end of this miniature concert, Previn suddenly appeared in the doorway clutching a hair comb. 'Was that you?' he haltingly enquired. Bashfully, Harwood answered in the affirmative. The conductor flicked a lock from his forehead: 'You're the worst pianist I've ever heard,' he coolly declared before returning to his ablutions. 'Well,' riposted the librettist through the partially-closed door, 'at least you rate me.'

It strains credulity to believe that less than thirty years later, the same lacklustre soloist would write the screenplay of perhaps the greatest film on an ebony and ivory theme. *The Pianist* starring Adrien Brody, Emelia Fox, Maureen Lipman and Ed Stoppard remains, without doubt, Harwood's single greatest contribution to cinema. 'It did wonders for me,' he reminisces, '– suddenly every studio in Hollywood wanted me. ... I wouldn't say that they were queuing up round the block, but they certainly came to me.'

The man who bears greatest responsibility for this happy metamorphosis is Roman Polanski. 'He had seen the wonderful French production of *Taking*

Sides,' recounts Harwood, 'and, from that, thought I might be right for *The Pianist*.' So perfectly was he suited for the project that he not only leapt at the offer, but even chided the Polish director for his lack of imagination. 'Everyone heaps praise on the director for choosing me to write the screenplay for *The Pianist*,' he jokes, '– *I* could have chosen me … Who else writes as much as I do about Nazis and musicians?'

The book from which Harwood was to base his screenplay was originally published in 1946, bearing the Polish title *Śmierć Miasta*: 'Death of a City'. In Spartan prose it tells the story of the deliverance of the book's author, Włladysław Szpilman, from the horrors of the Warsaw Ghetto. Formerly an acclaimed pianist on Polish Radio, Szpilman passed the war years confined to this sickeningly overcrowded apparition of Hell, firstly as a law-abiding prisoner of the Nazi regime and, latterly, as a gaunt fugitive from the death camps. His life was eventually saved by a 'good Nazi', Captain Wilm Hosenfeld, who provided him with food and shelter during the final months of 1944. Over fifty years later the book was finally translated into English as *The Pianist*.

No sooner had Harwood verbally accepted Polanski's offer than a copy of this nightmarish tome was dispatched to his Chelsea home. 'I couldn't put it down,' he recalls, '– I read it in one go in four or five hours.' What especially appealed to him was the author's decided lack of sentiment. 'He simply described the terror without comment,' he continues, 'without reference to his own suffering or courage; without saying, "Wasn't this appalling?" or, "Wasn't I lucky?"' One passage taken almost at random illustrates this point. As Szpilman was walking back into the ghetto one day, he saw a little boy running towards a checkpoint. 'He was very pale, and so scared', wrote Szpilman, 'that he forgot to take his cap off to a German policeman coming towards him.'

> The German stopped, drew his revolver without a word, put it to
> the boy's temple and shot. The child fell to the ground, his arms

flailing, went rigid and died. The policeman calmly put the revolver back in its holster and went on his way. I looked at him; he did not even have particularly brutal features, nor did he appear angry. He was a normal, placid man who had carried out one of his many minor daily duties and put it out of his mind again at once, for other and more important business awaited him.[65]

From this brutal tale of human woe and depravity, Harwood was to construct his epic. Before commencing, he flew out to meet the diminutive director of *Chinatown*, *Repulsion* and *Rosemary's Baby* in Paris. 'We had never met before,' recounts Harwood, 'but became friends at once and have remained so to this day.' Sharing a Jewish heritage and an almost overwhelming obsession with the Nazis and the Holocaust, the two men felt completely at ease with one another – and with their subject matter. Like Szpilman, the director had come of age as a denizen of a Jewish ghetto (in Kraków) and knew at first hand the moral rot that ensues from such inhumane segregation: his own mother was one of the six million individuals ethnically cleansed by the Nazis. Harwood, in his own way, has long felt the trauma of the same historical period. Never has he forgotten the day he went to the Reform synagogue in Sea Point with the other children in the congregation to see the gruesome Pathé newsreel images of the liberations of Bergen-Belsen, Auschwitz and the other death camps. This common vantage would prove invaluable in the making of the film.

Yet it was Polanski's and Harwood's common artistic sense that was especially vital in the construction of this poignant classic. During the course of their first meeting, both men agreed that they had to be completely faithful to Szpilman's memoir. 'We were not going to employ a voice-over,' explains Harwood, 'nor was I going to introduce some sort of companion to whom the pianist could talk. … We would invent only where the film demanded it.' Likewise, they were not going to preach to their audience. 'In the film,' continues Harwood, 'there are good Poles and bad Poles, good Jews and bad Jews, good Germans and bad Germans – just people, human beings caught up in the most terrible circumstances.' And, most importantly of all, the two men were going to trust each other implicitly. 'I later told Roman,' recounts Harwood conspiratorially, 'that I could not work with any of the "story-editors" from the studio … those people always have very predictable suggestions about how to develop a screenplay. …. [Polanski] very kindly agreed that we would not have any such external interference in future.' 'Story-editors,' continues Harwood with an unsettling little chuckle, 'should be chained up and starved.'

Harwood's justification for wanting complete control over his writing is easily understandable. Not an author ever to be paralysed by 'writer's-block' or want of certainty, he shares Polanski's incredible self-belief and inexhaustible creative energy. But when it came to beginning *The Pianist*, the British playwright was uncharacteristically lost for words. The difficulty was how to start. 'Roman would call me from time to time,' reminisces Harwood, 'and ask how I was getting on. I lied and said it was going swimmingly.' But after several such conversations, the screenplay-writer eventually came clean: 'I don't know how to begin,' he stammered. It took a director of Polanski's repute to devise a solution: 'For God's sake!' he exploded, 'the book's called *The Pianist*! Start with him playing the piano!' Harwood thought this a rather ingenious suggestion. 'It's so simple when you hear it,' he sighs airily, 'and from that moment the screenplay began its journey.'

The first draft was completed in a matter of weeks. But what gave *The Pianist* the edge over every other film that Harwood has written was Polanski's insistence that they spend an additional month and a half revising the text together. 'To do this,' recounts Harwood, 'we repaired to a house near Rambouillet, south-west of Paris, where we were locked up together and worked every day from 10 a.m. till 6 p.m.' It was an experience that Harwood fondly recalls as one of the most fruitful collaborations of his career. 'He's a great actor,' explains Harwood, '… and I'm an actor *manqué*, so we both acted out the scenes.' In this way the two men tested each line for authenticity, often drawing on the director's own experiences of life in the ghetto. 'There was one [contribution of Polanski's] in particular I remember,' recalls Harwood. 'I had accurately reproduced the moment in the book when a Jewish policeman saves Szpilman from boarding a cattle truck bound for Treblinka. Szpilman describes himself running from the scene. "No!" Polanski said. "I'll tell you what happened to me; it'll be better." Apparently he too was saved in a similar manner but when he'd been pulled out from the crowd and started to run, his saviour hissed, "Walk! Don't run!" And so we changed it.'

Harwood was far from shy in suggesting alterations of his own. These pearls were not, however, always gratefully received. 'When a problem arose,' he narrates, 'and I'd make a suggestion that wasn't to his liking, he'd react as though I'd insulted his wife. "You crazy? That's terrible!" he'd cry. "Let's have a coffee." And when I suggested something of which he did approve, he would be equally extreme: "That's great, my God, that's great. Let's have a coffee!" We drank a lot of coffee.' The two men also told a lot of jokes. 'If he suffered pain,' recounts Harwood of their conversations about Polanski's childhood, 'he did not show it … [he] tells you about his extraordinary life only if he remembers something funny.' This morbid banter could often get alarmingly out-of-hand. 'Roman used to say,' chuckles Harwood, '"How many Jews did we kill today?" I'd say, "About ten or twelve." "Not enough!" And then we'd fall about like children. It was our defence mechanism. The material was bleak.'

The filming took place between February and July 2001 in Warsaw, Berlin and the Babelsberg Studio, Potsdam. 'It was very important for Roman that the locations looked authentic,' recalls Harwood. To ensure that this ambition was fulfilled, the director conscripted the brilliant Polish set designer, Allan Starski, who had won an Academy Award in 1993 for his work on *Schindler's List*. With the utmost attention to detail, he and his team transformed the only surviving part of pre-war Warsaw into a near replica of its former ghetto. No one was more conscious than the director himself of the appalling memories that this particular set might evoke in this particular district. But in the event, the people of Warsaw were grateful for the production. 'I was aware that it could be annoying for some people,' recounts Starski, '… but old people were moved by the images from the war, and the young people were pretty excited by the name of Roman Polanski, so it was pretty good for us to work in this part of Warsaw.' Only Harwood, it seems, failed to be mesmerized by the magic of Starski's simulated world. 'I did not spend a great deal of time on the set,' he recalls, 'but I do remember watching the scene where the man in the wheelchair is thrown from the balcony … with all the ropes and so forth it really had no effect on me at all; but when I later saw it in the film I was overwhelmed by its power … *The Pianist* must have released something in him [Polanski].'

Another factor elevating *The Pianist* to the movie pantheon was the casting. After studying dozens of audition tapes, Polanski had the inspired idea of giving the lead to Adrien Brody. Relatively unknown at the time, the lean twenty-seven-year-old not only bore a striking resemblance to the young Szpilman, he was also able to play the part without the affectation of a 'star'. 'Brody's process might best be described as Method,' explains Polanski's biographer, Christopher Sandford, 'and broadly in the school of a young Al Pacino.' He was helped in conveying this flat sincerity by a script that, unlike those of many of Harwood's stage plays, did not demand any verbose speeches or jarring wisecracks. In Brody's own assessment, Szpilman was 'just a very outgoing and good-hearted young man [before the war] … a regular, not especially heroic guy.' But it was his willingness to submit completely to the demands of the production team that gave his performance legendary status. 'He's a darling man,' recounts Harwood of the actor, 'and he completely lived the part.' As well as selling his car and apartment, Brody starved himself in order to transform himself into a credible ghetto scavenger. When he finally ate a square meal again he vomited.[66]

The response of the major film studios to the proposed movie was not dissimilar. This was partly down to a fact that is easily forgotten: in the year 2000, Roman Polanski was considered by many big names in Hollywood to be a spent force. 'Had you sat a hundred industry chiefs in a room,' remarked the producer-director Stanley Kramer, 'and asked them if Roman was still a significant player, at least eighty of them would have said "no."' Moreover, he was widely considered to be 'difficult to work with' on account of the intrinsic force of his personality – on set he is only half-jokingly known as 'God'. The result was that *The Pianist* was made on a budget of $35 million: a modest sum by comparison to those of contemporary blockbusters such as *Titanic* ($200 million), *Gladiator* ($103 million) and *The Fellowship of the Ring* ($93 million). Most of the finance was eventually provided by the French cable television channel *Canal+*. Only at the eleventh hour did the Hollywood movie-men descend – and even then, with considerable ill-grace. At the film's premiere at the Cannes Film Festival in May 2002, Harwood was amazed to see one of movie's potential distributors, Harvey Weinstein of Miramax, 'very ostentatiously' stand up and leave the theatre after three or four minutes. When asked if this was because, as a Jew, he had been overcome with emotion watching Szpilman play Chopin to the accompaniment of a Nazi air-raid, Harwood shakes his head sadly. 'He didn't think it would make any money,' he explains: 'He was saying, "I am the great Harvey and you guys know nothing."' After being taken up by a far less prestigious studio, Focus Features, and subsequently showered with critical acclaim, it amused Harwood to see the same Hollywood bigwig at the film's New York premiere. 'Weinstein came ... and introduced himself to the film's principals,' records Sandford, 'telling them that he loved their work.' 'He'd forgotten all about [Cannes] by then, of course,' resumes Harwood with a dollop of that hard-earned smugness which is his own.

In the event, *The Pianist* outperformed nearly everybody's expectations. While the film's harrowing content prevented it from becoming a popular 'smash-hit', it was widely respected and moderately lucrative. After winning the Palme d'Or at Cannes, it went on to gross $32 million in the USA and roughly the same amount again worldwide. In Germany, where the film took $1.8 million in the first month, every secondary school child watched the movie as part of the History curriculum. These solid achievements were propped up by the hundreds of column inches devoted to the film and its director: one wag joked that there was more in the newspapers about 'little Roman' and his new movie than there was about the Iraq War. Harwood basked in the reflected limelight. Of the mountains of glowing notices that tumbled down upon him and his collaborator, Harwood particularly relished the learned panegyric which appeared in the columns of the *New York Times*. Admiring the film's 'bleak, acid humour', the paper's film critic A. O. Scott compared Brody's Szpilman to 'one of Samuel Beckett's gaunt existential clowns, shambling though a barren, bombed-out landscape clutching a jar of pickles. He is like the walking punchline to a cosmic jest of unfathomable cruelty.' Now that was more like it.

Surprisingly the film was much less admired in the United Kingdom, where it was released in March 2003. The veteran critic Alexander Walker, writing in the *Evening Standard*, was not convinced that the movie lived up to 'its pretensions or the responsibilities of history.' It was, he contended, merely 'a dispassionate inventory of ethnic slurs, personal humiliations and criminal acts committed by German forces on Warsaw Jews.' Of particular offense, in his view, was the fact that the Poles in the film spoke English 'like Hampstead bourgeoisie' – only the Germans spoke German. 'You cannot make a film with mature pretensions to authenticity,' he went on, 'by putting it into a language that strips the characters of their national identity.' 'Such a convention,' he concluded, 'has had its day.' While there were friendlier reviews in other papers – notably *The Times*, which bestowed four stars upon the picture – no British publication went out of its way to mention that the film was partly the result of home-grown talent. The reviewer in *Sight & Sound* even went so far as to contend that the 'least impressive aspect of the film is Ronald Harwood's English language script, which is frequently more functional than inspired.'[67]

Thankfully for Harwood these murmurings did not reach the influential ear of the Academy. Having already had his appetite whetted by his nomination for *The Dresser*, he knew exactly what was inside the comically large cloth envelope shortly dispatched by that august body to his Chelsea home. 'On behalf of the Academy,' he excitedly read one cold February morning,

> I am delighted to formally notify you that you have been nominated for an Academy Award in the Adapted Screenplay category for THE PIANIST. Congratulations!

Harwood did not begrudge the President of the Academy, Frank Pierson, the split infinitive. Breathlessly he read on that he and his wife were invited to the ceremony at the Kodak Theatre on 23 March 2003. In due course the Harwoods emerged from a sleek limousine at this temple of celluloid vitality to mingle with the other nominees, among whom were numbered no less than seven associated with the film. All seemed to be going extremely well until Harwood was finally ushered to his seat. 'I saw that they'd stuck me next to a fire exit,' he sulks, 'so assumed the Oscar must have gone to someone else.' Only the wisdom of a grey-bearded, kilted gentleman dared to demur: 'You're gonna win!' shouted the most famous of all 007s from the aisle. Harwood would not, however, succumb to premature euphoria: 'Fuck off, Sean!' he yelled over the top of his velvet lapel.

The playwright was no more put at his ease by one of Steve Martin's opening gags. 'Writers, directors, actors,' beamed the compere, '– if we're stuck in here tonight and run out of food, that's the order of whom we eat.' Then the waiting began – hour after hour of it. Harwood does not particularly recall whom he was applauding, but his hands were raw by the time that Garcia Gay Harden finally stood up to announce the nominees for Best Adapted Screenplay. His competitors were Bill Condon for *Chicago*, Charlie Kaufman for *Adaptation*, Peter Hedges for *About a Boy* and his fellow playwright David Hare for *The Hours*. This time, however, there was no mistake: the boy from Sea Point came out Number One. But it says something of his obscurity in the world of movies that his name was read as 'Ron Harwood'. 'No one calls me "Ron,"' he sniffs contemptuously.

There was, however, no uncertainty about his acceptance speech. Breezing past several cast members on his way to the podium, Harwood barely paused to acknowledge the proffered hand of his fellow Oscar-winner, Adrien Brody, who had just used his moment on the stage to deliver a touchingly rambling soliloquy about the rights and wrongs of the world. 'I gave the lad a little pat on the cheek,' says Harwood proprietorially ('I think that's the last time I saw him,' he adds with a note of surprise). Then, after embracing Garcia Gay Harden, the playwright received his trophy. The ensuing speech must rank among the briefest, funniest and most ostensibly humble ever delivered at the Academy Awards. 'When I was last here twenty years ago,' he coolly began,

> ... I'm not making a habit of it, don't worry [*laughs*]... Shirley MacLaine got Best Actress. When she got the statue she said, 'I deserve this.' [*silence*] ... Well, I wish I could say that, but I can't. Roman Polanski deserves this. [*subdued applause*]... He's a great director and a wonderful colleague. And I want to thank him, and indeed you, for this splendid honour. Thank you very much indeed. [*cheers*]

The reason for the audience's uneasy response to Harwood's heartfelt tribute was obvious. Due to an outstanding court order for his arrest for the rape of a thirteen-year-old child in 1977, the Polish director was *persona non grata* in Los Angeles. 'The warrant against him remains outstanding', the county sheriff's department had confirmed shortly before the ceremony. When Harrison Ford, with a noticeably curled lip, confusingly accepted Polanski's award for Best Director 'on behalf of the Academy', there was a sense that the ensuing applause and somewhat reluctant standing ovation was in reality a protest against the despised Bush government. After all, the nomination of a self-styled 'Bush-baiter' and fugitive from US justice was said by one trade weekly to be a 'defiant open letter' to an 'illegal regime'. His nomination was bracketed with that of Michael Moore for Best Documentary as Hollywood's way of raising two fingers to the White House.

When asked whether, as a writer fascinated by great moral dilemmas, Harwood was at all apprehensive of working with a director such as Polanski, he looks puzzled. 'No,' he says flatly. Pushed a little on the matter – was it not an unspeakable crime? – Harwood gravely intones a studied mantra: 'He's suffered enough.' A third attempt to elicit a credible defence for his decision to collaborate with the controversial director causes Harwood to squirm painfully: 'What do you expect me to say?' he says at last, '– I'm biased. He's my friend.'

This unswerving loyalty caused some embarrassment for Harwood in the immediate aftermath of his Oscars triumph. For it so happened that the hosts of the after-party, the owners of *Vanity Fair* magazine, were just then defending a multi-million dollar defamation claim brought against them by the Polish star. The result was that Harwood was shunned and reviled. 'I wasn't exactly inconspicuous,' he says with a sad smile, 'holding this great gold statuette, but no one said "hello" to me …' After downing a few glasses of champagne, Harwood suggested to his wife that they return to their hotel suite for chicken soup and a long-awaited cigarette. The next day they saw Peter O'Toole at breakfast: 'Why didn't you come into the back room?' he asked. No one had told them that this was where the stars coalesced.

And this was only the beginning of Harwood's sense of neglect. Within hours of his return to England he heard Jonathan Ross declare on the BBC that *The Pianist* had scooped up 'two major Oscars' – Best Actor and Best Director; not Best Adapted Screenplay. 'I'd like to see the profile of film writers raised,' says Harwood, '… we're not in the front rank. Even the Academy is pretty disparaging. You'll never see a writer present another writer with an Oscar. And that's pathetic.' Central to this grievance is the public's lack of appreciation that almost every line spoken on a television screen has been created by an unseen hand. 'It never occurs to anyone,' sighs Harwood, 'except those in the know that the wisecracking hosts did not make up all their jokes themselves. "You mean they're written!?" someone said to me in disbelief … believe me, that tends to be forgotten.' As if to remind the world of this awesome power, Harwood joined the Writers' Guild strike of 2007-8 and even boycotted the Golden Globes ceremony along with many of his confrères. The result was that the large studios agreed to give their writers a share of the gross profits for digital distribution for the first time in history.

Over the coming years this windfall would help boost Harwood's rapidly swelling income. A series of big budget films including *Love in the Time of Cholera, Oliver Twist* and *The Diving Bell and the Butterfly* fluttered across his writing desk. For the first time he was a man whom famous actors and producers wanted to meet. Harwood was not, however, so green as to be dazzled by this new-found adulation. As well as refusing to relocate to California – 'it's a fatality to go to Hollywood,' he smirks – the playwright maintains an icy hauteur whenever in the presence of household names. When Universal Pictures were trying to entice Johnny Depp to play the lead role in *The Diving Bell and the Butterfly*, the author was invited to meet the star at a screening of his latest film, *Finding Neverland*. 'I went over,' recounts Harwood, 'and he held my hand, looked me in the eye and said, "I love your screenplay and I can't wait to start filming."' That would have delighted any mere Hollywood hack – but not Harwood. 'I knew then,' he explains, 'that he wasn't going to do it. I've been around actors long enough to know that look. And I was right – he went off and made two pirate pictures.'

Only once has Harwood stooped to attempting a straightforward blockbuster. This was Baz Luhrmann's 2008 frontier epic, *Australia*. Costing $130 million to produce, it was both Harwood's most lucrative project to date, and also his most disappointing. The first problem was the storyline. Taxing the ingenuity of even the most brilliant Wikipedia encyclopaedist, the film concerns the fortunes of Lady Sarah Ashley, who travels to Australia with the intention of forcing her philandering husband to sell his ranch; subsequently, however, she falls in love with both the cattle drover who serves as her guide and a little Aborigine boy called Nullah, whom the drover later rescues from Mission Island, where he and other native children have been abducted by the government authorities. At the end of this knotty saga, Nullah's mysterious grandfather, the 'magic man' 'King George', appears at the harbour in Darwin to slay Lady Sarah's mortal enemy, Neil Fletcher. Lasting almost three hours – at the cinema there was need for an interval – the film meanders around these tangled subplots with no clear direction or sense of purpose. It was, in the words of one experienced British producer, 'unwatchable'.

The next problem was the casting. 'I like real actors,' says Harwood proudly. Baz, however, wanted stars. Initially desperate to interest Russell Crowe in the role of the drover, Luhrmann in the end had to settle for Hugh Jackman. The Wolverine was secured by the gentle persuasion of his no less mainstream co-star, Nicole Kidman. When these 'bankable' Hollywood actors met at a Super Bowl party during the pre-production phase, Kidman mentioned that she had overheard Jackman's name mentioned in relation to the movie. 'Hugh hesitated,' records his biographer, Anthony Bunko, 'and replied that he hadn't even read the script yet and didn't know anything about it.' The Australian beauty did not relent: 'Nor me,' she said coyly, 'but it's Baz ... just sign on.'

Jackman would live to regret not first reading Harwood's manuscript. When it eventually found its way into his straining arms, he was terrified. 'This is how they describe my character's horsemanship,' he gasped in one interview:

> 'The Drover, astride his horse, like a knight in shining armour corralling 100 wild horses at the back of the homestead, by himself.' That freaked me out to begin with, and on the day, of course, it was 200 wild horses, not 100! Then the next page said, 'The Drover rides along on the saddle, pursuing a bull across the plains. He leaps down, grabs his tail and, with one fluid movement, he heaves his weight down upon it to throw the massive beast onto its side. The Drover takes out a bush knife, grabs the bull by the balls and slices them.'[68]

It wasn't exactly *Gone with the Wind*. But many reviewers admitted to a sneaking sympathy for the film. 'Have you seen everything *Australia* has on offer a dozen times before?' asked Richard Schickel in *Time*. 'Sure you have. It's a movie less created by director and co-writer Baz Luhrmann than assembled, Dr Frankenstein-style, from the leftover body parts of earlier movies. Which leaves us asking this question: How come it is so damnably entertaining?' Similarly, Ann Hornaday of the *Washington Post* admitted to succumbing to Harwood's and Luhrmann's wizardry: 'A wildly ambitious, luridly indulgent spectacle of romance, action, melodrama and revisionism, *Australia* is windy, overblown, utterly preposterous and insanely entertaining.' Most critics, however, sided with the *West Australian*, whose chief critic, Mark Naglazas, lamented the film's 'unrelenting awfulness': 'it lurches drunkenly from crazy comedy to Mills and Boonish melodrama in the space of a couple of scenes.' As Bonnie Malkin of the *Daily Telegraph* echoed:

> Local critics had worried that the much anticipated film *Australia* would present to the world a series of time-honoured Antipodean clichés. Their fears were well founded.[69]

And yet the film was not a commercial disaster. Taking $211 million in receipts worldwide, it remains the third highest-grossing Australian film of all time, behind *Crocodile Dundee* and *Mad Max*. Perhaps the best way of explaining this anomaly is to realize that *Australia* is the kind of film that most people will watch – once. With a legion of big names, fantastic scenery and buckets of goodwill from an entire continent, there was never any danger of anyone losing money on the project. But it did little good for the film-making credentials of either Harwood or Luhrmann. To this day, Harwood struggles to come to terms with the sheer dreadfulness of his creation. 'They got two Aussies to muck about with the script after I'd finished with it,' he explains on one occasion. Another time the film's flaw is said to be the dire performance of Nicole Kidman as a titled English lady: 'She's a [*inaudible*] actress!' he huffs. Yet another time, the playwright bubbles with discontent for the director: 'Baz isn't really ... [*mumble mumble*].'

Maybe Harwood came closest to the truth when asked point blank about it by Richard Eyre before a large audience of drama students at RADA: 'I needed the money...' he grinned helplessly, '... for my kids.'

It would be tempting to suppose that, by the early 2000s, Ronald Harwood was principally a writer of films, not plays. This, however, was not the case. While his reputation in the theatre remained largely dependent on *The Dresser* – which continued to be frequently revived, most notably by Sir Peter Hall in 2005 and subsequently by Sean Foley in 2016 – he has never ceased to be a proud, unashamed scribbler of plays.

These new dramas, no less than his previous works, stubbornly refused to conform to the canons of the 'fashionable theatre'. They stood little chance of appearing at the National Theatre, and even today the visitor will be fortunate to find even a single edition of Harwood's works in the bookshop of that cherished eyesore. Their absence from the lists of the Royal Court goes almost without saying. More tellingly, perhaps, Harwood's name was conspicuously absent in Michael Billington's 435-page survey of post-war British theatre, *State of the Nation* (2007). And yet, in small playhouses from Bradford to Bournemouth, from Chichester to Watford and from Stirling to Richmond, thousands of regular theatregoers have delighted in these well-crafted dramas, which even now seem as much part of the scenery of theatrical history as the drawing-room thrillers of Noël Coward and Terrence Rattigan.

One of Harwood's most underrated plays from this late period is *Equally Divided*, which was first performed at the Yvonne Arnaud Theatre, Guildford, on 15 September 1998. Like nearly all of Harwood's most enduring works, the compass is small; the dialogue taut. The narrative revolves around two sisters, Renata and Edith, the first comfortably off, the latter not. Their recently-deceased mother, whom Edith has nursed for many years, has left her modest fortune and a lifetime's collection of (surprisingly valuable) bric-à-brac to both daughters in equal portions. At the heart of the story is the poorer sister's dilemma over whether to accept the terms of her mother's will, or to succumb to the alluring blandishments of an 'honest rogue' (an antiques dealer named Fabian) who offers to replace all of her mother's possessions with cheap imitations in return for a share of the proceeds. 'I know I've done the right thing,' says Edith after giving in. 'You think so, too?' she pathetically enquires of her new friend just before the curtain falls – 'Don't you?'

The play did not proceed to the West End – not, at least, for another fifteen years – but was favourably reviewed by the local critics. Of greater national significance was Harwood's next play at the Yvonne Arnaud Theatre: *Quartet*. The tale of a medley of retired opera singers who conspire to return to the stage in order to save their magnificent nursing home from sale, it is a poignant story of love, vanity and what Harwood calls 'the triumph of old age'. After going on to enjoy a successful run at the Albery Theatre (renamed in 2006 The Noël Coward Theatre), it was suggested to Harwood by his old friend Sir Tom Courtenay that it would make a terrific film. 'When we did the concert scene at the end of the play,' recalls Sir Tom of the West End production, 'I could tell that the audience was incredibly moved – there was a real connection. ... I knew that it would work brilliantly for cinema.'

Courtenay's presentiment was proved absolutely correct when Harwood's adaptation was eventually made into a film by Dustin Hoffman in 2012. 'He was after a script,' explains Harwood, 'and mine was suggested to him by the producer Kathleen Kennedy.' Shortly thereafter the seventy-five-year-old veteran of *The Graduate*, *Rain Man* and *Kramer vs. Kramer*, paid a visit to Drayton Gardens for a tête-à-tête with the British playwright. 'He's a very talented man,' says Harwood as though confiding a great secret, 'and we got on together very well ... working our way through the script on the roof terrace of the Chelsea Arts Club.' Linked both by long experience and a decidedly unfavourable view of most Hollywood studios, the two men enlivened their toil by exchanging cinematic tales. One that particularly stands out in Harwood's memory was Hoffman's recollection of the first screening of *The Graduate*. At the end of the film, the 'big cheese' from the studio was heard to mutter, 'Well, of course, the problem is the boy.' Sadly, however, Harwood saw little more of his distinguished friend once all the changes had been approved by the film's eventual producer, Finola Dwyer. 'It wasn't his fault,' he explains sombrely, '… it was the producer who kept me shut out.' 'Miserable cow,' he adds quietly.

Harwood's next play, *Mahler's Conversation*, was an attempt to crown the glory of *Taking Sides* with a drama of even grander proportions. Based on the life of Gustav Mahler, it centres on the dilemma he faced in 1897: would he convert from Judaism to Catholicism in order to secure the position of Director of the Vienna Court Opera? That his eventual decision is never in doubt does not detract from the potency of the drama. For while the composer is adamant from the outset that the transition is a matter of negligible importance, it becomes clear during the course of the play that it has affected him deeper than he envisaged. 'My worst nightmare is now a reality,' he wails when he realizes that his conversion has transformed him into the Wandering Jew. 'And that's what I've become,' he continues,

> sailing the ocean back and forth to the new world, and finding nothing but sterility, yes, and impotence. There will only be one resting place for me, one true, still centre. Oblivion.

When he finally dies in the arms of his shrewish and anti-Semitic wife it is clear that he has sold himself and his faith for the bauble of cheap popular acclaim.

The play had a deep personal significance for Harwood. Firstly, it was closely based on some of his own experiences. 'Shortly after my marriage,' he explains, 'I briefly considered converting to Catholicism.' Visited on a regular basis by a priest, it was only at the last minute that Harwood resolved to remain true to the faith of his fathers. This was largely because of a careless phrase uttered during the course of his counsellor's final visit: 'I have converted many people,' he said proudly, 'Lutherans, an Orthodox priest, and even two Muslims.' Far from putting Harwood at his ease, it brought an end to the entire project then and there – 'I wasn't going to be the Jew on his list!' he fumes. The clergyman's tactless boast appears in Act One of the play.

But *Mahler's Conversion* had an even deeper personal significance for Harwood. The reason was that he wrote the main part for his cousin, Sir Antony Sher. 'It was the first time that we worked together,' recalls Harwood of his maternal aunt's grandson. The two men had barely been in contact since Sher first arrived in Britain in 1968 in an attempt to follow in the footsteps of his acclaimed cousin. 'Growing up in Sea Point,' remembers Sher, 'I was aware of this legend who had gone to England and made a great success as an actor and author.' After briefly serving as babysitter to the family of the older man, Sher found his way into repertory theatre. 'I only saw Ronnie from time to time,' he continues, 'but he always tried to help and offer encouragement.' On one occasion while Sher was working at the highly-regarded Everyman Theatre Company, Liverpool, his distinguished relation took him aside to deliver a hushed word of warning: 'The Liverpool Rep.,' he whispered, 'is very socialist.' Only with Sher's triumphant performance as Richard III for the RSC in 1984 did the two men really start to correspond on level ground. *Mahler's Conversion* was envisaged as the vehicle for their artistic union: 'I read the script,' recalls Sher, 'and could see that this was a story with which we could both strongly identify.'

Alas, *Mahler's Conversion* was savaged by the reviewers. Writing in the *Jewish Chronicle*, John Nathan dismissed the production as a 'dirge of a play', and the critics of nearly every other publication happily echoed the same sentiment. 'He doesn't seem so much to have written this play,' fumed Charles Spencer in the *Daily Telegraph*, 'as to have phoned it in … the theatrical equivalent of hack journalism.' What particularly irked many of these reviewers was the sense that Harwood had simply sewn together a patchwork of clichés relating to Mahler and the Vienna of his day. '[W]e don't need the appearance of Freud in a park (yes, really),' sniffed Benedict Nightingale in *The Times*, 'to twig that he's in conflict about God the Father, whom he sees partly as a force from whom his music pours, partly as a punitive old man in the sky.' Such tricks left Nicholas de Jongh of the *Evening Standard* feeling physically 'disgusted'. Old friends of Harwood's including Michael Billington, Sheridan Morley and Michael Coveney, meanwhile, found themselves collectively longing for the unashamedly silly Hollywood version directed by Ken Russell as a happier alternative.[70]

It was the missed opportunity of a lifetime, as theatrical success at this moment would have undoubtedly hailed a triumphant new phase for Harwood. Instead, he would struggle over the coming years to have new plays considered by West End theatre managers. 'It was a massive, crushing moment,' he sighs, 'for both Tony and me.' Yet neither Harwood, Sher, nor the actor's partner, Greg Doran (who directed), regret the project. 'We still talk about it,' explains Harwood, who suspects that the timing of the production – it opened six days after the terrorist attacks on the World Trade Centre – played a part in the calamity ('They weren't to know' as Norman consoles 'Sir' over the bombing of the theatre where he made his debut in *The Dresser*). In the wake of the play's premature demise, Sher touched on this theme in a poignant letter to his cousin: 'It is said that special relationships are born of adversity,' he wrote.

> [W]e had a fine play and a fine production crash into a solid wall
> of critics and become destroyed. But out of those ashes a great
> warmth arose, the friendship between you, the Harwoods, and us,
> the Doran/Shers.[71]

In the event, Harwood would not have a new play on in the West End for almost a decade. For the playwright's legion of friends and admirers, including such diverse personages as the Prince of Wales, the Conservative

Party leader Michael Howard, the Pinters and the England football manager, Roy Hodgson, the wait was not in vain. Anticipated by the success of a play about the British fascist John Amery, *An English Tragedy*, which was staged at the Watford Palace Theatre in the Spring of 2008, Harwood went on to have two plays running simultaneously at the Duchess Theatre in the early months of 2009. These productions were a revival of *Taking Sides* and a new play, *Collaboration*, about the relationship between Richard Strauss and his Jewish librettist, Stefan Zweig. While there was an element of *déjà vu* about the latter of these productions, the critics found Michael Pennington's Strauss even more captivating than his stiff-backed, brooding Furtwängler. The veteran actor was, in the words of the *Daily Telegraph's* Dominic Cavendish, 'mesmerising … full of rheumy dignity, his tufty snowy-white hair makes him resemble some lonely Alpine peak.' Even *The Guardian's* critic, Lyn Gardner, confessed that this masterclass of acting owed something at least to the playwright. 'This is old-fashioned drama with a capital D,' she wrote, 'but it is so beautifully upholstered and acted you don't worry about the fact that the plays are more smart than subtle. *Taking Sides* is so full of tension that you forgive Harwood for conveniently rigging the argument by making the Major so crudely philistine; *Collaboration* is very slow to come to simmering point but when it does, it boils over.'[72]

While such begrudging recognition was as much as Harwood had come to expect from Fleet Street, he basked in the recognition of a far more exalted quarter. This began with the arrival of the sort of missive he had not seen since his days with Wolfit. 'The Prime Minister,' wrote Mr J. H. Holroyd of the Cabinet Office in the final weeks of 1998,

> has asked me to inform you, in strict confidence, that he has it in mind on the occasion of the forthcoming list of New Year's Honours, to submit your name to The Queen with a recommendation that Her Majesty may be graciously pleased to approve that you be appointed a Commander of the Order of the British Empire.[73]

The announcement of the honour drew forth scores of letters from the faithful. The General Secretary of the Society of Authors, Mark le Fanu, spoke for the entire literary community in celebrating the fact that such recognition had been bestowed on a playwright at a time 'when the honours system seems to favour performers, celebrities and "personalities."' With equal pride, Sir Richard Attenborough, David Suchet, Sir Peter Hall and Adrian Noble each wrote expressing their unreserved admiration and satisfaction at the decision – 'And about bloody time too!' exclaimed the first mentioned of these theatrical worthies. Similar sentiments were expressed by Harwood's ever-diminishing circle of friends from his youth. 'I was so glad,' wrote seventy-nine-year-old Lionel Bowman in a fax from Sea Point, 'that you have been honoured by The Queen and as your sister rightly says, we hope the next honour will be SIR, and then I'll bow to you when we next meet.' 'You can be sure,' wrote another ancient comrade, 'that Sir Donald Wolfit is looking down on you with delightful approval!'[74]

But more precious than all of these generous testimonials was the gradual thawing of the Wolfit clan itself. 'Have you practised kneeling and getting up again?' wrote Wolfit's daughter Margaret, 'Or don't you have to? … At any rate, we are delighted, it is much merited. You have done a lot for theatre worldwide, and we were really pleased at the news.'[75]

In due course, Harwood would indeed follow in the footsteps of his unsurpassable Lear. For the summer of 2010 brought forth a second invitation from the Palace. It would transform the playwright's beloved Princess into a gracious Lady, and himself into a proud Knight of Old England.

12

Arise, Sir Ronald

At the back of my mind an idea hovers, a memory,
a ceremony, a great crowd –
After the Lions, *Act One.*

When Harwood woke at his customary hour of 7 a.m. on Thursday 27 January 2011, he knew that it was to be an unusual day. Sixty years since he disembarked from the *Edinburgh Castle* with nothing in his pockets but bags of ambition and unripe talent, he was going to the home of his sovereign to be conferred with one of the greatest honours that can be bestowed upon a subject. Later the same evening, he was due to return to Buckingham Palace for a special performance of a short piece he had devised in collaboration with the Royal Opera House, *Beloved Friend*, based on the correspondence of Tchaikovsky and his patron Madame Nadezhda von Meck.

As he reclined in the low armchair in his study contemplating this heady moment, the playwright gazed at three photographs hanging on the wall above his writing desk. From left to right they were of his younger self, embracing his mother, circa 1954, amid the pigeons of Trafalgar Square; the next was of his wife, Natasha, captured unawares by Marigold Johnson at Lady Antonia Fraser's seventieth birthday party, and, finally, his parents posing on the occasion of their engagement: 'With love from Ike and Bella, 16/10/18' his mother had written across the bottom.

He wondered what the unlikely couple would have thought of their son today. All their years of patiently nurturing him, indulging his fantasies and cultivating his faculties, had brought forth a spectacular harvest. He regretted that neither they, nor his two siblings, had lived long enough to share in this triumph. But their images would cling to his memory throughout the remainder of the day like the haunting apparition of the King of Denmark.

Harwood's only doubt was how he would carry the thing off. During his last visit to the Palace he had been struck by the cool nonchalance of his former acting partner, Sir Nigel Hawthorne, who had held himself aloof from his fellow dignitaries with an almost regal condescension. Others, he believed, had treated the ceremony as a kind of extended cocktail party, chatting to all and sundry as if their new titles brought with them an instant kinship and familiarity. In the event, Harwood resolved that he would end his journey just as it had commenced. 'I decided,' he explains, '… [that] I should make every effort both to observe and partake, as though I were an actor asked to play a role for which I was only partly suited.'

At nine-thirty sharp an elegant Mercedes mounted the curb outside the apartment block. The playwright, his pink-coated spouse and their twenty-year-old grandson, Isaac, piled in. Their driver, accustomed to transporting individuals of quality, took every junction and traffic light with a deliberation befitting the occasion. At length the limousine glided through the security gates of the Georgian palace and followed the discreet road markings into the inner courtyard. Here, garbed in a hired morning suit, Harwood emerged to lead his party through the massive double doors of the Palace.

The room into which they entered filled the visitors with wonder. Guests and officials mingled amenably, exchanging small talk and pleasantries in a cacophony of anticipation. Rows of erect Life Guards, gleaming in their brass breast plates, stood by like statues in a museum. And, at the far end of the room, a magnificent sweep of red carpeted stairs loomed invitingly.

In a few moments the guests and the recipients of honours were divided. First in line, Harwood presently found himself proceeding down a long corridor directly behind a serene equerry. Having passed a great portrait of King Charles I astride a horse, he soon found himself alone in the vast Green Drawing Room. As his companions joined him, he admired the exquisite furniture, the huge cabinets displaying porcelain and glass, and the noble portraits and landscapes adorning the walls. Once the entire contingent had arrived he spent a moment surveying their chattering faces. 'I recognized none of the others,' he confesses, 'and none of the others, needless to say, recognized me.'

After acknowledging this fact with the dignity befitting his new station, Harwood's attention was diverted by the appearance of Lieutenant Colonel Alexander Matheson of Matheson, the Secretary of the Central Chancery of the Orders of Knighthood. Tall and slim, with a playful twinkle in his eye, Harwood saw at once that this veteran courtier was perfectly cast for his position. Every detail of the imminent ceremony was quickly explained to the onlookers with the utmost clarity: they would be led to the doors of the Ballroom where an official would tell them when to enter; once inside they were to stand by the first Gentleman Usher, and when their surname was called they were to march to the centre, turn and bow to the Prince of Wales by inclining just their heads – and then boldly go forth to receive their honour.

At this moment it was pointed out that the sole recipient of a Knighthood at this investiture would have to undergo an additional formality before respectfully beating a retreat: to bend on one knee and be touched on both shoulders by the Prince's royal sword. A velvet Investiture Stool was reverently produced just as these words were spoken. Matheson of Matheson then proceeded to demonstrate: 'quickly down on one knee, head down while the sword makes contact with the right shoulder, then the left, and then up, walk backwards, bow from the neck, and follow the awaiting usher,' he explained in one breath. 'Nothing will be said,' he concluded, 'no "Rise, Sir Galahad" or anything like that. You rise immediately and step to the side of the stool.'

A flash of anxiety passed beneath Harwood's steely brow. For although he had said nothing of it to the Palace officials, he had recently been diagnosed with tendonitis in his left ankle. He knew that he would be able to kneel down, but would he be able to stand up again? Casually he studied the Investiture Stool. It looked significantly lower than he had envisaged – he would have to do that which Wolfit's daughter had teased him about. 'May I practise?' he asked Matheson of Matheson as blithely as he could. 'Of course,' the courtier replied with a tinge of impatience, 'that's why the stool is here.' To the amusement of the gaping assemblage, Harwood slowly dropped onto one knee and then repeated the process in reverse. A spontaneous patter of applause disturbed his thoughts. He knew that he would be able to fulfil his part in the ceremony, but the terror had still not abated.

A few minutes later, an equerry commanded the guests to proceed to the side entrance of the Ballroom. Standing here behind the three Dames to be created at the investiture, Harwood peered through the open door at the expectant rows of guests. For a moment his eyes met those of his wife. A smile no less radiant than the one that had first captivated him on the stage of the Stephenson Memorial Hall spread across her glowing face. Then the Orchestra of the Band of the Royal Artillery struck up Men of Harlech. This was the cue for five Yeomen of the Guard to process up the central aisle in their ancient uniforms. No sooner had they taken up their places than the tall double doors on the far side of the Ballroom swung gently open to reveal the Prince of Wales and his entourage. Harwood's heartbeat now reached crescendo. 'He looked so splendid and handsome,' he recalls of his friend and patron: 'Uniforms suit him.'

After choking back the tears during the National Anthem, Harwood's waiting was finally at an end. 'The three dames were damed,' he explains without embellishment – '[then it was] my turn.' Following a subtle nod from an elegant young page, Harwood walked purposefully towards the Gentleman Usher, who smiled encouragingly while they awaited his name to be announced. No sooner were those magic syllables uttered than the great playwright was in a pose of reverent submission before his liege lord. Heavily he felt the cool steel pressed onto his right shoulder and then his left. This completed, he stood up and froze. He realized that he had made an oversight. 'I'm sorry, Sir,' he said with a tentative step forward, 'I forgot to bow.' The Prince smiled wryly. 'Never mind,' he replied as an attendant handed him the badge and ribbon of Knight Bachelor, 'you can make up for it tonight.' The two men shared a knowing laugh before the Prince placed the ribbon around Harwood's neck. 'You are a national treasure,' he said as he completed the action. 'I feel like one now,' added Sir Ronald with an impish chuckle.

Having been escorted out of the room, divested of his medallion, which disappeared into a large leather box, and interviewed by an awaiting journalist from the Press Association, Harwood re-entered the Ballroom through the back door to watch the rest of the investiture. While the countless public servants and deserving local worthies received their honours, he found himself daydreaming of Sea Point and South Africa. Then, as suddenly as it had begun, the solemn ritual came to an end. 'The ceremony was due to end at 12.15 p.m.,' recalls Harwood, 'and at 12.15 p.m. precisely the Prince handed out the last decoration.' Everybody stood as the heir to the throne gracefully departed. 'The organization,' rounds off Harwood exultantly, 'was breathtaking.'

Half an hour later, Harwood was surrounded by his family at his favourite restaurant, Lucio on the Fulham Road. This was perhaps the most special moment of all for the newly minted theatrical knight: through years of hardship and steady toil, his wife and children had borne the brunt of his tremendous achievement. 'Everyone was on great form,' reminisces Harwood, 'there was much chatter and fun – it was delightful.' In the spirit of the occasion, the maître d' laid on a complementary bottle of champagne. Once that – and several more – had been polished off, the party bade farewell to their resplendent star. By quarter past three he was back at the Palace in his more customary attire. Upstairs, in a luxurious changing room, was hung the dinner jacket that he was to wear for the evening's entertainment.

In the original production of *Beloved Friend* at the Royal Opera House, Dame Helen Mirren read the part of Madame von Meck, Toby Stephens played Tchaikovsky and Charles Dance narrated. For this encore at the Palace, Harwood had the privilege of seeing his work performed by the no less distinguished ensemble of Dame Harriet Walter, Simon Russell Beale and David Suchet. Overseeing the vocalists and musicians at the piano, was the Royal Opera House's Antonio Pappano, who had also wielded the conductor's baton in the original production. Harwood's only cause for disquiet was the venue: the Ball Supper Room. Specially designed in 1856 for large scale entertainments, this richly coloured chamber, crested with a stately dome and underlain by a gleaming parquet floor, was slightly too roomy for his intimate Russian melodrama. 'It was not,' says Harwood, 'the ideal shape for our performance.'

Despite lamenting this inconvenience, the show was a great success when performed before the Prince and his guests later that evening. Interspersed with extracts from *Swan Lake* and some of the Russian composer's other works, the audience was gripped by the fascinating true story of Tchaikovsky's friendship with the generous noblewoman whom he never actually met in the flesh. When it was over, Pappano hauled up the playwright to share the applause and adulation. They were shortly followed by Prince Charles himself, who mounted the stage to announce that the evening's performance had raised a highly impressive £500,000 for the Royal Opera House Education Fund. After congratulating the musicians for their accomplished performances, he heaped praise upon Harwood, adding that he had knighted him only that morning. With excessive deference, the playwright slowly inclined his head. The Prince, understanding the joke, smiled delightedly.

This remarkable day was capped off by a large banquet in the glorious surroundings of the Picture Gallery. Here Harwood caroused beneath the approving gaze of portraits by Titian, Rembrandt, Vermeer, Rubens, Frans Hals and Canaletto. His dining companions were scarcely less exalted. They included Lord Chichester, Lady Solti, Leopold de Rothschild and, on the playwright's immediate right, the Duchess of Cornwall herself. 'She is wonderful company,' confides Harwood, 'witty and interesting and clever.' Yet the food did not appeal: 'I had no appetite,' he goes on, 'all I wanted was a cigarette, but Her Royal Highness kept my mind off my craving and we chatted non-stop.'

Just as the flow of truffles and Château Mouton Rothschild began to abate, the Prince appeared to collect his Duchess. Proudly Harwood stood up and, reminding his host of his earlier lapse, proceeded to bow again. 'You've bowed enough already,' replied the Prince before sweeping away his royal companion. But a moment later he was back. This time it was the Prince who had made an oversight: he had forgotten to say farewell to Lady Natasha. Kissing her on both cheeks, he apologized for not being able to see her earlier or at all during the evening. 'As a result,' continues Harwood with undisguised satisfaction, 'Natasha was the centre of much whispered attention.' 'Prince Charles,' concludes the merry playwright, 'is one of the nicest and politest men I have met.'

Upon returning home Harwood crept into his study for a victory cigarette. On the wall his eyes rested on a picture: 'With love from Ike and Bella, 16/10/18,' he read. He wondered what they would have said about their son and this unusual day in his life.

CURTAIN CALL

13

At Home

If only I could find a good, catchy title.
I think My Life *a little plain, don't you?*
The Dresser, *Act One*

'What was the question again?' asks Sir Ronald over the top of his smart phone. He has sunk deep into his high-backed armchair, an image of weariness.

'Oh yes,' he resumes absent-mindedly, 'my first television play, *The Barber of Stamford Hill.*'

He shuffles back into position and gives a faint smile. 'It's about a Jewish barber from Stamford Hill,' he says triumphantly. 'He is enchanting to his customers, but has this lonely, miserable life…'

There is a pause. Sir Ronald's smile temporarily vanishes.

'You know, I really don't remember that much about it,' he says at last, '– it's over fifty years ago. You'll be able to find a copy of it somewhere, I expect.'

Sir Ronald lights another ultra-slim cigarette. He has been answering questions about his life all morning and is conscious that he must shortly prepare himself for an important lunch date.

'How much longer is this thing going to take you?' he bellows unexpectedly into a cloud of exhaled smoke.

My expression vaguely resembles that of Garrick's nightmare-haunted Richard III which hangs on the wall behind the distinguished playwright. 'Not long now,' I improvise: 'Not too long at all.'

Sir Ronald nods approvingly before casting an eye at his wristwatch. Then, without warning, he roars: 'Bonnie!' In a few moments a young Australian woman is panting in the doorway. 'Fetch me my navy-blue blazer,' he says softly.

'Keep going,' he whispers indulgently to me: 'We have a little time yet.'

I return to one of the frayed edges of our earlier conversation by asking if success has changed him.

'Not in the least,' he calmly bats away: 'People treat me differently, that's all.'

Another silence. The girl returns with a jacket.

'No, no!' he fumes, '– I said my *blazer*. That's a sports jacket.'

I laugh nervously before resuming the interview. Does he ever find all the fame and adulation oppressive?

'Well,' he sighs, 'to tell you the truth, the only time members of the public ever approach me directly is when I am with J….. D….. or T….. C….. – people only ever want to meet actors!'

The young lady returns with another garment. 'Still wrong,' he grins, '– you know, the navy one I wore to lunch with J….. le C…..'

Sir Ronald catches me looking more than slightly impressed. 'Sorry,' he interjects, 'I really must stop name-dropping. I got a ticking off about that from Prince Charles the other day.'

I shake my head compassionately before firing another hard question at my subject: does he find it surprising that a man such as himself who has won an Oscar and a host of other awards should be so comparatively unknown?

'Ah, well,' he goes on, 'that's partly down to my own life choices. I was always very faithful to my dear wife – a director friend of mine told me that an affair with a famous actress would really raise my profile, but I was never tempted by that sort of thing.'

Another item of clothing is added to the growing collection on the far side of the room. 'For God's sake!' explodes the playwright: 'We'll have to get you on the boat back to Oz – let me *show* you what a blazer is!'

Sir Ronald grabs his walking-stick and gestures for me to follow. The three of us proceed down the passageway to his bedroom. 'There,' he says drawing a rather nondescript flannel jacket from the wardrobe. Bonnie and I exchange sympathetic glances while she holds the blazer aloft for him to throw his arms through.

'While we're down here,' he says to me in his more customary tone, 'there's something I want to show you.'

Sir Ronald leads me into a small, book-lined study. Solemnly, he glides open a mahogany case. 'The key to the city of Guadalajara,' he says brandishing the toothy lump of gold within.

'Very fine; very fine,' I murmur before it is hastily returned to its place between a portrait of the playwright and his gleaming Academy Award.

In a few moments we are back in the entrance hall discussing his lunch companion.

'She *is* a very beautiful woman,' he replies to my thoughtless use of the past tense. 'Occasionally,' he continues while I put on my scruffy coat, 'we invite a guest to join us – they are very honoured to be asked.'

But the ensuing silence is filled only by Sir Ronald's enormous smile.

'Goodbye, Will,' he says soberly: 'Do please send me a text if you have any other questions about my life – but do ... *gert on wi'd it!*'

Acknowledgements

My first debut of gratitude is to Sir Ronald Harwood. From our first meeting in January 2014 until our final informal interview in August 2016, he has tolerated my questioning (and occasional pestering) with the utmost good humour, patience and understanding. As well as respecting my complete independence as a biographer, he has given up many hours of his time to help make this book as detailed and interesting as possible. For this, and for so generously granting me full access to his life without so much as a hint of editorial oversight, I can only imperfectly express my deepest thanks.

In addition to Sir Ronald's invaluable assistance, I have been aided by many persons whom have shared in his journey. As much the subject of the book as Sir Ronald himself, I extend my thanks to the following individuals, without whom this book would not have been possible: Sir Timothy Ackroyd, Sir Tom Courtenay, Lady Antonia Fraser, Antony Harwood, Kit Hesketh-Harvey, Gerald Masters, Sir Ian McKellen, Sir Antony Sher, Sir Tom Stoppard, the late Sir Arnold Wesker and Misha Williams. Several other sources have requested to remain anonymous. To all I am immensely grateful.

For answering letters and queries, as well as sustaining my commitment to this project over the past three years, I am especially grateful to the following individuals: Oladipo Agboluaje, Lisbeth Bartlett, Neville Bass, Maurice Bourcier, Sonia Bourcier, David Cornwell (John le Carré), Dr Christine L. Corton, Jonathan Acton Davis QC, Tim Day, Marianne Elliott, Michael Freedland, James Gillam, Professor Sir Antony Kenny, Rosalind Knight (Mrs Michael Elliott), Professor Antony Lentin, Janet Mackam (on behalf of Albert Finney), Claudio Macor, Isabel Marks, Andrew Morse, Phil Porter, Simon Raison, Julia Raybould, Fletcher Robinson, George Robinson, Rachel Rogers, Amy Rosenthal, Judith Scott, Jonathan Smith, Rachel Smith, James Stitt, Sir Roy Strong, Joe Sutcliffe, Sarah Treanor, Fleur Wadley, Ann White,

James Woodcock and all of my colleagues and students at Rugby School, Malcolm Arnold Academy and Winchester House School.

For reading through the manuscript and making invaluable suggestions about style, form and content, I am especially grateful to Sir Ronald's son, Antony, and also to Neville Bass and my father, Fletcher, all of whom have saved me from many solecisms. Judy Daish has kindly assisted with the compilation of Sir Ronald's major works in the appendix. For what errors remain, I am entirely responsible.

For permission to quote extensively from Sir Ronald's publications, I am grateful to the executive boards of Faber and Faber, Harper Collins Publishers Ltd and the Amber Press. For permission to quote from letters relating to Sir Ronald's knighthood and CBE, I am grateful to the Minister for the Cabinet Office, Ben Gummer MP. Similarly, I am grateful to the governors of the British Library for permission to quote from Sir Ronald's collected papers. To the staff of that indispensable institution, as well as those of the London Library, the Bodleian Library, the Cambridge University Library and the Buckingham University Library, I express my sincere thanks for their unfailing assistance and expertise.

And for believing so strongly in this project from the time of our first meeting in July 2016, I am hugely grateful to James Hogan. Both he and his superlative chief editor, George Spender, have invested huge amounts of time and resources into ensuring that this book is worthy of its subject. To them, and all of their colleagues at Oberon Books, my debt is incalculable.

Major Works by Ronald Harwood

Plays (title: opening night venue: date first performed: director)

March Hares: Royal Court Theatre, Liverpool: 9 March 1964: Casper Wrede

Country Matters: University of Manchester Theatre: 16 October 1969: Casper Wrede

The Ordeal of Gilbert Pinfold: Royal Exchange Theatre, Manchester: 15 September 1977: Michael Elliott

A Family: Royal Exchange Theatre, Manchester: 11 May 1978: Casper Wrede

The Dresser: Royal Exchange Theatre, Manchester: 6 March, 1980: Michael Elliott

After the Lions: Royal Exchange Theatre, Manchester: 18 November 1982: Michael Elliott

Tramway Road: Lyric Theatre, Hammersmith: 23 October 1984: David Jones

The Deliberate Death of a Polish Priest: Almeida Theatre, London: 17 October 1985: Kevin Billington

Interpreters: The Queen's Theatre, London: 19 November, 1985: Peter Yates

J. J. Farr: Theatre Royal, Bath: 27 October 1987: Ronald Eyre

Ivanov (from Chekhov): Yvonne Arnaud Theatre, Guildford: 20 February 1989: Elijah Moshinsky

Another Time: Theatre Royal, Bath: 22 August 1989: Elijah Moshinsky

Reflected Glory: Vaudeville Theatre, London: 8 April 1992: Elijah Moshinsky

Poison Pen: Royal Exchange Theatre, Manchester: 13 May 1993: Ronald Harwood

Taking Sides: Minerva Theatre, Chichester: 18 May 1995: Harold Pinter

The Handyman: Minerva Theatre, Chichester: 24 September 1996: Christopher Morahan

Equally Divided: Yvonne Arnaud Theatre, Guildford: 15 September 1998: Christopher Morahan

Quartet: Yvonne Arnaud Theatre, Guildford: 13 July 1999: Christopher Morahan

Mahler's Conversion: Yvonne Arnaud Theatre, Guildford: 5 September 2001: Gregory Doran

An English Tragedy: Watford Palace Theatre: 14 February 2008: Di Trevis

Collaboration: Minerva Theatre, Chichester: 16 July 2008: Philip Franks

Heavenly Ivy: The Ivy, London: 8 November 2010: Sean Mathias

Entartete Kunst ('Degenerate Art'): Renaissance Theatre, Berlin: 5 October 2015: Torsten Fischer. Translated into German by Max Faber.

Fiction

All the Same Shadows (London: Jonathan Cape, 1961)

The Guilt Merchants (London: Jonathan Cape, 1963)

The Girl in Melanie Klein (London: Methuen, 1969)

Articles of Faith (London: Secker and Warburg, 1973)

The Genoa Ferry (London: Secker and Warburg, 1976)

One. Interior. Day. – Adventures in the film trade (London: Secker and Warburg, 1978)

César and Augusta (London: Methuen, 1978)

Home (London: Weidenfeld and Nicolson, 1993)

Biography

Sir Donald Wolfit: his life and work in the unfashionable theatre (London: Secker and Warburg, 1971)

Edited by

A Night at the Theatre (London: Methuen, 1982)

The Ages of Gielgud: an actor at eighty (London: Hodder and Stoughton, 1984)

Dear Alec: Guinness at 75 (London: Hodder and Stoughton, 1989)

The Faber Book of Theatre (London: Faber and Faber, 1983)

Film

The Barber of Stamford Hill (with Casper Wrede), 1961

Private Potter (with Casper Wrede), 1961

A High Wind in Jamaica (with Stanley Mann and Denis Cannan, adapted from the novel by Richard Hughes), 1965

One Day in the Life of Ivan Denisovich (adapted from the novel by Aleksandr Solzhenitsyn), 1971

Evita Peron, 1981

The Dresser (adapted from the play by Ronald Harwood), 1983

Mandela, 1987

The Browning Version (adapted from the play by Terrance Rattigan), 1994

Cry, The Beloved Country (adapted from the novel by Alan Paton), 1995

Taking Sides (adapted from the play by Ronald Harwood), 2001

The Pianist (adapted from the memoir by Wladyslaw Szpilman), 2002

Being Julia (adapted from the novel *Theatre* by W. Somerset Maugham), 2004

Oliver Twist (adapted from the novel by Charles Dickens), 2005

The Diving Bell and the Butterfly (adapted from the memoir by Jean-Dominique Bauby), 2007

Love in the Time of Cholera (adapted from the novel by Gabriel García Márquez), 2007

Australia (with Baz Lurhmann, Stuart Beattie and Richard Flanagan), 2008

Quartet (adapted from the play by Ronald Harwood), 2012

Television

The Barber of Stamford Hill (with Casper Wrede), 1960

Private Potter (with Casper Wrede), 1961

The Guests, 1972

Read All About It (host), 1978-79.

Tales of the Unexpected (adapted from the stories by Roald Dahl), 1979-80

All the World's a Stage (presenter), 1984

Breakthrough at Reykjavik, 1987

Countdown to War, 1989

Other

Radio: *Kaleidoscope* (host), 1973; *Goodbye Kiss*, 1997

Musical libretto: *The Good Companions* (adapted from the novel by J. B. Priestley), 1974.

Historical: *All the World's a Stage* (London: Little, Brown, 1984)

Further Reading

Billington, Michael, *State of the Nation: British theatre since 1945* (London: Faber and Faber, 2007)

------------, *Harold Pinter* (London: Faber and Faber, 2007 [1996])

Bunko, Anthony, *Hugh Jackman: the biography* (London: John Blake, 2014)

Clare, George, *Berlin Days* (London: Macmillan, 1989)

Courtenay, Tom, *Dear Tom: letters from home* (Oxford: ISIS, 2002)

Coveney, Michael, *Maggie Smith: a biography* (London: Weidenfeld and Nicolson, 2015 [1992])

Dench, Judi, *And Furthermore: Judi Dench as told to John Miller* (London: Phoenix, 2010)

Donaghy, H. J., *Conversations with Graham Greene* (London: University Press of Mississippi, 1992)

Eberts, Jake, and Ilott, Terry, *My Indecision is Final: the rise and fall of Goldcrest Films* (London: Faber and Faber, 1990)

Elsom, John, *Theatre Outside London* (London: Macmillan, 1971)

Falk, Quentin, *Albert Finney in Character: a biography* (London: Robson, 2002 [1992])

Figes, Orlando, *A People's Tragedy: the Russian Revolution, 1891-1924* (London: Jonathan Cape, 1996)

Fraser, Antonia, *Must You Go?: my life with Harold Pinter* (Oxford: ISIS, 2010)

Goodman, Jonathan (ed.), *The Master Eccentric: the journals of Rayner Heppenstall, 1969-1981* (London: Allison and Busby, 1986)

Gross, John, *The Rise and Fall of the Man of Letters: aspects of literary life since 1800* (London: Weidenfeld and Nicolson, 1969)

Hobson, Harold, *Theatre in Britain: a personal view* (Oxford: Phaidon, 1984)

Maschler, Tom, *Publisher* (London: Picador, 2005)

Miller, John, *Judi Dench: with a crack in her voice: the biography* (Rearsby: W. F. Howes, 2007 [1998])

Murphy, Robert, *Sixties British Cinema* (London: BFI Publishing, 1992)

Murray, Braham, *The Worst it can be is a Disaster: the life story of Braham Murray and the Royal Exchange Theatre* (London: Methuen Drama, 2014)

O'Connor, Gary, *Paul Scofield: the biography* (London: Sidgwick and Jackson, 2002)

Roth, Joseph, *The Wandering Jews* (trans. M. Hofmann, London: Granta, 2001 [1927])

Sandford, Christopher, *Polanski* (London: Century, 2007)

Sher, Antony, *Beside Myself: an autobiography* (London: Hutchinson, 2001)

Szpilman, Wladyslaw, *The Pianist* (London: Gollancz, 1999 [1946])

Wansell, Geoffrey, *The Garrick Club: a history* (London: The Garrick Club, 2004)

Wilkinson, David Nicholas, and Price, Emlyn (eds.), *Ronald Harwood's Adaptations: from other works into films* (London: Guerilla, 2007)

Wright, Adrian, *West End Broadway: the golden age of the American musical in London* (Woodbridge: Boydell Press, 2012)

Ziegler, Philip, *Olivier* (London: MacLehose Press, 2013)

Endnotes

1   *The Times*, 31.8.16 & 1.9.16.

2   J. Roth, *The Wandering Jews* (trans. M. Hofmann, London, 2001 [1927]), pp. 99-100.

3   A. Wright, *West End Broadway: The Golden Age of the American Musical in London* (Woodbridge: Boydell Press, 2012), p. 115.

4   H. Hobson, *Theatre in Britain: a personal view* (Oxford: Phaidon, 1984) pp. 146-7.

5   RADA Report, Spring 1953. BL Add MS 88881/6/27.

6   For this and following see R. Harwood, *Sir Donald Wolfit CBE: His life and work in the unfashionable theatre* (London: Secker & Warburg, 1971), pp. 222-41.

7   J. Elsom, *Theatre Outside London* (London: Macmillan, 1971), pp. 27, 31.

8   For this and following see O. Figes, *A People's Tragedy: the Russian Revolution, 1891-1924* (London: Jonathan Cape, 1996), pp. 666-70 and *passim*.

9   For this and following see R. Harwood, *Home* (London, 1993), pp. 204-8, 365-9.

10   *Times Literary Supplement*, 17.3.61; *The Guardian*, 31.3.61; *The Sunday Times*, 5.3.61.

11   For this and following see *The Barber of Stamford Hill* typescript. BL Add MS 88881/2/1

12   *Daily Mirror*, 6.4.61; *Daily Express*, 6.10.62.

13   T. Maschler, *Publisher* (London: Picador, 2005), pp. 9-50.

14   T. Maschler to R. Harwood, 18.6.62. BL Add MS 88881/4/9.

15   *The Observer*, 23.5.65.

16   *The Sunday Times,* 23.5.65.

17   R. Harwood, *One. Interior. Day: Adventures in the film trade* (London, 1978), pp. 9-10.

18   Harwood, *Sir Donald Wolfit*, pp. 252, 260.

19   *The Guardian*, 14.9.71; *Times Literary Supplement*, 16.10.71; *The Sunday Times*, 31.10.71.

20   *The Sunday Times*, 5.12.71.

21   *The Guardian*, 16.10.69.

22   *The Guardian*, 10.3.64 & 17.10.69.

23   E. Waugh, *The Ordeal of Gilbert Pinfold and Other Stories* (London: Chapman & Hall, 1975 [1957]), pp. 126-27.

24   *The Sunday Times*, 12.1.69.

25   *Daily Telegraph*, 10.4.05.

26   *The Sunday Times*, 18.9.77.

27   J. Goodman (ed.), *The Master Eccentric: the journals of Rayner Heppenstall 1969-1981* (London: Allison & Busby, 1986), pp. 219-20.

28   A. Fraser, *Must You Go?: my life with Harold Pinter* (London: Weidenfeld & Nicolson, 2010), pp. 47, 98.

29   M. Elliott to R. Harwood, 15.10.77. BL Add MS 88881/5/5.

30   *The Guardian*, 7.7.78.

31   G. O'Connor, *Paul Scofield: the biography* (London: Sidgwick & Jackson, 2002), p. 278.

32   J. Dench, *And Furthermore* (London: Phoenix, 2010), p.109; For following see BL Add MS 88881/1/10 and 88881/4/54.

33   I. McKellen to author, 18.7.16.

34   J. Abineri to R. Harwood, 30.11.80. BL Add MS 88881/6/32.

35   P. Scofield to R. Harwood, 13.2.78. BL Add MS 88881/6/37. *Daily Telegraph*, 10.10.16.

36   *Illustrated London News*, 31.5.80.

37   *The Sunday Times*, 26.2.84.

38   Diary of K. Hesketh-Harvey, 9.11.84.

39   Ibid.

40   L. Bartlett to R. Harwood, 24.5.85. BL Add MS 88881/6/32.

41   J. Shepard to R. Harwood, 16.8.89. BL Add MS 88881/6/37.

42   J. Eberts & T. Ilott, *My Indecision is Final: the rise and fall of Goldcrest Films* (London: Faber and Faber, 1990), pp. 128-30.

43 Q. Falk, *Albert Finney in Character* (London: Robson Books, 2002 [1992]), pp. 164-66.

44 *Mail on Sunday*, 9.5.93; J. Macklam to W. Robinson, 12.4.16.

45 Eberts & Ilott, *My Indecision is Final*, pp. 159-60.

46 *The Sunday Times*, 11.3.84.

47 *Daily Mail*, 20.4.84.

48 For this and following see BL Add MS 88881/6/26.

49 *The Sunday Times*, 21.11.82.

50 *The Times*, 25.10.84; *The Guardian*, 24.10.84.

51 *Cape Times*, 26.4.85.

52 Lecture by R. Harwood about *Taking Sides*. BL Add MS 88881/1/56.

53 *The Sunday Times*, 24.11.85; *The Guardian*, 21.11.85.

54 M. Coveney, *Maggie Smith: a bright particular star* (London, 1992), p. 160.

55 *The Spectator*, 28.11.87.

56 A. Guinness to R. Harwood, 6.5.88. BL Add MS 88881/4/30.

57 *The Observer*, 16.5.93; *The Times*, 17.5.93.

58 G. Clare, *Berlin Days* (London: MacMillan, 1989), p. 89.

59 *The Daily Telegraph*, 24.5.95; *The Guardian*, 23.5.95.

60 H. Cudlipp to R. Harwood, 16.5.95; C. Fry to R. Harwood, 6.6.95; L. Rainer to R. Harwood, 25.5.95; Y. Cloetta to R. Harwood, 21.7.95. BL Add MS 88881/1/63.

61 See BL Add MSS 88881/1/63.

62 R. Harwood to E. Furtwängler, 28.4.95. BL Add MSS 88881/1/63.

63 D. Gillis to E. Furtwängler, 11.10.95. Add MSS 88881/1/63.

64 *The Sunday Times*, 4.5.97.

65 W. Szpilman, *The Pianist* (London, 1999 [1946]), p. 129.

66 C. Sandford, *Polanski* (London, 2007), pp. 411-14.

67 *Evening Standard*, 22.1.03; *Sight & Sound*, Feb., 2003.

68   A. Bunko, *High Jackman: The biography* (London, 2014), pp. 204, 213.

69   *Time*, 25.11.08; *The Washington Post*, 26.11.08; *The Western Australian*, 19.11.08; *The Daily Telegraph*, 18.11.08.

70   *Jewish Chronicle*, 4.3.05; *The Daily Telegraph*, 4.10.01; *The Times*, 4.10.01; *Evening Standard*, 3.10.01; *The Guardian*, 3.10.01; *The Spectator*, 13.10.01; *Daily Mail*, 3.10.01.

71   *Jewish Chronicle*, 28.8.2014.

72   *The Daily Telegraph*, 31.7.08; *The Guardian*, 30.5.09

73   J. H. Holroyd to R. Harwood, 19.11.98. BL Add MS 88881/6/29.

74   M. le Fanu to R. Harwood, 8.1.99; L. Bowman to R. Harwood, 25.1.99; BL Add MS 88881/6/29.

75   M. Wolfit to R. Harwood, 1.1.99.

Index

231

WWW.OBERONBOOKS.COM